THOMAS HARDY ANNUAL No. 1

The *Thomas Hardy Annual* will make available some of the most important critical and scholarly work arising from the new recognition of Hardy's status and significance, and this opening volume reflects a wide variety of approaches and an international interest. Among the topics covered in the essays in this volume are Hardyan biography, the sociological approach to Hardy, Hardy and feminism, Hardy's notebooks, and the metrics of Hardy's poetry; among the contributors are such well-known scholars as John Bayley, Tom Paulin, Arthur Pollard and Merryn Williams. In addition to the essays there are reviews of recent books; a reconsideration of Donald Davie's important study of Hardy's poetry; and a survey and bibliography of recent Hardy studies (the first instalment of what will become a continuous and comprehensive listing).

The editor

Norman Page is Professor of English at the University of Alberta, Canada. A graduate of the Universities of Cambridge and Leeds, he has held a Guggenheim Fellowship and is a Fellow of the Royal Society of Canada.

He has lectured widely on Hardy and other authors, and his publications include *The Language of Jane Austen*, *Speech in the English Novel*, *E. M. Forster's Posthumous Fiction* and *Thomas Hardy*, as well as edited volumes on Dickens, Wilkie Collins, Tennyson, Hardy, D. H. Lawrence and Nabokov.

In the same series

O'CASEY ANNUAL Nos 1 and 2
Edited by Robert G. Lowery
YEATS ANNUAL Nos 1 and 2
Edited by Richard J. Finneran

Further titles in preparation

THOMAS HARDY ANNUAL No. 1

Edited by Norman Page

© Norman Page 1982

Softcover reprint of the hardcover 1st edition 1982

All rights reserved. No part of this publication may be reproduced or transmitted, in any form or by any means, without permission

First published 1982 by
THE MACMILLAN PRESS LTD
London and Basingstoke
Companies and representatives
throughout the world

ISBN 978-1-349-16971-9   ISBN 978-1-349-16969-6 (eBook)
DOI 10.1007/978-1-349-16969-6

Typeset by
Scarborough Typesetting Services

Contents

Editor's Note	vi
The Contributors	vii
Editor's Introduction	ix
'Old Tom and New Tom': Hardy and His Biographers *Peter J. Casagrande*	1
Hardy and Rural England *Arthur Pollard*	33
Hardy and 'the Woman Question' *Merryn Williams*	44
The Love Story in *Two on a Tower* *John Bayley*	60
The Experimental and the Absurd in *Two on a Tower* *Rosemary Sumner*	71
Fifty Years On *Christopher Wiseman*	82
'Words, in all their intimate accents' *Tom Paulin*	84
Hardy's Use of the Hair Motif *Peter W. Coxon*	95
Hardy and His 'Literary Notes' *Lennart A. Björk*	115
Three Unpublished Letters by John Addington Symonds	129
Thomas Hardy, Donald Davie, England and the English *John Lucas*	134
A Survey of Recent Hardy Studies *Richard H. Taylor*	152
Dennis Taylor: *Hardy's Poetry, 1860–1928* and Patricia Clements and Juliet Grindle (eds): *The Poetry of Thomas Hardy* *P. N. Furbank*	172
Jeannette King, *Tragedy in the Victorian Novel* *Juliet McMaster*	177
R. L. Purdy and M. Millgate (eds), *The Collected Letters of Thomas Hardy*, vol. 2 *Norman Page*	181
Reviews in Brief *Norman Page*	188
A Hardy Bibliography, 1978–81 *Richard H. Taylor*	190

Editor's Note

Contributions for future volumes of the *Annual* are welcome at any time. There is no limit on length, and illustrations may be included where appropriate. Contributions should be typewritten (double-space throughout, including quotations and footnotes). References to Hardy's novels should be identified by chapter-number, thus: (*The Woodlanders*, Ch. 10). Footnotes should be kept to a minimum and brief references worked into the text wherever possible.

All contributions, correspondence and books for review should be sent to the editor at the Department of English, University of Alberta, Edmonton, Alberta, Canada T6G 2E5; or at 41 Trent Road, Oakham, Rutland LE15 6HE, UK.

The Contributors

John Bayley is Warton Professor of English Literature at Oxford and a Fellow of St Catherine's College. His books include *The Romantic Survival* (1956), *The Characters of Love* (1961), *The Uses of Division* (1976) and *An Essay on Hardy* (1978).

Lennart A. Björk is Professor of English at the University of Stockholm and editor of *The Literary Notes of Thomas Hardy*.

Peter J. Casagrande is Professor of English at the University of Kansas. He is the author of *Unity in Hardy's Novels* (1982) and of many articles on Hardy.

Peter W. Coxon is a lecturer in the Department of Hebrew and Old Testament at the University of St Andrews. He has published widely on Semitic philology and Biblical criticism, and his interest in the nineteenth-century novel has resulted in several articles on Hardy.

P. N. Furbank is Reader in English at the Open University. He is general editor of the New Wessex Edition of Hardy's novels and has published a selection of Hardy's poems. His other books include *Samuel Butler, 1835–1902* (1948), *Reflections on the Word 'Image'* (1970), *Italo Svevo: The Man and the Writer* (1966), and *E. M. Forster: A Life* (1977–8).

John Lucas is Professor of English at Loughborough University of Technology. His books include *Arnold Bennett* (1974), *The Literature of Change: Studies in the Nineteenth-Century Provincial Novel* (1977), and *The Melancholy Man: A Study of Dickens' Novels* (1970). He has also edited *Literature and Politics in the Nineteenth Century* (1971) and *The 1930s* (1978).

The Contributors

Juliet McMaster is Professor of English at the University of Alberta. Her books include *Thackeray: The Major Novels* (1971) and *Trollope's Palliser Novels: Theme and Pattern* (1978), and she is the editor of *Jane Austen's Achievement* (1976).

Tom Paulin is Lecturer in English at the University of Nottingham. He has published *Thomas Hardy: The Poetry of Perception* (1975) as well as various collections of verse, including *The Strange Museum* (1980).

Arthur Pollard is Professor of English at the University of Hull. He has published *Mrs Gaskell* (1965), *Charlotte Brontë* (1968), *Satire* (1970) and *Anthony Trollope* (1978), and has edited *Crabbe: The Critical Heritage* (1972) and (with J. A. V. Chapple) *The Letters of Mrs Gaskell* (1966).

Rosemary Sumner is Principal Lecturer at the University of London Goldsmiths' College. She is the author of *Thomas Hardy: Psychological Novelist* (1981).

Richard H. Taylor is Senior Lecturer in English at the University of London Institute of Education, currently on secondment to the University Teaching Methods Unit. He is the author of *The Neglected Hardy* (1982) and the editor of *The Personal Notebooks of Thomas Hardy* (1978). He is currently at work on a bibliography of Hardy criticism.

Merryn Williams was formerly a Lecturer in English at the Open University. She is the author of *Thomas Hardy and Rural England* (1972) and of *A Preface to Hardy* (1976), and has edited *Revolutions, 1775–1830* (1971).

Christopher Wiseman is Professor of English at the University of Calgary and has published poetry and criticism, including *Beyond the Labyrinth: A Study of Edwin Muir's Poetry* (1978).

Editor's Introduction

Hardy once said that, although he was not a best-seller, he was a long-seller. It is true that he published no book that had the instant and prodigious success of, say, Mrs Humphry Ward's *Robert Elsmere*, which appeared one year later than *The Woodlanders*; but, half a century after his death, while Mrs Humphry Ward and her works are almost forgotten, his popularity stands higher than ever – at least if one can judge by paperback reprints, television serials, fan clubs, tourist publicity, and other manifestations of widely diverse kinds, including such unlikely phenomena as a map of Hardy's Wessex distributed gratis by a generous brewer and the recent alliance of Hardy's talents with those of Mr Roman Polanski. In the week in which I write these words, I have chanced to come across a publisher's announcement of a new and lavishly illustrated selection of Hardy's poems; some references to his novels in Q. D. Leavis's lecture on 'The Englishness of the English Novel'; a poem by Brian Aldiss titled 'Thomas Hardy Considers the Newly-Published Special Theory of Relativity' (*The Times Literary Supplement*, 25 September 1981); and a review of a recent novel, Philip Rock's *Circles of Time*, in which a character suffering from shell-shock is cured by reading the poems of Hardy – four quite different and not altogether predictable manifestations of the wide currency now enjoyed by Hardy's work and by what he is seen as having stood for. Not long ago a survey of sixth-formers' tastes in books showed Hardy to be top of the list; and while such surveys may invite insincerity, the result is so striking as not to be easily discounted.[1] Hardy, it is clear, is too big to belong only to the academic establishment; if there are great writers who are kept alive by being studied rather than by being read, Hardy is not one of them. His work continues to possess a life – a vitality that, in Johnsonian phrase, preserves it from putrefaction – quite independent of the classroom and the seminar, the learned journal and the examination paper.

And yet Hardy belongs to the scholars and critics too; and *they* are showing nowadays a livelier interest in him than ever before. The rehabilitation of Hardy as novelist and poet is one of the most remarkable examples of the way in which the map of modern literature has been redrawn in the last generation or so. Venerated in his later years as Grand Old Man of letters, and assigned the reassuring role of countryman-sage, with one eye fixed on the boundless universe and the other on the darkling thrush, Hardy suffered a posthumous decline in reputation that is the common fate of widely-loved authors. Speaking for myself, so far as I recall I read no Hardy at school except for a poem or two in anthologies; and when I was an undergraduate thirty years ago I do not remember anyone lecturing on Hardy; there was, it is true, a young schoolmaster called Douglas Brown who was said to be writing a book on him, but it seemed a distinctly odd thing to be doing. A rough seismographic record of the convulsions of critical or at least academic taste is provided by the periodic variations in the author prescribed for special study in Part II of the English Tripos at Cambridge. Thirty years ago it was George Eliot; somewhat later it was Dickens; in 1981 it was Thomas Hardy.

It is in this context, popular and academic, that the *Thomas Hardy Annual* has been established. As Richard Taylor's bibliography in the present volume makes abundantly clear, a vast amount of material, on a great variety of topics and on different levels of sophistication, is now being published every year on Hardy, who promises (or threatens) to rival Dickens one of these days as the most-written-about novelist in the English language. (Who would have guessed, for instance, that in the short period surveyed no fewer than twenty-five separate items on *Jude the Obscure* appeared, not to mention numerous discussions of the same novel in books devoted to Hardy?) Much of this material is in relatively out-of-the-way publications, not always readily accessible to those who might wish to read it; periodicals, too, are often forced to impose strict limits on length. The *Annual* will be hospitable to a wide variety of approaches to Hardy and to contributions ranging from notes and queries, reviews and short articles, to substantial essays and even monographs. It aims to be international in scope (this opening volume includes the work of scholars of several countries) and to make available some of the best of the current scholarship and criticism devoted to Hardy.

In the present volume are brought together a group of essays that exemplify between them a great variety of approaches. Peter J. Casagrande assesses some of the trends in Hardyan biography – a field in which there has recently been considerable, and often controversial, activity. Arthur Pollard offers a critique of the influential sociological approach to Hardy. Merryn Williams examines Hardy's handling of 'the woman question' against the background of other contemporary writings, once widely read and eagerly debated but now largely forgotten, on the same topic. The essays by John Bayley and Rosemary Sumner commemorate the first appearance of *Two on a Tower* exactly one hundred years ago (it was serialized in the Boston magazine *Atlantic Monthly* from May to December 1882 and appeared in volume form in October of that year); it is to be hoped that their discussions will find new readers for this curious and haunting story, and will prompt those who have read it and found it wanting to give it, and themselves, another chance.[2] Tom Paulin analyses the metrical delicacy of Hardy's verse, and pleads that it should above all be *listened to*. Peter W. Coxon shows the extraordinary frequency and prominence of Hardy's references to what his contemporaries would no doubt have referred to as a woman's crowning glory. Lennart A. Björk describes and illustrates his ongoing work on Hardy's notebooks – and in doing so provides a glimpse into the writer's workshop and the processes of the creative mind. John Lucas's essay is the first of what will become a series of revaluations or reconsiderations of works of Hardy criticism or scholarship that have been widely influential, Professor Lucas's starting-point being Donald Davie's *Thomas Hardy and British Poetry*, first published in 1973. Other features planned to reappear in future volumes will be reviews of recent books and a Hardy bibliography and survey, the latter to be regularly contributed by Richard H. Taylor. As indicated elsewhere, contributions for future volumes of the *Annual* will be warmly welcomed, and I shall also be grateful to receive from readers any suggestions relating to the *Annual*.

My thanks are due to Dame Janet Vaughan for kind permission to print three letters written to Hardy by her grandfather, John Addington Symonds, and previously unpublished; to Charles Tomlinson for permission to quote his poem 'On the Hall at Stowey' from his collection *Seeing is Believing*, published by Oxford University Press; and to Routledge & Kegan Paul Ltd, for permission to quote Donald Davie's 'Thanks to Industrial Essex' from *Essex Poems* (1969). I should also like to acknowledge the invaluable work done in connection with this volume by Paul Kelly, the very model of a research assistant. Those irresistibly tempted to punning by the title of this volume may like to know that 'Thomas Hardy Annual' is also the title of an etching by Graham Clarke that depicts Hardy's birthplace (I owe this information to Professor Lloyd Siemens).

Since editions of Hardy's novels are now proliferating rapidly, quotations are identified by chapter number rather than by page number. All references to Hardy's autobiography, originally published in two volumes, are to the single-volume edition, *The Life of Thomas Hardy 1840–1928* (London: Macmillan, 1962), designated throughout as *Life*.

NOTES

1. Hardy's score as a novelist was 194, beating Jane Austen (165) as well as D. H. Lawrence (158); as a poet, he did conspicuously less well (24 votes), being beaten not only by Eliot (104) and Wordsworth (69) but by Dylan Thomas (39) and Philip Larkin (28).
2. Among earlier critics A. J. Guerard, Harold Child and Irving Howe have some good things to say about *Two on a Tower*; Douglas Brown finds it 'the best of the lesser novels' but accords it only seven lines. Most recent critics pay little or no attention to 'the lesser novels', so that Richard Taylor's recent study of them – the first of its kind – is long overdue.

N.P.

'Old Tom and New Tom': Hardy and His Biographers

Peter J. Casagrande

> I am more than ever convinced that persons are successively various persons, according as each special strand in their characters is brought uppermost by circumstances.
> Thomas Hardy, 4 December 1890.

I

No one has ever pretended that the biographer's art is anything but one of the most difficult. And its particular difficulty probably lies, as Paul Murray Kendall has said, with its need to achieve authenticity, an elusive quality that stems not just from what the biographer gives his reader, but from what he persuades his reader to accept. No one has ever found Thomas Hardy an easy subject for biography. The efforts of life-writers from Frank A. Hedgcock in 1911 to Robert Gittings in 1975–8 have been made difficult both by Hardy's notorious secretiveness and by a deceptive simplicity in his make-up. He is apparently a man difficult to come to know, or better, a man easy to mistake. So in Hardy's case, perhaps more than in most, an authentic portrait must do more than uncover all the available facts. And it must do more than arrange those facts so as to serve a particular view of Hardy. It must persuade its readers to accept the view set forth. In this, the attitude of the biographer toward his subject is all important. If he writes with clinical detachment, he may sacrifice his reader's sympathy. If he writes with partisan ardour, he may sacrifice his reader's trust. The best approach for a biographer then, especially the biographer of so elusive a man as Thomas Hardy, may well be the charitable one – the approach that forgives at the same time that it dissects, the approach that asserts and judges at the same time that it allows that some things in the personality of a man or a woman, especially a man or a woman of genius, are bound to remain a mystery. This same charity, but in the form of respect, can be extended to the subject's opinions about himself, or in the case of a novelist and poet like Hardy, to the elements of self-depiction in his writings. Though the biographer will beware of reading back into the artist's life from the self-probings of his art, he *can* consult his subject's autobiographical writings. He can attempt to discern both his subject's changing sense and his changing use of himself and certain of his experiences. A writer's perceptions of himself are at least as important as the perceptions of him of those around him. A critical reverence, a slightly sceptical affection and respect, a certain humility, a willingness to listen to what his subject has said or projected of himself – is that not what one finds in the best of modern biographers, in an Edel, a Troyat, an Ellmann, or a Haight?

It seems to be so, and it seems also, at least to this reader, that not enough of these things are to be found in Robert Gittings' recent life of Thomas Hardy.[1] Although Gittings' portrait is new and in some of its details revelatory, it is "inauthentic" because unbalanced and incomplete in a way it need not be, even when it is judged strictly on its own terms. The problem can be stated briefly in the following way: Gittings is strongly critical of Hardy at the same time that he is strangely silent about the acuity and persistence of Hardy's self-criticism. Gittings unveils a troubled and difficult personality, points out with varying degrees of completeness the presence of similarly troubled personages in a number of the novels and poems, but then fails to take a next, and logical, step – to show how and perhaps why Hardy frequently used his novels and poems as instruments of self-study, and self-censure. If Gittings had taken this second step, wholly appropriate within the premises guiding his study, he might well have portrayed Hardy as a troubled man and artist struggling toward an emotional maturity he only partially achieved and toward an artistic maturity (as poet) he completely achieved, rather than as a "perpetual adolescent" without, in Edward Clodd's regrettable phrase, "largeness of soul" (*The Older Hardy*, pp. 66, 211).

Perhaps one explanation is that Gittings simply dislikes Hardy – for his alleged snobbishness, for his "peasant" origins, for his agnosticism, for his nympholept's attraction to women, and in particular for what Gittings describes as a persistent heartlessness toward his wives. This seems possible, though it is unlikely that a biographer of Gittings' stature would succumb to bias of this kind.[2] What seems probable is that Gittings' censoriousness is one result of the fact that his life of Hardy is in several important ways strongly revisionary. First, it is an attempt to correct and complete Hardy's evasive self-portrait in *The Early Life* (1928) and *Later Years* (1930), the autobiography that Hardy arranged to have written and published as though it were a life of him by his second wife, Florence. Secondly, Gittings' life is a startling departure from Carl J. Weber's hagiographic *Hardy of Wessex* (1940; revised edition 1965). Gittings is as insistently critical as Weber was insistently eulogistic, and one important result of this is that Gittings, in censuring Hardy, finds frequent occasion to praise, even champion, Emma and Florence, Hardy's wives; so that we gain from Gittings not just a new view of Hardy, but of his wives as well, and particularly of Emma.[3] Finally, Gittings' portrait corrects if it does not wholly rebut Lois Deacon's account of Hardy, *Providence and Mr Hardy* (1966), as a man and artist tormented during much of his career by guilt over an incestuous liaison with a first cousin (perhaps a niece) named Tryphena Sparks.

Gittings' portrait is indeed revisionary, and if it can be said to be somewhat out of focus, it if tends too relentlessly to give us Hardy at his worst, if it too frequently neglects the achievements of the self-critical artist in its zeal to show the failures of the man, it is perhaps because he was in reaction against both Hardy's disguised self-portrait and Weber's saint's-life. And yet, Gittings' critical view of Hardy is not without precedent. Not only the fundamentally reductive portrait by Lois Deacon but also many of the seventy-two *Illustrated Monographs on the Life, Times, and Works of Thomas Hardy*, edited and published by J. Stevens Cox between 1962 and 1971, can be seen as antecedents for Gittings' debunking life. The *Monographs* are undoubtedly a hodge-podge, running the gamut from serious scholarship to local gossip, and constituting, in the words of George Wing in the last of them, "a valuable, if a curious and slightly fey, biographical addendum to existing biographies".[4] Though vastly more erudite than most of the *Monographs*, Gittings' view has many roots in the generally unflattering view of Hardy that emerged bit by bit in the *Monographs* between 1962 and 1971.[5] There can be little doubt that the diminished and unheroic Thomas Hardy extracted from interviews with his servants, his barber, his physician, and with other associates in Dorchester is nearer the difficult and troubled Hardy of Gittings' portrait than the retiring and noble Hardy of Weber's, where he is called, among other highly complimentary things, 'one of the great spiritual leaders of the modern world.'[6]

Reviewers of Gittings' life have agreed almost unanimously that he has painted a new Thomas Hardy, a snobbish, ambitious, devious, morbid, stingy, sexually troubled Thomas Hardy, a Thomas Hardy cruelly insensitive to the wants and needs of both his wives.[7] Some reviewers accept this view of Hardy, some do not; but all find it amply documented.

No one, at least to date, has been able to refute or substantially alter it. Bernard Bergonzi's somewhat tongue-in-cheek review (*Observer*, 5 March 1978) is fairly representative:

> Mr Gittings provides a sober, compelling, even-handed narrative; if it has a somewhat lowering effect, that is because he does not try to hide Hardy's less agreeable personal characteristics. Hardy appears here as a perpetual adolescent. Throughout his life he was falling rapidly in and out of love, increasingly with fashionable literary ladies. This in itself may have been an engaging characteristic, but it caused much irritation and some grief to Emma Hardy, whom he treated with steady neglect, not even dedicating a book to her. . . . Hardy had not only an adolescent's susceptibility but also an adolescent's insensitivity and self-centredness. After Emma's death, of course, he made magnificent reparation in the great poems of 1912–13, expressing his depth of grief and regret and renewed love. But when he was writing them he was compromisingly involved with Florence Dugdale, 39 years his junior, who became the second Mrs. Hardy in 1914. She, understandably, was disturbed by this flare-up of posthumous passion for her predecessor. Hardy undoubtedly loved Florence, but once they were married she was treated with similar lack of consideration. Her health was poor and when she had to undergo a disagreeable operation on her nose Hardy let her pay the surgeon's and nursing home fees out of her personal savings. After many years of literary success he was wealthy, but he habitually displayed what Mr. Gittings calls a "peasant meanness". After Hardy's death, Edward Clodd, who had been a friend for many years, wrote, "he was a great author: he was not a great man; there was no largeness of soul".[8]

Clodd's phrase, "no largeness of soul", echoes through Gittings' second volume like the death-knell of the noble, courageous, and generous Thomas Hardy of Carl Weber's portrait of thirty-five years before. Gittings seems as intent on deflating Hardy as Weber was on elevating him, and though one might wish for something else, there seems little doubt that Gittings is often close to something like the unvarnished truth. Gittings has dug more deeply than any previous biographer, and students of Hardy are heavily in his debt. And yet, as suggested in my opening remarks, Gittings cannot, finally, persuade because he has not gone far enough along his own line of analysis; he has failed to see or chosen to ignore Hardy's serious and persistent efforts at critical self-portraiture, both in certain of the novels and poems and in the *Life*.

For example, Hardy understood himself well enough, and was candid enough, to state in the *Life* that he was late to develop in "virility" and that this lateness of sexual development was "a clue to much of his character and action" throughout his life.[9] Though Gittings notes this clue and develops its implications quite convincingly as one of the governing factors of Hardy's temperament and in particular of his attitude toward women, he says nothing about the significance of Hardy's awareness of it or of Hardy's willingness to speak of it, especially in so cautious a document as the *Life*. Similarly, Gittings seems not to see that in many of the novels and poems Hardy was carrying on close, critical study of himself in terms much like those he used, so unexpectedly, in the early pages of the *Life*. It would seem worth exploring the possibility that the intimate revelation Hardy allowed to break surface in the highly discreet *Life* is related to certain elements of self-portraiture in the novels and poems.

In the novels, for example, are to be found a series of important characters, all arguably author-figures, who are precocious in intellect, hampered in their sexuality, and – this goes beyond the portrait in the *Life* – often cruelly fastidious in love as a result. I refer in particular to Henry Knight of *A Pair of Blue Eyes*, Clym Yeobright of *The Return of the Native*, Angel Clare of *Tess of the d'Urbervilles*, Sue Bridehead of *Jude the Obscure*, and Jocelyn Pierston of *The Well-Beloved*. What Hardy, speaking of himself in the *Life*, called "immaturity" and "lateness of development in virility" is a salient characteristic of these important figures in his fiction.[10] Henry Knight is, we are told, "not shaped by Nature for a marrying man" (*A Pair of Blue Eyes*, Ch. 30). Clym Yeobright remains, to the end of his story, tragically divided between a mature man's love for a passionate wife and a boy's rebellious devotion to his mother. Angel Clare, seeking in Tess a way of recovering his own lost purity, cannot forgive her impurity, abandons her, then returns too late in forgiveness. Sue Bridehead, a woman at once frigid and flirtatious, is driven to self-loathing by marriage and motherhood. Jocelyn Pierston loves an Ideal that he pursues from mother, to daughter, to granddaughter, much as Thomas Hardy, according to Gittings, loved in sequence his maternal cousins, Martha, Rebecca, and Tryphena Sparks, all of whom resembled his mother, Jemima. Elfride Swancourt, Tess Durbeyfield, Jude Fawley, Eustacia Vye, and the Caros pursued by Jocelyn Pierston are, in different ways, victims of a peculiar kind of idealist, a desperately nostalgic man (or woman) who looks to the beloved for a lost truth and beauty associated with childhood and its innocence. It seems altogether reasonable to suggest, on the evidence of this self-scrutiny, that if Hardy did not develop "in virility" until after 1890, it was because he had not until after 1890 completed the tortuous trek toward maturity worked out in part through the partial self-portraits in Knight, Yeobright, Clare, and Pierston.[11]

The fruit of this process of self-scrutiny between the ages of about thirty and fifty-five, of this attempt to understand through his art the consequences of late sexual development, is not simply a portrait of the troubled artist. First of all, there is the outpouring of poetry that came hard on the heels of the revision of *The Well-Beloved*. Second, and nearer our concern here, there are Hardy's greatest characters – not the sexually inhibited Knight, Yeobright, Clare, and Sue Bridehead, but their partners in love and therefore their victims – Elfride, Eustacia, Jude, and especially Tess. If *Tess of the d'Urbervilles* is Hardy's greatest novel and its heroine his greatest achievement in character-creation, may that not be because she is the fullest embodiment of Hardy's understanding of the human consequences of a defect (Angel Clare's in the novel) much like his own? And if this is so, that is, if Hardy's greatest fiction stems at least in part from his perception of the possible consequences for humanity of human defects like his own, then are we not, as we read his novels and think about his life, in the presence of something quite other than a man without "largeness of soul"? Hardy's soul may have been without "largeness", but it was also, if my suggestion that his art is simultaneously self-critical and altruistic is at all correct, a soul that strove for largeness. The inhumanity and pettiness of the man seem to be the sources of the humane sympathy of the art. The diminished Hardy we find in Gittings', Deacon's, and the *Monographs'* accounts did not write *Tess of the d'Urbervilles*. A man and novelist striving against his defects, a man wretched in his way but striving against his wretchedness by projecting the tragic mischief of his own defect, by turning it to art, wrote *Tess of the d'Urbervilles* – and *Jude the Obscure*, *The Mayor of Casterbridge*, and *The Return of the Native* – and then, a personal and creative equanimity having been achieved, *The Dynasts* and the eight volumes of poems. Hardy reached maturity, one suspects, when he became what he said he had always wanted to be, a poet. A responsible biographer will avoid of course the fallacy of inferring the man from the artist's partial self-portraits, but he surely will not wish to ignore the help in understanding the man to be derived from those self-portraits.

Gittings indeed recognizes the connections between Hardy and some of his people: the resemblance (mentioned by Hardy himself) between Henry Knight and Hardy; the tie between "intolerable" personal strain and "the disoriented nature of all the actors" in *The Return*; the origin of *Tess* and *Jude* in "a remote yet intimate past, of people, events, and family traits"; the origin of *The Well-Beloved* in Hardy's sense of his own artistic constitution.[12] Gittings can even mention something he calls Hardy's "penetrating power of self-knowledge or self-criticism''. But he does not work to connect the two things: the penetrating power of self-criticism and the frequency of critical self-portraiture. In fact, on at least one notable occasion, he makes what seems to be a pointed attempt to belittle Hardy's efforts.

I have in mind his discussion of Hardy's poem "Surview", a poetic self-study that illustrates in clear and deeply moving terms the alternation in Hardy between self-criticism and human sympathy I have described. I quote the poem in full, along with Gittings' remarks on it:

> A cry from the green-grained sticks of the fire
>   Made me gaze where it seemed to be:
> 'Twas my own voice talking therefrom to me
> On how I had walked when my sun was higher –
>   My heart in its arrogancy.
> '*You held not to whatsoever was true*,'
>   Said my own voice talking to me:
> '*Whatsoever was just you were slack to see*;
> *Kept not things lovely and pure in view*,'
>   Said my own voice talking to me.
> '*You slighted her that endureth all*,'
>   Said my own voice talking to me;
> '*Vaunteth not, trusteth hopefully*;
> *That suffereth long and is kind withal*,'
>   Said my own voice talking to me.
> '*You taught not that which you set about*,'
>   Said my own voice talking to me;
> '*That the greatest of things is charity* . . .'
> – And the sticks burnt low, and the fire went out,
>   And my voice ceased talking to me.

The poem is an unwavering self-indictment. Leaning heavily on the language of St Paul, and echoing passages from his own *Tess* and *Jude*,[13] Hardy exhibits his "own voice" condemning his failure to teach what he had "set about" teaching: truth, justice, "things lovely and pure", and most important, charity. He depicts himself a failed moral teacher and a hypocrite. He makes no excuse, only marks his failure through arrogance to value and to do what a part of him insists he ought to have valued and done. "Surview" is not an isolated instance of critical self-scrutiny. In the "Poems of 1912–13" he depicts himself an uncharitable, unfeeling husband, in "The Impercipient" a man perversely unable to share the beliefs of his fellows, in "Dead Man Walking", "Wessex Heights", and the "In Tenebris" poems a man "shaped awry". In each of these poems, as in the novels mentioned above, one finds confession of personal weakness without apology, self-censure untainted by self-pity or masochism. One finds Hardy trying to see and to present a version of himself not unlike the Thomas Hardy, troubled and difficult, that Gittings helps us to see. One wonders at times if Gittings does not derive his critical sense of Hardy from Hardy's critical sense of himself. It is difficult to say, but it is clear that Gittings places little or no value on, even actively distrusts, Hardy's unselfpitying self-portraiture. His lack of sympathy with Hardy's effort to project the worst in himself, an effort at work in some of Hardy's most important novels and poems, is clear from the slanted language of his remarks on "Surview":

> Hardy, for all the tortuous deceptions of his outward life, was seldom anything but honest in poetry. Stress of poetic utterance forced the truth from him. As he approached the final stages of the book [*Late Lyrics and Earlier*, 1922], he faced the problem of which poem to put last. . . . Mean or even uncharitable as many of his recent actions were, he had not lost the penetrating power of self-knowledge, or self-criticism. He could realize in poetry what he would not admit in life. In a mood only approached by W. B. Yeats, in his old age, Hardy faced himself and his betrayals [and described his own hypocrisy]. He used an image centred on the cottage fireside, now more real to him than any other scene. He recalled his mother's saying, as the green and wet wood sighed and muttered in the flames, that it was his own voice talking to him. The primitive fancy, together with that other childhood echo, the resounding texts of the New Testament, mingled into the message of humility that spanned his experience, as he comprehended it in the title of the poem, "Surview".

Gittings' acknowledgement that Hardy was capable of self-knowledge and self-criticism occurs too late in his biography (the second-from-last chapter of the second volume) to change very much the portrait he has built up of Hardy as a strange, morbid, gloomy, habitually deceptive, obsessive, and mean individual.[14] In fact, that negative view intrudes even here, though he seems inclined to praise Hardy, in the weighted language of the first five sentences quoted above: "tortuous deceptions of his outward life", "seldom anything but honest in poetry", "forced the truth out of him", "mean or even uncharitable as many of his recent actions were", "what he would not admit in life". This is hardly the language of a disinterested observer, and its presence here, where Gittings seems inclined to soften some of his previous harshnesses, prevents him from providing the important insight that his tough-minded approach can offer – that Thomas Hardy was not merely a mean and uncharitable man, not merely a man without "largeness of soul", but rather, as "Surview" suggests in its portrait of the poet calling himself to account, that more complex, that really human thing – an at times mean and uncharitable man who saw his shortcomings and, most important, understood their strength. That is, Hardy not only recognized his faults, he understood their irresistible authority. Though he did not find them incapacitating, he did find them incurable, and his acceptance of the incurable in himself made him the tragic visionary he was. If he had been capable of being a better man, he might well have been a quite different kind of writer, perhaps one with a taste for happy endings. And though we can only wish he had been kinder and gentler to his wives, we cannot but take him as we find him, and try to understand him as a man who saw his own imperfections, who knew that "he kept not things lovely and pure in view", and who found it necessary to commit to his art that incurably defective nature he believed he had been dealt. "O doth a bird deprived of wings go earthbound wilfilly"? That agonized question by the unbelieving poet in "The Impercipient" might well be Hardy's question about his own capacity to hold to the true, the pure, and the beautiful. Hardy wanted to be a better man than he found himself at the same time that he believed he possessed an unalterably defective character.

The view a reader is probably left with upon completing Gittings' life is something like this: "Although Hardy sometimes told the truth about himself, he was usually mean, deceptive, and uncharitable, a man without 'largeness of soul'." But the view can more sensibly, and I think more fruitfully, be this: "Although Hardy was frequently mean-minded and uncharitable, he depicted repeatedly in his novels and poems, with a 'penetrating power of self-knowledge', the plight of persons victimized by the mean and emotionally troubled persons who love them." For the truth seems to be that Hardy kept before his readers, and before himself, the plight of unfortunates led to ruin by persons much like the poet of "Surview", much like the Thomas Hardy of Gittings' portrait. Surely it is possible to approach Hardy with some of the charity he tells us he himself did not practise. Surely it is not necessary to deny him the charity he allegedly denied others in order to catch a glimpse of his troubled personality. And is not this very much the request of the poet in "The Impercipient", in which the speaker wishes that he, an unbeliever surrounded by believers, were treated with more charity than the believers whose love-centred faith he has been *denied* seem able to muster on his behalf: "Since heart of mine knows not that ease / Which they know; since it be / That he who breathes All's Well to these / Breathes no All's-Well to me / My lack might move their sympathies / And Christian charity!".[15]

A satisfactory account of the self-probing, self-critical, and self-creating Thomas Hardy remains to be written. I do not pretend to write it here, but rather to try to show, in the remarks that follow, why it is an account of Hardy that deserves to be written. These remarks fall naturally into two parts. First, I will give a brief account of eight biographical studies of Hardy written between 1910 and 1971, including a selection from some revealing notes Hardy made in the margins of his personal copies of the three earliest of these lives. Attention will be given to (1) F. A. Hedgcock's *Thomas Hardy: Pensuer et Artiste* (1911); (2) Ernest Brennecke's *Life of Thomas Hardy* (1925); (3) Samuel Chew's *Thomas Hardy* (1921); (4) Florence Hardy's *Early Life* (1928) and *Later Years* (1930); (5) Carl J. Weber's *Hardy of Wessex* (1940; revd. 1965); (6) Evelyn Hardy's *Thomas Hardy: A Critical Biography* (1955); (7) the *Monographs on the Life, Times, and Works of Thomas Hardy*, ed. J. Stevens Cox (1962–71); and (8) Lois Deacon and Terry Coleman's *Providence and Mr Hardy* (1966).[16] Secondly, and with reference mainly to Gittings' *Young Thomas Hardy* (1975) and *Thomas Hardy's Later Years* (1978), I will discuss the self-elaborating impulse in the novels. I shall give particular attention in the discussion of Gittings and of the earlier biographers to their handling of *The Return of the Native*, both because it was for Hardy a truly pivotal novel and for other reasons that will emerge, the most important being that Gittings, I believe, neglects it because the presence of critical self-portraiture in it contradicts his view of Hardy as a "perpetual adolescent" of deceiving ways. If Hardy is somehow incurably adolescent, it may well be in his capacity for covert self-criticism, the expression of a profound uncertainty about the self rooted in what he himself described as a late sexual development. It is the assumption throughout that Hardy's extreme sensitivity to biographical speculation was caused not just by snobbishness, guilt, or deviousness, as has usually been argued, but also by his strong wish to preserve the integrity of the autobiographical drama he knew to be central to his writing of fiction.

II

Though the first book-length life of Hardy, Ernest Brennecke's *Life of Thomas Hardy*, was not published until 1925, three years before its subject's death, biographical speculation had been a prominent, for Hardy a distressingly prominent, element of reviews of his books from the very beginning. From the moment in 1871 when a review of *Desperate Remedies* in the *Spectator* made him wish himself dead, to his angry turn from pastoral romance in 1874 because a reviewer thought *Far From the Maddening Crowd* might be the work of a house-decorator, to his even more angry turn in 1896 from prose fiction to poetry because of attacks on *Jude the Obscure*, to his deathbed epithets aimed at George Moore and G. K. Chesterton, Hardy responded to criticism that touched on his personality with a peculiar animus. In what was probably the last piece of critical prose he ever wrote, the introduction to *Winter Words* (1928), he is found to be as bitter towards those he there called "licensed tasters" as he had been fifty-seven years before. The note with which Florence Hardy prefaced the *Early Life* reveals the same uneasiness:

> Mr. Hardy's feeling for a long time was that he would not care to have his life written at all. And though often asked to record his recollections he would say that he 'had not sufficient admiration for himself' to do so. But later, having observed many erroneous and grotesque statements advanced as his experiences, and a so-called 'Life' [probably Ernest Brennecke's *Life*] published as authoritative, his hand was forced, and he agreed to my strong request that the facts of his career should be set down for use in the event of its proving necessary to print them (*Life*, p. vii).

What this preface does not reveal, of course, is that the *Early Life* and *Later Years* (perhaps this preface as well) are almost entirely the work of Hardy, even though Florence Hardy's name appears on the title page as author.[17] By using Florence as his narrator, so to speak, Hardy wrote a most discreet account of himself. He merely hinted at his modest beginnings as the son, conceived out of wedlock, of a rural stonemason and a woman who had been a charity-child and for a time a servant; at his troubled relations with women and his hampered sexuality; at his unhappy first marriage. Peering out from behind his spokeswoman – in a relationship reminiscent of his relationship to the third-person narrators of the novels – he could present the Thomas Hardy he at the time wished to present, an unambitious and retiring man born to write poetry, then diverted from his calling by a career in architecture and another in fiction-writing, but finally fulfilling his dream and coming to maturity as the author of *The Dynasts* and eight volumes of poems.

But before Hardy could play his own Boswell, before he could erect a public self that would enable him to go on chiselling away at a private one, the critics were about him again, and this time with real vigour. Books by a French scholar, Frank A. Hedgcock, and by two Americans, Ernest Brennecke, Jr, and Samuel C. Chew, confirmed Hardy's worst fears of biographical intrusion. Hedgcock's *Thomas Hardy: Penseur et Artiste*, first published in Paris in 1911, was being considered for translation and publication by Oxford University Press in 1922, and Hardy dreaded it. Chew's *Thomas Hardy: Poet and Novelist* appeared in 1921, Brennecke's *Life of Thomas Hardy* four years later. These are books we might well set aside as limited in scope and method if we were not furtunate enough to have Hardy's copies of them, complete with his written comments in the margins, in the Hardy Memorial Library of the Dorset County Museum. In the margins of the three books, in his neat, draftsman's hand, Hardy wrote down his angry objections to the probing commentaries on his life and art he found there. Though space permits mention of only a few of these remarks, it is possible to see from them that Hardy's greatest fear was that his personality and character would be inferred from the words and acts of figures in the novels thought to resemble their author. At the same time, however, he can be found capitulating – almost against his will – to his biographical critics' demonstration that self-portraiture played a large part in his fiction. It must be remembered in this that during the period 1921–5, when Hardy read and dissected Hedgcock, Chew, and Brennecke, he had been at work for some five years on his own carefully wrought version of himself in the *Early Life* and *Later Years*. His most ambitious effort at self-portraiture (and self-concealment) was suddenly in jeopardy. Here are some of his remarks (six of a total of twenty-six) in the margins of Hedgcock's book:

(1) On page 1 he wrote, "Note: Biographical details imagined from details in the novels, and gathered from newspapers, are *mostly wrong*" (italics mine).
(2) On page 17, where Hedgcock suggests that Hardy might have drawn on his own experience as an architectural draftsman for characters like Owen Graye of *Desperate Remedies* and Stephen Smith of *A Pair of Blue Eyes*, Hardy wrote "incorrect (both drawn from others)".
(3) On page 19, where Hedgcock suggests that Thomas Hardy, like Stephen Smith of *A Pair of Blue Eyes*, studied the classics by correspondence with a learned friend like Henry Knight of the novel, Hardy wrote: "misleading and invidious – and *mostly incorrect* – T. H. never learnt the classics by correspondence; or of any person like Knight – who was not drawn from any friend of his." (Italics mine;

note that Hardy wrote his marginalia in the third person, just as at this time he was writing his autobiography in the third person. He would later insist that these notes were not his but Florence Hardy's.)

(4) On page 29 of *Thomas Hardy: Penseur et Artiste*, in response to Hedgcock's statement that *Desperate Remedies* shows in Edward Springrove a growing distaste for architecture probably based on Hardy's own increasing distaste for it in the early 1870s, Hardy replied: "Fiction is here used as if it were about an author's life – *a quite unauthorized proceeding*" (italics mine).

(5) Hedgcock (p. 31) continues his argument that certain people and events in *A Pair of Blue Eyes* were drawn from Hardy's experiences, and to this Hardy objected at some length: "The same unwarranted assumption as before – Stephen Smith was drawn from another pupil – the personal description of him is not the least like Hardy. Stephen Smith's father is not at all like Thomas Hardy's (who was a journeyman) but was suggested by a workman in Cornwall. The whole page is *too knowing*, and is *somewhat impertinent and unmannerly in its personalities concerning a living writer*" (italics mine). To Hedgcock's extension of his argument to Clym Yeobright of *The Return of the Native*, Hardy objected even more vehemently: "All this is too personal, and in bad taste, even supposing it were true, which it is not. It is surprising that a good critic would print it. It betrays the cloven foot of the 'interviewer'." (Hedgcock had indeed interviewed Hardy, but some twenty years before, in 1910). Then again: ". . . These criticisms of the fictitious characters may be right enough: but to quiz the author through them is unmannerly" (pp. 33–4).

(6) Hedgcock's argument (p. 265) that *Jude the Obscure*, like *The Return of the Native*, *Desperate Remedies*, and *A Pair of Blue Eyes*, had its origins in personal experience, drew this response from Hardy: "In this page and onwards the arguments of the characters in *Jude* are often alluded to as if they were the author's. Of course, the author's bias is perceptible, but the characters' words should not in strictness be used as his own. The criticisms of this book much resemble those of reviewers when *Jude* appeared, but they have been abandoned by the best critics for many years."

As these six examples show, Hardy did *not* argue that Hedgcock was wholly wrong to connect details from his movels with details from his life. "Mostly wrong", "mostly incorrect", "misleading and invidious", or, less damningly, "quite unauthorized", "unwarranted", "impertinent and unmannerly", "too personal, and in bad taste" – these were the strongest denials he could make. In part, Hardy did not offer categorical denials because it must have been obvious to him, as to Hedgcock, that some aspects of himself and his experiences had indeed found their way into his novels – that Smith's and Graye's work in architecture resembled his, that Henry Knight resembled his friend and mentor, Horace Moule, if not himself, that the events of *Blue Eyes* recalled his courtship of Emma in Cornwall in 1870–3, that Clym Yeobright's dilemma resembled his own between 1873 and 1878. But Hardy makes more than a mere acknowledgement of resemblances in his replies to Hedgcock. Not only does he admit that his characters derive from actual persons, he also reveals a growing understanding that he had indeed put something of himself into his novels – perhaps more than he realized – for the strength of his denials wanes visibly between the first and the last note; so much so in fact that in the last (p. 265) he is found admitting that his biographer-critic is right after all: "Of course, the author's *bias* is perceptible, but the character's words should not *in strictness* be used as his own" (italics mine). If not "in strictness", then precisely how? In a highly perceptive passage unfortunately ignored by later biographers of Hardy, Hedgcock suggests how. He describes Springrove, Smith, and Yeobright as "three portraits of the same person, taken at three different periods" ("trois portraits de la même personne, pris à trois périodes différentes" [p. 34]); and as "three men marking the different stages through which Thomas Hardy passed between 20 and 30" ("ces trois hommes marquent les differentes étapes par lesquelles M. Hardy passa entre vingt et trente ans" [p. 35]). But Hedgcock went no further, either in his discussion of Hardy's life or his discussion of the novels of the 1870s. And his insight, validated in a sense by the qualifications in Hardy's objections to it, would not be taken up by later biographers, not even by those, like Carl Weber, Evelyn Hardy, and Robert Gittings, who would address themselves, in various ways, to autobiographical elements in the novels.

In a sense, then, Hedgcock had prevailed over his "critic". But Hardy's view as critic in this matter cannot be ignored. His fiction, his remarks suggest, is not a mere selection of facts from his experiences; it is a product of his "bias", and is by no means a simple or strict imitation of that "bias". This is consistent with his view, stated repeatedly in the 1880s and 1890s, that "the seer should watch that pattern among general things which his idiosyncrasy moves him to observe, and describe that alone", and that such a seer's art is "a changing of the actual proportions and order of things, so as to bring out more forcibly than might otherwise be done that feature in them that appeals most strongly to the idiosyncrasy of the artist . . ." (*Life*, pp. 153, 228–9). These often-quoted remarks are seldom viewed as

Hardy's defence of an autobiographical fiction, though in the present context they can plausibly be seen as such – as Hardy's attempt, characteristically cautious, to describe his peculiar way of being present in his fiction.

Samuel Chew's *Poet and Novelist*, complimentary, discerning, and in every way judicious, received from Hardy a welcome much like that given Hedgcock's *Penseur et Artiste*.[18] Hardy's note beside Chew's mention (p. 106) of Hedgcock's study – that Hedgcock made "errors of attribution in efforts to discern realities under fictional disguises" – marks the drift of his response to Chew. The word "disguises", however, may in fact be a slip on Hardy's part, for by using "disguises" (counterfeit semblances created for deception) where the word "guises" (semblances, appearances) is called for, Hardy seems unknowingly to admit what he will deny throughout his annotations to Chew – that his fiction "disguises" certain personal "realities". His perhaps unwitting use of "disguises" may suggest that though Hardy objected strongly to Chew's method, he could not, as he could not with Hedgcock, be brought to reject entirely Chew's conclusions. I have selected for illustration five (of a total of twenty-one) of Hardy's notes in Chew:

(1) To Chew's description of Hardy's father as a mastermason much like Stephen Smith's father in *A Pair of Blue Eyes*, Hardy responded: "His father was a small master-builder and mason, employing about half a dozen workmen – sometimes several more. His condition, etc., had no resemblance to Smith's father in 'A Pair of Blue Eyes', this being the invention of journalists" (p. 1).

(2) To Chew's statements (p. 8) that there is self-portraiture in Clym Yeobright, Angel Clare, and Jude Fawley, and to his suggestion that Horace Moule may have been the original for Henry Knight of *A Pair of Blue Eyes*, Hardy responded: "Quite inaccurate. There would have been no insuperable difficulty in his going to Cambridge, and it was discussed, but was thought unnecessary for an architect (Jude was a working man, not at all in Hardy's position)." Then, in response to Chew's remarks on Knight: "Quite inaccurate. Knight was an absolute invention.[19] S. Smith was drawn from a pupil 8 or 9 years younger than T. H., and 'A Pair of Blue Eyes' is only autobiographical as to some of the accessories at the beginning (after the first 2 or 3 chapters there is not a word of autobiography, even in accessories). It is only in the character of the heroine that there is some resemblance.[20] As for 'Jude the Obscure', there is not a word of autobiography in it."[21]

(3) To Chew's continued remarks on the autobiographical element in *A Pair of Blue Eyes*, Hardy responded waveringly (p. 8). As in his responses toward the end of Hedgcock's book, he seems to be willing to concede his biographical critic's point. Though he rejects the statement that in *A Pair of Blue Eyes* Smith's courting of Elfride is based on his courtship of Emma Gifford, he is willing to concede that Smith resembles him "in a few external adventures", though "not at all in person", a concession that must cast doubt on his note in *Penseur et Artiste* (p. 31) that "the personal description of [Smith] is not the least like Hardy".

(4) Hardy made yet another concession when, in response to Chew's suggestion that there may have been a Shakespearean source for the scene in the church-vault in Chapters 25 and 26 of *Blue Eyes*, he wrote: "The scene in the church-vault, whatever it may resemble, was drawn from one witnessed by Thomas Hardy when he was a boy of 15." If Hardy disliked biographical probing, he disliked even more any suggestion of plagiarism.

(5) At the beginning of Chew's discussion of *Jude the Obscure* (pp. 95ff.), Hardy wrote: "It may be mentioned here that as stated [on p. 8 of Chew] there is not a page of autobiography in this book as frequently asserted."

Hardy rejected Chew's study, as he had rejected Hedgcock's, because he found it established connections between him and certain of his characters; and yet his rejection is qualified, partial, self-contradictory, by no means absolute. As suggested above, through his biographical critics Hardy seemed to be discovering elements of self-portraiture in his novels that he did not know, or perhaps had forgotten, he had put there. Some years before, he had contemplated just such an exasperating possibility: "How strange that one may write a book without knowing what one puts into it – or rather, the reader reads into it" (*Life*, p. 246).

Brennecke's *Life of Thomas Hardy*, the closest thing to a full-blown biography among the three early studies, seems to have worried Hardy more than either Hedgcock's *Penseur et Artiste* or Chew's *Poet and Novelist*; and for good reason, for Ernest Brennecke, Jr, was ruthless in his determination to publish a life of Hardy. Hardy wrote to C. B. M. Childs in March 1925 to warn him against reading Brennecke's "large biography of me" as if "it were an authorized life". It is nothing, Hardy complained, but "a mass of unwarranted assumptions and errors that are at times ludicrous, and has been published in New York in the face of my protests against such an impertinence".[22] One can hardly blame Hardy for shrinking before the prospect of Brennecke's study, for this American scholar, already the author (in 1924) of a study of Hardy's philosophy titled *Thomas Hardy's Universe*, had ridden roughshod over all Hardy's protests against the projected life. Brennecke had interviewed Hardy in the summer of 1923, and a little over a year later, in October 1924, had asked Hardy for permission to publish a biographical sketch as an "authorized biography, at least so far as the main facts are concerned". Hardy's reply, via Florence and dated 1 November 1924, was strongly negative: "He cannot authorize anything in the nature of a biography of himself to be published." Hardy had refused a second time, in a telegram dated 24 January 1925, probably sent in response to another request from Brennecke: "Disapprove of biography altogether." But Hardy's refusal and disapproval only brought from Brennecke, surely one of the most persistent and, to use one of Hardy's favourite epithets for literary detectives, "impertinent" of men, a letter, dated 27 January 1925, expressing regret at Hardy's refusal to endorse the biography, and informing Hardy that though "a biography in the ordinary sense of the word" had not been written, a biography of Thomas Hardy was none the less in proof. As if this were not impertinence enough, in March 1925 Hardy received from Greenburg Publishers of New York not one but *two* books by Brennecke, one titled *The Life of Thomas Hardy*, and another, of which Hardy knew absolutely nothing, titled *Life and Art: By Thomas Hardy*. The former was the authorized life he had so dreaded, the latter a collection of Hardy's non-fictional prose, edited by Brennecke and destined to be the only collection of its kind for some forty years. Of *Life and Art*, Hardy, who by this time must have thought himself the victim of an international conspiracy, wrote to Childs in April 1925: "I have had no hand in compiling any such book, and know nothing of it, or its title, though the announcement reads as though it were a book by me published under my own direction." He remarked also that Macmillan had been thinking of publishing a similar collection as a part of a uniform edition of his works. Brennecke's manoeuvre undoubtedly did Hardy out of more than a few pounds.

As might be expected, Hardy scoured Brennecke's *Life* with blood in his eye. He wrote down sixty-seven objections of a substantial nature in the book's 260 pages, with the result that his copy of Brennecke's *Life* resembles nothing so much as an examination on the life and works of Thomas Hardy that the learned author has failed badly. Hardy seemed determined to correct every error, even the slightest. In addition to the usual objections to the association of him with his characters, there are many others.[23] Perhaps the most revealing (and humorous) was the note he jotted alongside Brennecke's account of how, during his visit with Hardy, Hardy had shown him his (Hardy's) heavily annotated copy of Hedgcock's *Penseur et Artiste*. Hardy was clearly trying to warn Brennecke against Hedgcock's biographical method, but Brennecke was equal to the occasion. "'Now here,' said Hardy, handing Brennecke Hedgcock's book, 'is a fellow who has written about me with some enthusiasm. Only he has gone to my novels instead of to *Who's Who* for his facts. He's been impertinent in spots, you see. We've corrected him; I've penciled some notes in his margins. Perhaps you'd care to look at them, if you're interested'" (p. 7). Brennecke obediently copied out several of Hardy's complaints against Hedgcock, at the same time muttering to himself, "A quaint preoccupation, this." At least this is Brennecke's account in his *Life of Thomas Hardy* of what occurred (probably in the summer of 1923). Hardy saw it in somewhat different terms by the time he got round to reading this episode in the same book some two years later. He wrote "garbled" in the margin beside it and probably winced under the satire in the circumstance that his attempt to discourage biographical criticism had somehow become part of yet another biography of him. He also denied telling Brennecke that he himself had written the notes in Hedgcock: "not written by T. H. but by Mrs H.," he scrawled. But the marginalia in Hedgcock's *Penseur et Artiste* and in Brennecke's *Life* (as well as in Chew's *Poet and Novelist*) are almost certainly Hardy's. He had merely disguised them as the third person commentary of Florence, just as he was, at this very time, disguising his autobiography as a third person account of him by the same compliant writer.[24]

Hardy's notes in Chew, Hedgcock, and Brennecke might seem of little or no value to our understanding of Hardy and his writing if the attitude they reveal were not all of a piece with his attitude, throughout his life, toward critics who sought to uncover a personal element in his writing.[25] The usual explanation for Hardy's secretiveness is that he had something to hide. His modest beginnings, his love for a first cousin, his unhappy marriage, this argument goes, had to be concealed. And so, probing critics had to be kept at bay; his autobiography had to be written in such a way as to make it seem a biography by his second wife. As has been suggested, however, if this was true, it was also true – on the evidence of his inability to deny completely the autobiographical element of his novels – that biographical critics were not just trespassing on Hardy's private life. They were also intruding on the process of self-examination and self-formation central to his art. But let us continue here with our brief account of the history of Hardy biography, henceforth with particular attention to the years 1876–8, years that produced *The Return of the Native*, in which the tragic handling of autobiographical materials resulted in Hardy's first major novel and one of the great novels of the nineteenth century.

First, the autobiography *qua* biography Hardy was writing when the poachers appeared on his preserve. Hardy's account of himself in the *Early Life* (1928) and the *Later Years* (1930), as is well-known, was highly discreet: "He wrote his own life, or what he cared to tell of it, in the third person, to be passed off as a biography written by her [Florence]. No author can have taken more care that the future should know only what he wanted it to know...."[26] Hardy's ruse would produce the very opposite of his intent – a riot of biographical speculation, often of the most uncomplimentary kind, the kind he might well have called "impertinent", "quizzing", or worse if he had lived to read it. But his disguise would hold, and hold well, for nearly half a century.

Signficantly enough, the segment of the *Life* that treats *The Return of the Native* (pp. 110–24) is one of the richest in the entire book. Here are found some of Hardy's earliest ruminations on the Napoleonic theme one day to become *The Dynasts*. Here are found some of his most passionate and penetrating remarks on life and art: on the evolution of man and culture (p. 111), on the vanity of things and that blindness to misery that fosters laughter (p. 112), on those defects of nature that it is the artist's duty to transform into a new kind of beauty (p. 114), on the peculiar worth of an object made by man when it is found in nature (pp. 116, 120–1). The period from June 1876 to April 1878 seems, on the evidence of the *Life*, to have been a critical one for Hardy. Though his marriage in September 1874 and the success of *Far from the Madding Crowd* in the same year must have given him some hope for a bright future, happiness was not to be his, at least not for long. Undoubtedly the death by suicide of Horace Moule in September 1873 (not recorded in the *Life*) still oppressed him. Certainly, as has been noted, he was stung by the remark in one review that its author was a "house-decorator". Possibly he was still pained by his failure to establish himself as a poet, and by the need that novel-writing imposed on him to live life as "a science" rather than "an emotion". Surely he was disturbed, and disturbed deeply, by Emma's failure to conceive a child ("We hear that Jane, our late servant, is soon to have a baby. Yet never a sign of one is there for us" [*Life*, p. 116]). And quite clearly, his two-year-old marriage (for reasons not mentioned in the *Life*) was faring badly.[27]

Taken together, these things go some way toward suggesting a personal crisis that may have occasioned the tragic view of things in *The Return of the Native*. Hardy's thought and experience between 1876 and 1878 (and before) come to fruition in his vision in *The Return* of a new kind of beauty, "a beauty of association . . . entirely superior to the beauty of aspect" – a beauty exhibited in both the novel's setting and in its central action, Clym Yeobright's failure to return to his beginnings, his futile attempt to reconcile his devotion to a possessive mother and his love for a passionate wife.[28] Clym's situation is not unlike Hardy's, of course, for Hardy in 1867 had returned to his native place after five years in London, and by 1883 would be permanently established in Dorchester. What's more, a genuine rivalry seems to have existed between Hardy's wife, Emma, and his strong-minded mother, Jemima. *The Return* can be seen as an expression of Hardy's powerful need in the middle and late 1870s to see a "beauty" in the "ugliness' of a situation much like his own from his marriage in 1874 on. But what is peculiar in this is that after 1917, when Hardy wrote this account of his life some fifty years before, he chose to say far less about Clym and *The Return* than about *A Pair of Blue Eyes, Far From the Madding Crowd*, or *The Hand of Ethelberta*, possibly because Hedgcock, Chew, and Brennecke were making connections between Clym and his author that Hardy did not wish to see developed further. And so he mentions in the *Life* only the connection between discovery of a "hitherto unperceived" beauty and his story of return, and goes no further. But there seem to have existed other, more intimate, connections between *The Return* and its reticent author. In April 1912, for example, while correcting proofs for the Wessex Edition of *The Return*, he wrote: "I got to like the character of Clym. . . . I think he is the nicest of all my heroes, and *not a bit like me*" (*Life*, pp. 357–8). The italics are Hardy's, and they suggest his continuing need, more than thirty years after writing his novel, to deny an autobiographical element in the novel. In a sense, he was correct. Based on his own account of his development – "a child till . . . sixteen, a youth till . . . five-and-twenty, and a young man till . . . nearly fifty" – by 1912 and age seventy-two he was "not a bit" like Clym Yeobright (*Life*, p. 32). But in 1878, as Carl Weber and Evelyn Hardy would see, Hardy and his homecoming hero had a good deal in common.

In *Hardy of Wessex* (1940), his highly complimentary and even worshipful account of Hardy, Carl J. Weber described a distinctly autobiographical element in both *The Return of the Native* and *The Hand of Ethelberta* (1876). He noted similarities between Ethelberta and her author: both value a tragic art, both write poetry and are constrained by modest incomes. Similarities between author and protagonist continue in *The Return*, in which Clym Yeobright's intimacy with Egdon is seen to resemble Hardy's fondness for the heath that surrounded his birthplace at Higher Bockhampton. And for this novel, as Weber observed, Hardy made a detailed sketch-map of Wessex and proceeded in other ways with great fidelity to personal experience and local detail. Weber remarked also that Hardy adopted the five-part structure of Greek tragedy and made frequent allusions to Sophocles and Aeschylus, to the Old Testament, and to

Shakespeare's *Lear* and *Hamlet* to lend his narrative tragic form and effect. Though Weber barely suggests it, it seems possible that Hardy's allusive manner in *The Return* was in part an attempt to distance himself from his hero and to exhibit the condition of all men in the tragic condition of a protagonist founded on himself. But exact or nearly exact correspondences between Yeobright and Hardy – Weber's main interest here – are less important than the strong signs that in 1876–8 Hardy was using a tragic fiction for the purpose of self-portraiture, and self-portraiture for the purpose of discovering tragedy. In his revised *Hardy of Wessex* (1965), Weber would expand his view of the autobiographical significance of *The Return* (see especially p. 105). But aware as he must have been by 1965 of the work of Evelyn Hardy and Lois Deacon, and disconcerted perhaps by the deprecatory view of Hardy advanced by the latter, Weber continued to look only to correspondences between Hardy's life and his art, and not to the way Hardy perhaps used his art to study and shape his own life. What one misses in Weber's account of the fiction and the life between 1876 and 1878 is a perception that Hardy's turn to a tragic fiction with personal overtones was a highly self-conscious, and self-critical, response to inner imperatives. Hedgcock's view of Hardy's characters as men marking different stages through which Hardy himself was passing might have served Weber well.

Evelyn Hardy's *Thomas Hardy: A Critical Biography* (1954) moved nearer to Hedgcock's undeveloped insight in her treatment of Hardy's life in the mid-1870s. She noted that with the death of Horace Moule in 1873 Hardy's mentor became Leslie Stephen, editor of the *Cornhill*, who was to give Hardy much valuable advice in the course of editing *Far From the Madding Crowd* and *The Hand of Ethelberta* for publication in his magazine. One bit of Stephen's advice is preserved in a letter Stephen wrote to Hardy in May 1876: "You have a perfectly fresh and original vein and I think the less you bother about critical canons the less chance there is of your becoming self-conscious and cramped" (*Life*, p. 109). This advice, coming from the man whose thought Hardy himself said influenced his own "more than that of any other contemporary" (*Life*, p. 100), coming too when he was on the verge of beginning *The Return*, may well have given Hardy the confidence he needed to turn toward a kind of self-portraiture in *The Return* even more candid than that in *Ethelberta* (or *A Pair of Blue Eyes*). Evelyn Hardy in fact describes a deepening process of self-delineation in *Ethelberta* and *The Return* – the reliving through Ethelberta of "some of his troubles in joining London society" (p. 149); the recollection throughout the whole of *Ethelberta* of his mother's, or grandmother's, tales of the difficulty of life in a large family in his account of the Chickerels;

then, quite suddenly, in *The Return* "an *explosion* into the truth and reality of his own nature and idiosyncrasy" (italics mine):

> Here [in *The Return*] he was fully himself: the mood, the setting, and the philosophy implied by that setting which it interprets, are peculiarly his. Yet he keeps himself in abeyance, his character does not over-intrude: a perfect balance is kept between the parts played by the characters and by Fate, or Chance, as well as a balance between creator and creations. (p. 162)

This is penetrating and yet not definite enough. What, one wonders is 'the truth and reality' of Hardy's nature and idiosyncrasy? Into what particular truth and reality did Hardy explode in 1876–8? Evelyn Hardy does not say, perhaps because her "cataclysmic" view of his growth impedes her. Her view of Hardy's development as a sudden event, as an "explosion into the truth and reality of his own nature and idiosyncrasy", invites a simplistic explanation where a complex, developmental one is called for; for in a sense, in 1876–8, Thomas Hardy, though nearly forty, was without what might be called a clear sense of his literary calling. He was then, and until 1898 – when he became the poet of *Wessex Poems* – continued to be, a man in process of becoming, an artist repeatedly studying and forming himself through his self-critical autobiographical fiction. "I am more than ever convinced," he wrote in December, 1890, "that persons are successively various persons, according as each special strand in their characters is brought uppermost by circumstances" (*Life*, p. 230).

Evelyn Hardy's *Thomas Hardy* was moving in a right direction, toward an understanding of Hardy's self-formative use of his art, when biographical study of Hardy took the path of the *Monographs on the Life, Times, and Works of Thomas Hardy* (1962–71) and Lois Deacon's *Providence and Mr Hardy* (1966). Given the frequently lowering effect of both, an almost insurmountable difficulty arises: how to salvage the writings, especially their humane philosophy, in the face of the view that Hardy was a diminutive man; how to explain the way a mean, snobbish, even cruel man, a man haunted by memories of an incestuous love affair, could write novels and poems of deep moral seriousness. Hardy's kind of fiction – humane, moral, at times satiric, frequently self-reflective – seems the expression of a sensibility far sounder, far better attuned to "the still, sad music of humanity", than the sensibility implied by Deacon and some of the other authors of the *Monographs*. And, as has been suggested, Robert Gittings does not correct this difficulty because, though he unveils Hardy's shortcomings, thereby correcting the hagiography of Weber, and though he corrects the more reckless speculations of Lois Deacon and some of her followers, he seems unable to show Hardy at his best – as an imperfect man who faced his imperfections in an art at once inward-turning and representative, at once expressive and mimetic. In this context, Gittings' handling of the period 1876–8 and *The Return of the Native* becomes extremely interesting.

III

For Gittings, the period 1876–8 was clearly pivotal in Hardy's life. This is silently evident in the fact that Gittings chose to end his first volume (*Young Thomas Hardy*) with the events of the year 1875 and begin his second (*Thomas Hardy's Later Years*) with 1876, when Hardy was on the threshold of *The Return of the Native*. Like Evelyn Hardy some twenty years before him, Gittings dwells on Hardy's transfer of allegiance from Horace Moule (to whom Gittings gives a whole chapter) to Leslie Stephen, whose influence on Hardy he regards as decisive. Stephen's firm editorial hand, according to Gittings, was the determining reason for the quality and the success of *Far From the Madding Crowd*.[29] At this point, however, as at others, Gittings becomes patronizing and even derogatory: "The writing of *Far From the Madding Crowd* seems to show that Hardy wrote his best under the guidance of a trained but sympathetic mind. He had always need of this, in a pathetic and almost Coleridgean want to supplement his own self-taught judgment." This is an odd statement to make about a writer who by 1874 had completed three novels and a fairly large number of poems almost wholly without editorial guidance of the kind Stephen gave – a writer, moreover, who would complete the remainder of his works usually free of, at times in defiance of, editorial and other opinions. In writing *The Return of the Native*, for example, Hardy would turn away, with firmness and resolve, from Stephen and the prestigious *Cornhill* because Stephen, a bit of a Grundyite in spite of his free-thinking, objected to the passionate sexuality of Eustacia Vye. Even earlier, Hardy had remonstrated with Stephen about Stephen's unease with the seduction of Fanny Robin of *Far From the Madding Crowd* (*Life*, pp. 98–9). Gittings seems to ignore some of the facts, to be sure; yet he is wholly consistent with his general view of Hardy as deeply flawed, frequently hapless, perpetually adolescent, as at best a "tragi-comic contrast between mean and noble".[30]

But if Gittings' bias at times distorts, it also leads to some genuine insights. He gives one a deep and clear sense of Hardy's dependency, even after his marriage, on "the scenes and the people of his boyhood home, mother, father, brother, sisters, and . . . cousins down the road"; of Hardy's need for the "reassurance of the familiar", especially the support of his mother, whose profound influence Gittings is the first of Hardy's biographers to sharply define; of Hardy's fear of revealing to his middle-class wife that this adored mother had been the subject of Poor Law charity and that many of his Dorset kinfolk had been servants and labourers; and of Hardy's dissatisfaction with Emma, who soon appeared somewhat provincial alongside many of the women he came to know in London after 1874.[31] But perhaps Gittings' most useful contribution to our understanding of Hardy in 1876–8 is his detailed account of *The Hand of Ethelberta* as a disguised rendering of Hardy's own dilemma in the first half of the 1870s. In the story of Ethelberta Chickerel Petherwin, a gifted Wessex girl who marries above her station (like Hardy), writes then gives up the writing of poetry (like Hardy), takes up prose fiction (like Hardy), then finally abandons her origins and her poetic ambitions to marry a wealthy and unscrupulous nobleman (here the novel departs from experience), one undoubtedly finds a covert account of what Gittings, in a fine phrase, calls "the violence that [Hardy's] uprooting from the past had done to his essential being".[32] Gittings' account of *Ethelberta* – though somewhat inconsistent with remarks elsewhere in his study[33] – enables one to see this seriously flawed novel of 1876 as an important personal document, an effort in self-criticism and self-formation.

Given this detailed and searching criticism of *Ethelberta*, one hardly knows what to make of the absence of a comparable account of *The Return of the Native*, the novel written between 1876 and 1878 in which Hardy exhibits Clym Yeobright's return to his native place after a long absence abroad (like Hardy's return to Dorset in 1867 after five years of architectural work in London). Clym insists he returns to recover a simpler life and to educate the unlettered denizens of Egdon, but this conscious purpose seems much less important than his nostalgia for the scenes and sensations of his boyhood and for the company of his strong and domineering mother. This attachment to his mother is soon in deepest conflict with his love for the passionate Eustacia Vye, with the death of both mother and lover the tragic result. As Gittings himself suggests (see note 36 below), it is not difficult to recognize in *The Return of the Native* some of the qualities of a novel like Lawrence's *Sons and Lovers*. Given this, it is difficult to understand why Gittings, centrally concerned as he is with Hardy's strong attachment to Jemima Hardy, should give merely cursory treatment to that major novel in which Hardy, at a pivotal moment of his career, took up the story of a young man's hopeless struggle to choose between mother and wife, between prolonging adolescence and moving into manhood. It seems a curious oversight, or choice, especially in light of the heavily autobiographical interpretation of *Ethelberta*, the novel that immediately preceded *The Return* and that, probably not coincidentally, bears several striking resemblances to it.³⁴

An answer may lie in Gittings' argument that in *The Hand of Ethelberta* Hardy snobbishly and heartlessly declared an end to his attachment to the Hardys of Dorset: "In [*The Hand of Ethelberta*], Hardy wrote out of his system the Hardy who was one of the people who toiled and suffered."³⁵ To argue that *Ethelberta* is Hardy's rejection of his personal past may well be to oversimplify the novel's achievement. What Gittings neglects in his account of Ethelberta as a projection of his social and personal dilemma is the honesty in Hardy's depiction of the self-doubt and self-contempt Ethelberta suffers in coming to the decision to break with her origins. Ethelberta is no cold-hearted, self-centred snob; she deeply regrets the loss of family-feeling that accompanies her rise in society. She knows the cost of choosing social gain over loyalty to family and origins. One of the most memorable scenes of the novel is that in which Ethelberta, in her last public performance as a "teller" of novels, suddenly decides to tell the truth about herself, to substitute a sincere autobiographical "I" for the fabricated "I" of the naive first-person narrative. She does this because she has decided, in a moment of guilt and candour, "to show herself as she really was . . . and so get rid of that self-reproach which had by this time reached a morbid pitch" (Ch. 38). What Ethelberta feels obliged to reveal is that by birth she is not a lady but the child of servants. Far from writing out of his system "the Hardy who was one of the people who toiled and suffered", Hardy seems bent on confessing, at least to the few who might understand, an undying but troubled allegiance to them.

That same allegiance is revealed again in *The Return of the Native*. In *The Return*, however, and particularly in the portrait of Clym Yeobright, the element of self-portraiture is more severely self-critical than in *Ethelberta*; for Clym, much more than Ethelberta, is the target of Hardy's irony. He is made to exemplify the folly of nostalgia, of the wish to turn back the clock, to be a boy again, to recover the simplicities of rustic life. Clym is a man of 33 who cannot choose his wife over his mother, and he is depicted as suffering the most terrible consequences as a result — loss of wife, loss of mother, loss of vocation, loss of a stable sense of self. He ends an attendant to his mother's memory, determined to live out his life in her house on the maternal heath.³⁶

Given his view of Hardy as a snob, a habitual deceiver, and a perpetual adolescent, Gittings is ill-equipped to assess the serious and searching self-criticism projected by Hardy in his portrait of Clym Yeobright. To do so would be to contradict his consistent view of Hardy as egotistical, immature, even unstable. Gittings unfortunately has little room in his sceptical and frequently demeaning account of Hardy for extended discussion of a novel in which Hardy exhibits the tragic division of love, the hampering emotional immaturity, that allows Clym to be neither a loyal son nor a loving husband, but rather a strained and strange creature trying at once to grow up and to recover a lost childhood joy. Gittings himself argues, and most persuasively, Hardy's profound attachment to people and places associated with his earliest days. He describes, better than any other biographer of Hardy, Hardy's fixation on his mother. But Gittings, for reasons not clear, has no place for a considered view of Hardy as a troubled genius struggling through *The Return* (and other novels) to both understand himself and, through this understanding, proclaim the tragic nature of things. Gittings prefers the snob, the nympholept, the heartless husband of occasional "peasant" meanness. It seems wholly reasonable to expect that Gittings apply to *The Return* the searching method he applied to *Ethelberta*. Is it possible that he does not because *The Return* — in its critical self-portraiture — confutes his basic view of Hardy? Because he does not, and because the same difficulty exists in his treatment of other novels, the completeness and soundness of his portrait of Hardy must remain in question. For example, though he recognizes in *Desperate Remedies* Hardy's projection of two sides of himself into the brother and the lover of the heroine, and of qualities of Mary Hardy (Hardy's favourite sister) into the heroine, he chooses to dwell on the book's clumsy melodrama, its self-conscious style, and its highly derivative plot. Though he recognizes Hardy's heavy dependency in *A Pair of Blue Eyes* on Hardy's experiences in Cornwall from 1870 to 1873, and the repetition in it of the technique of "splitting" discovered in *Desperate Remedies* Gittings sees this not as another step in a process of self-exploration but merely as the clumsy manipulation of the conventions of melodrama. Though he notes the power and originality of *Far From the Madding Crowd*, he suggests, as noted above, that Leslie Stephen was the decisive factor in Hardy's coming to artistic maturity. Even while recognizing the highly personal nature of *The Well-Beloved*, Gittings sees it not for its attempt at self-study and self-understanding, but as a book whose "wrongness" lies in its coming "uncomfortably near to self-revelation of some of the less attractive sides of Hardy's character and physical make-up". And though he recognizes the deeply personal origins of *Tess* and *Jude*, particularly the self-reflective element in *Jude*, his emphasis falls not on the function of Hardy's attempts at self-examination, but on the incongruity between Hardy's seriousness in these novels and his behaviour ("his aristocratic literary infatuations") in real life. It indeed seems true, as John P. Farrell has remarked, that "Gittings has marred his important book by turning it at times into soap-opera. . . . Hardy the writer sometimes seems to matter merely in his role as cad."[37] Though Gittings gives us Hardy at his worst, he does not show him at some of his best moments, at those times when in his autobiographical art he subjects himself, however obliquely, to the eye of judgment. Surely the literary biographer is obliged to attend to the self-portraits of his subject, especially those enshrined in his best books. Hardy's projection of himself in his fiction is at least as important as Edward Clodd's opinion of him.

Hardy was indeed more harsh and hardhearted than Weber's *Hardy of Wessex* had led us to believe. One can hardly doubt Gittings in this. But Hardy's weaknesses are not the whole, or even the dominant part, of Hardy's story. What must be included, if a balanced, sober, and convincing account of Hardy's life is to be written, is that this harsh and at times heartless genius knew his shortcomings and carried on a programme of self-study and self-censure in many of his novels and poems. In characters like Henry Knight of *A Pair of Blue Eyes*, Clym Yeobright of *The Return of the Native*, Angel Clare of *Tess of the d'Urbervilles*, and Jocelyn Pierston of *The Well-Beloved*, in the poet-husband of the expiatory "Poems of 1912–13", in the personae of self-probing lyrics such as "The Impercipient", "Dead Man Walking", "Wessex Heights", "Surview", and the "In Tenebris" trilogy,[38] we find self-censure without self-pity or moral masochism. In a word, we find attempts at self-disclosure and self-formation. Such an effort is beyond the reach of a phrase such as "no largeness of soul". If Hardy's effort in this did not produce an exemplary man and husband, it can certainly be seen as preferable to mere egotism or arrogance. And in any case it became the occasion for an art of true distinction. For after all, if perfection is the measure, if anything more than imperfect self-knowledge and fitful self-mastery is the measure, who shall 'scape hanging?

Some words of J. Hillis Miller are perhaps worth quoting by way of conclusion, words in which Miller describes what he calls the "proper model for the relation of the critic to the work he studies". He could as easily be describing, I believe, the proper model for the relation of the biographer to the man or woman he sets out to portray:

> The end of literary study is still elucidation of the intrinsic meaning of poems, plays, and novels. In the effort toward such elucidation the proper model of the critic to the work he studies is not that of scientist to

physical objects but that of one man to another in charity. I may love
another person and know him as only love can know without in the least
abnegating my own beliefs. Love wants the other person to be as he is,
in all his recalcitrant particularity. As St Augustine puts it, the lover says
to the loved one, *"Volo ut sis!"* – "I wish you to be."[39]

Hardy, in all his "recalcitrant particularity", was neither the saint of
Weber's portrait nor the cad of Gittings'. He was, as recognition of the
autobiographical drama in many of his novels and poems can help one see, a
writer who made the study, and the display, of faults like his own, as well
as the terrible consequences for others of just such faults, one of the central
concerns of his fiction. If he found it impossible to remedy in life what he
depicted as irremediable in his art, it was because he held to an unpleasant
but verifiable truth that the age of Spencer and Mill often chose to ignore
– that more often than not imperfect and erring men and women and
their imperfect world cannot be amended, redeemed, or made good. After
all, he himself had said that he took as his artistic task not the correction of
"Nature's defects", but the honest fronting of them in order that they
might become the basis of "a hitherto unperceived beauty". It was in the
context of a distressed self-survey in "In Tenebris, II" that he urged that
"If way to the Better there be, it exacts a full look at the Worst". Hardy
understood, with Ruskin, that all too often "the best that is in us does not
manifest itself but in company with much error". Robert Gittings' *Young
Thomas Hardy* and *Thomas Hardy's Later Years*, for all its merit as a
revisionary biography, might have taken better account than it does of that
bit of Gothic wisdom.[40]

NOTES

1. *Young Thomas Hardy* (London: Heinemann, 1975); *The Older Hardy* (London: Heinemann, 1978). The remark by Kendall in the previous paragraph is from his *Art of Biography* (London: Allen & Unwin, 1965) p. 8.
2. Gittings is also the author of *John Keats* (1968) and the recent *Nature of Biography* (1978). The second volume of his life of Hardy (published in the USA as *Thomas Hardy's Later Years*) received the Royal Society of Literature Award (under the W. H. Heinemann Bequest) in 1978, as well as the James Tait Black Memorial Prize for the best biography of 1978. With Jo Manton, Gittings has recently published *The Second Mrs. Hardy* (London: Heinemann, 1979).
3. See also Gittings and Manton, *The Second Mrs. Hardy*; also Denys Kay-Robinson, *The First Mrs. Thomas Hardy* (London: 1979).
4. *Old Tom and Young Tom: A Commentary on the Monographs* (Guernsey, C. I.: Toucan Press, 1971) p. 509. A strong connection exists between Deacon's *Providence and*

Mr. Hardy and the *Illustrated Monographs*. Deacon's *Tryphena and Thomas Hardy*, the germ of her 1966 study, first appeared as Monograph, no. 3, in 1962; she also contributed eight other monographs to the series, six of them on Hardy or Tryphena (nos 29, 31, 32, 38, 46, 62). Her view of Hardy as a guilt-haunted man not only struck a major chord in the series, it also influenced important work by scholars such as F. R. Southerington (*Hardy's Vision of Man* [London: Chatto & Windus, 1971]) and J. O. Bailey (*The Poetry of Thomas Hardy: A Handbook and a Commentary* [Chapel Hill: University of North Carolina Press, 1971]). Southerington went so far as to publish a photograph of Hardy's supposed son by Tryphena (p. 137). Gittings' refutation of Deacon and Southerington, reprinted in *Young Thomas Hardy*, pp. 222–9, first appeared in *TLS* (April 1973).
5. Gittings draws on the *Monographs* over forty times, usually as reliable sources.
6. *Hardy of Wessex* (New York: Columbia University Press, 1940) p. 231. In his revision of this sentence for the 1965 edition of *Hardy of Wessex*, Weber wrote, somewhat more temperately, as follows: "He has taught [men and women all over the world] how the spirit of man can persist through defeat, and he continues today to inspire readers to strive towards noble conduct in an imperfect world."
7. Gittings' harsh view is taken up and extended in both Kay-Robinson, *The First Mrs Hardy* and in Gittings and Manton, *The Second Mrs. Hardy*.
8. The phrase occurs on pp. 173 and 211 of *Later Years*. For a view similar to Bergonzi's see Claire Tomalin, "Thomas Hardy and the Life-Long Search for Love", *The Sunday Times* (5 March 1978). For a hostile view see Anna Winchcomb, *Thomas Hardy Society Newsletter*, XXIII (June 1975) p. 4. John P. Farrell (*Studies in the Novel*, X [1978] pp. 368–9) notes certain elements of melodrama in Gittings' treatment.
9. *Life*, pp. 32, 405.
10. This does not apply literally to Sue Bridehead, of course, though in her (she is in several ways the female counterpart of Angel Clare of *Tess*) Hardy attempts to exhibit a woman's experience of slowness of sexual development, intellectual precocity, and extreme fastidiousness.
11. Hardy's complete account of his "immaturity" is as follows: "His immaturity . . . was greater than is common for his years, and . . . a clue to much of his character and action throughout his life is afforded by his lateness of development in virility, while mentally precocious. He himself said humorously in later times that he was a child until he was sixteen (1856), a youth till he was five-and-twenty (1865), and a young man till he was nearly fifty (*c*. 1890). Whether this was intrinsic, or owed anything to his having lived in a remote spot in early life, is an open question" (*Life*, p. 32).
12. *Young Thomas Hardy*, pp. 166, 211, 217; also *The Older Hardy*, pp. 67, 190.
13. Lines 1, 3, and 4 of stanza 2 paraphrase Philippians 4–8; lines 1, 3, 4 of stanza 3, and lines 1 and 3 of stanza 4 echo I Corinthians 13: 4, 7, and 13. The poem's motto is from Psalm 69: 59 in the King James Bible. The voice from the fire may derive from Psalm 39: 3. See also *Tess of the d'Urbervilles*, Chs 31, 36; and *Jude the Obscure*, Part VI, Ch. 4; also *Life*, p. 405.
14. Gittings relies heavily on the repetition of deprecatory words throughout his two volumes. For example: "strange" (or "weird", or "bizarre"), in *Young Thomas Hardy* (pp. 12, 26, 51, 55, 64, 198, 210); "obsessive" (or "literal-minded"), in *Young Thomas Hardy* (pp. 61, 64, 79, 151, 211, 212), and in *The Older Hardy* (Foreword, pp. 3, 12, 26, 52, 106, 191, 192, 205, 209); "morbid" (or "perverse" or "grotesque"), in *Young Thomas Hardy* (p. 60), and in *The Older Hardy* (pp. 12, 22, 177, 182, 205); "peasant" in *Young Thomas Hardy* (pp. 104, 217), and in *The Older Hardy*

(pp. 1, 183, 195); "abnormal", in *Young Thomas Hardy*, (pp. 1, 199, 203, 216), and in *The Older Hardy* (Foreword); "devious" (or "disingenuous", or "secretive"), in *Young Thomas Hardy* (pp. 1, 205, 215), and in *The Older Hardy* (pp. 93, 137, 177, 183). The cumulative effect of these litanies, especially when combined with Gittings' insistence on Hardy's "perpetual" adolescence, his "susceptibility", his "gloom", his attraction to dying or dead women, is to form not an objectively negative portrait but an insinuatingly negative one. A reader is confronted with repeated suggestions that Hardy was even worse than the facts might suggest – that he was ghoulish as well as a cad. This suggestion of hidden evil is capped, in a manner worthy of melodrama, on the last page of *The Older Hardy* with a remark by Hardy's sister Kate, made on 10 May 1939 after the opening of the reconstructed Hardy study at the Dorset County Museum: ". . . Kate threw down her bonnet on the sofa, laughed heartily, and referring to the complimentary speakers, exclaimed 'If they only knew!' The last 'Hardy born', she too was about to take his secrets to the grave." The source of this insidious and strategically placed anecdote is apparently a still-living cousin of Hardy.

15. Cf. Hardy's half-humourous plea in "The Profitable Reading of Fiction" (1888) for a reader who will swallow his author whole, believe in him "slavishly" and "implicitly", and never doubt for a moment "his coincidences, his marvellous juxtapositions, his catastrophies, his conversions of bad people into good people at a stroke, and vice versa". The reader's aim, he continues, should be "the exercise of a generous imaginativeness" (in *Thomas Hardy's Personal Writings*, ed. Harold Orel [Lawrence: University of Kansas Press, 1966] pp. 111–12).

16. These are the major biographical studies. There are of course others, some of them segments of critical studies (e.g. J. I. M. Stewart's provocative first three chapters in *Thomas Hardy* [London: Allen Lane, 1971]); some of them full length but with little new to add to the record (e.g. F. E. Halliday, *Thomas Hardy: His Life and Work* [Bath: Adams & Dart, 1972]; Timothy O. Sullivan, *Thomas Hardy: An Illustrated Biography* [New York: St Martin's Press, 1976]).

17. The suggestion that the publication of (probably) Brennecke's *Life* forced his hand is probably unfounded. Hardy seems to have begun work on an autobiography as early as 1917. See R. L. Purdy, *Thomas Hardy: A Bibliographical Study* (Oxford: Clarendon Press, 1954) p. 266.

18. Florence sent Chew three pages of typed notes, extracts from Hardy's notes in the margins of *Poet and Novelist*.

19. This is perhaps Hardy's strongest denial. But compare *Life*, pp. 73–4, where, making the usual disclaimers about *A Pair of Blue Eyes*, Hardy says he was "ever . . . shy of putting his personal characteristics into his novels", then partially contradicts himself by stating that "Henry Knight the reviewer . . . was really much more like Thomas Hardy as described in his future wife's diary" than Stephen Smith was. It seems altogether possible that this remark was designed to refute the claims of Hedgcock, Chew, and Brennecke.

20. Cf. *Life*, p. 174: "The character and appearance of Elfride have points in common with those of Mrs. Hardy in quite young womanhood, a few years before Hardy met her (though her eyes would have been described as deep gray, not blue); more-over, like Elfride, the moment she was on a horse she was part of the animal. But this is all that can be asserted, the plot of the story being one that he had thought of and written down before he knew her."

21. But cf. *Life*, pp. 207–8: "April 28 (1888). A short story about a young man – 'who could not go to Oxford' – his struggles and ultimate failures. Suicide. (Probably the

germ of *Jude the Obscure*). There is something in this the world ought to be shown, and I am the one to show it to them — although I was not altogether hindered going, at least to Cambridge, and could have gone up easily at five-and-twenty.''

22. In the Dorset County Museum, from a rough draft in Hardy's hand on the back of another letter from Childs to Hardy dated 31 March 1925. The four letters referred to in the sentences that follow are also in the Dorset County Museum.

23. Against an account of some remarks by Hardy on America — that its climate shaped the character of its people, that it is a tragic nation, that he felt its difficulties only distantly — Hardy wrote "incorrect", "false", respectively (p. 4). He wrote "false" again beside the statement, attributed to him, that Tennyson and Browning had lived near him in London in the 1860s (p. 5); "false" even again beside another statement attributed to him, that he disliked the intellectual revolutionaries of the 1860s and 1870s (p. 6); "false" beside Brennecke's statement that poetry was essential to Hardy's existence (p. 9); "garbled" beside Brennecke's remark that Hardy's war poem, "The Pity of It", brought down the wrath of some English jingoists (p. 10); "*suggestio falsi*" beside the remark that the name "Henry Knight" was borrowed from a Dorchester draper (p. 14); "incorrect" beside Brennecke's statement that the literary interests of Jemima Hardy were superficial (p. 43); "impertinent invention" beside the observation that Emma Gifford expected Hardy to make a mark in the world; "untrue impertinence" beside the statement that Hardy and Emma decided to risk marriage on the success of *Far From the Madding Crowd*.

24. One cannot help wondering why Hardy, given his aversion for personal gossip, should have left the "annotated" lives in his library. Perhaps it was mere oversight, perhaps a calculated attempt to influence the views of later biographers.

25. Space permits only brief mention of yet another episode in Hardy's struggle with biographers and interviewers. Several letters in the Dorset County Museum reveal that in June 1926, about a year after the publication of Brennecke's *Life*, R. Thurston Hopkins, a free-lance journalist, sent to the *Westminster Gazette* an account of Hardy's domestic life that so angered Hardy that he initiated legal action against Hopkins through the Dorchester firm of Lock, Reed, and Lock. Hardy was offended by three things in Hopkins' article: the statement that he had a half-brother who was a gardener; the statement that Mrs Hardy managed Max Gate with the help of just one maid-of-all-work; the statement that Hardy's silence was a byword in Dorchester. Hopkins was required to make complete withdrawal of his statements in the *Gazette*, to cease to annoy Hardy in the future, and to pay Hardy's legal expenses (Hardy later withdrew this last). Earlier in 1926 Hardy had written as follows to Captain J. E. Acland, then curator of the Dorset County Museum: "Would you be so kind as to caution the attendant Kibby [the Museum's porter] . . . against letting strangers who visit the museum draw from him any particulars about myself?"

26. Gittings, *Young Thomas Hardy*, p. 1. See also J. I. M. Stewart, *Thomas Hardy*, pp. 1–16, where the *Life* is described as a work "full of fibs" but "reflecting Hardy's personality and vision in a manner which would otherwise be lacking to us" (p. 5).

27. See the note dated 1 January 1879 (*Life*, p. 124): "The poem 'A January Night. 1879' in *Moments of Vision* relates to an incident of this new year (1879) which occurred here at Tooting, where they (the Hardys) seemed to feel that 'there had past away a glory from the earth.' And it was in this house that their troubles began."

28. Cf. the note in the *Life* (p. 114) dated June 1877: "Art lies in making these defects (in nature) the basis of a hitherto unperceived beauty . . ."; and the speculation at the beginning of *The Return of the Native* on the beginning of the reign of a new kind of

beauty: "Indeed, it is a question if the exclusive reign of this orthodox beauty is not approaching its last quarter. . . . The time seems near, if it has not actually arrived, when the chastened sublimity of a moor, a sea, or a mountain will be all of nature that is absolutely in keeping with the moods of the more thinking among mankind" (Bk I, Ch. 1).

29. *Young Thomas Hardy*, p. 190.
30. ibid., p. 191.
31. ibid., pp. 191–2.
32. ibid., p. 211.
33. After an illuminating discussion of the ways in which "this synthetic character [Ethelberta] and her dilemmas were meant to express, in secret guise, Hardy's own", Gittings concludes that the novel is Hardy's rejection of the class from which he derived (*Young Thomas Hardy*, p. 207). But elsewhere Gittings allows that in Hardy's case a complete break with beginnings was unlikely: "The process of cutting himself off from his family origins seemed complete [by the 1920s]; yet the poems, his inner life, tell a different story, a story of how the happenings of his young days were still as vivid and deeply-felt as when they had first occurred" (ibid., p. 221).
34. In addition to several verbal echoes, *Ethelberta* anticipates *The Return* in its use of Egdon Heath for a setting, and in its concern with a domestic drama centring on the results of the social rise of a talented child. Ethelberta, like Clym, has outstripped her origins; even more than Ethelberta, Clym seeks to recover them, with a tragic crisis the result. *Ethelberta* is a comedic, *The Return* a tragic, rendering of the dilemma of the uprooted.
35. *Young Thomas Hardy*, p. 209.
36. Eleanor McCann, "Blind Will or Blind Hero: Philosophy and myth in Hardy's *Return of the Native*", *Criticism*, III (1961) pp. 140–67, has described *The Return* as the story of Clym's failure to achieve knowledge of his "instinctive motivations", that is, of the influence on him of his natural mother and his archetypal mother, nature, embodied in Egdon Heath. "Psychologically speaking," McCann writes, "Clym is a sick man who projects onto his environment a solace for the halfway solution to an Oedipal conflict" (p. 157). Cf. Gittings (*Young Thomas Hardy*, p. 175): "For Hardy had returned [in 1874], just like some man in a D. H. Lawrence story, to the world of his mother, a fortress against the vagaries of other women."
37. Farrell's review appeared in *Studies in the Novel*, X (1978) pp. 368–9. For Gittings' remarks see *Young Thomas Hardy*, p. 217, and *The Older Hardy*, pp. 63–78.
38. I have described elsewhere (in a lecture to the 1978 Thomas Hardy Summer School) the striking similarities between the harried self-portrait in the "In Tenebris" poems of 1895–6 and characters such as Pierston, Clare, and Sue Bridehead in the novels of the 1890s.
39. From "Literature and Religion" (1967), in *Religion and Modern Literature: Essays in Theory and Practice*, ed. G. B. Tennyson and Edward E. Erickson (Grand Rapids, Mich.: Ferdman's, 1975) p. 45.
40. This study was completed with the aid of a grant from the General Research Fund of the University of Kansas for the summer of 1979. Quotations from the marginalia in Hardy's copies of the works by Hedgcock and Chew are made by kind permission of the Trustees of the Thomas Hardy Memorial Collection in the Dorset County Museum, Dorchester.

Hardy and Rural England

Arthur Pollard

Arnold Kettle has written that 'The history and geography of southern England are not just a necessary background to Tess's story, they are integral to it, entering at every turn and level into the essence of the situation that Hardy describes'.[1] I agree with Kettle.

It used to be the case that Hardy was seen, in Chesterton's phrase, as 'the village atheist cursing and blaspheming over the village idiot'. The key sentence was 'Justice was done, and the President of the Immortals, in Aeschylean phrase, had ended his sport with Tess', and the key questions centred around cosmic determinism. The change of direction was marked first by writers like Kettle and Douglas Brown, the latter proclaiming that the central theme of Hardy's novels is 'the tension between the old rural world and the new urban one'[2] and the former that 'the subject of *Tess* is the destruction of the peasantry'.[3] Later writers such as Merryn and Raymond Williams have refined and expanded these views, modifying and sophisticating without radically altering. Marx has succeeded to the inheritance of Schopenhauer. One sort of determinism has supplanted another.

In this essay I want to look at the importance of history and geography, at the exhibition of time and place, to trace change and to consider Hardy's feelings about it and his interpretation of it, and, finally, to ask whether his modern critics interpret it as I think he did.

Hardy wrote of Dorset in Dorset. Indeed, he could settle nowhere else, as his short stay in and early departure from London made clear. I must therefore begin with Wessex, a name that signifies not only geography but history, and history, moreover, spanning aeons of time. It is a place on which time has had little or no impact. The Australian poet Judith Wright's ancient cycad trees are relevant, which

> sullenly
> keep the old bargain life has long since broken;

and, cursed by age, through each chill century
they watch the shrunken moon, but never die,

for time forgets the promise he once made,
and change forgets that they are left alone.

Put alongside this Hardy's description of Egdon:

> The sombre stretch of rounds and hollows seemed to rise and meet the evening gloom in pure sympathy, the heath exhaling darkness as rapidly as the heavens precipitated it. And so the obscurity in the air and the obscurity in the land closed together in a black fraternization towards which each advanced half-way.
>   The place became full of a watchful intentness now; for when other things sank brooding to sleep the heath appeared slowly to awake and listen. Every night its Titanic form seemed to await something; but it had waited thus, unmoved, during so many centuries, through the crises of so many things, that it could only be imagined to await one last crisis – the final overthrow. (*The Return of the Native*, Book First, Ch. 1)

– a place all its own, a place in silent and eternal communion with night, a place in which man is an intruder, microscopic in size and ephemeral in his presence.

But that is only one part of Wessex; there are others – places like Stonehenge and Casterbridge; Stonehenge, one of those 'finally negative images of an empty nature and the tribal past', to use Raymond Williams' phrase,[4] and Casterbridge which 'announced old Rome in every street, alley and precinct' (*The Mayor of Casterbridge*, Ch. 11). Hardy is telling us that geography is history, that the land exhibits the marks of men long dead and of their pursuits both noble and less so. That way he proclaims the fleetingness of man's presence, just as in another, the lonely traveller, whether Venn on the Heath or Tess travelling across those 'white flinty rods [that] can be distinguished for miles' as James Caird described them,[5] he shows the minuteness of man in the landscape. Dorothy Van Ghent makes much of the incessant journey of isolated individuals in Hardy. Even the more hospitable areas of Wessex like Farmer Crick's lush watermeadows are seen first from the panoramic standpoint of the nearby hills. I would not wish, however, to mislead by excessive emphasis in one direction. These lands are 'a fertile and sheltered tract of country, in which the fields are never brown and the springs never dry', and it is true that with poetic intention Hardy often matched environment to the mood of his character, and thus Froom Vale is the locale of Tess's happiness as Flintcomb-Ash is of her desolation. One tendency of what I may perhaps call the socio-literary criticism of Hardy has been to miss the broad sweep of history and the poetic significance of landscape that are as much part of 'Hardy and rural England' as a narrower band of time and a more limited socio-economic analysis of the novels.

To look now at this narrower band of time. In *The Mayor of Casterbridge* Hardy looked back for his whole story from the mid-1880s to the mid-1840s, to agricultural England in the years just before the repeal of the Corn Laws. In *Tess* the date of his story is apparently much nearer the time of writing, but there is also much emphasis on an older generation and the ways things had changed. Before publishing either of these novels Hardy had written of an earlier time in his essay on 'The Dorsetshire Labourer'. What strikes the reader about this essay is its sense of intimacy and affection. Hardy knew the Dorsetshire labourer. He can describe him 'at his worst and saddest time . . . a wet hiring fair at Candlemas, in search of a new master. His natural cheerfulness bravely struggles against the weather and the incertitude; but as the day passes on, and his clothes get wet through, and he is still unhired, there does appear a factitiousness in the smile which, with a self-repressing mannerliness hardly to be found among any other class, he yet has ready when he encounters and talks with friends who have been more fortunate.' A man who knew such men so well was in no danger of failing to recognise individuals by submerging them in a class. There is much in this essay to remind us of *Tess*: the account, for example, of the rigours of working with the threshing machine, or the reference to the children with their National School education mixing 'the printed tongue as taught therein with the unwritten, dying, Wessex English that they had learnt of their parents'; but above all there is the rejection of a stereotype rustic, Hodge, in terms not unlike those which Hardy uses about Angel Clare's realisation that his fellows at Farmer Crick's establishment were all individuals, 'beings infinite in difference; some happy, many serene, a few depressed . . . men every one of whom walked in his own individual way the road to dusty death'. We need to remember that also when we incline to read *Tess* as some sort of socio-economic allegory, 'the destruction of the peasantry' or whatever else.

Hardy regretted the passing of the past and not least he regretted the migration of the labourers. He dwells on it in 'The Dorsetshire Labourer':

> It is the common remark of villagers above the labouring class, who know the latter well as personal acquaintances that 'there are no nice homely workfolk now as there used to be'. . . . It is only natural that,

now different districts of them are shaken together, once a year, and redistributed, like a shuffled pack of cards, they have ceased to be so local in feeling or manner as formerly.

The consequences of this last Hardy developed more specifically elsewhere. In a letter to Rider Haggard he wrote:

> Village tradition – a vast mass of unwritten folk-lore, local chronicle, local topography, and nomenclature – is absolutely sinking, has nearly sunk, into eternal oblivion. . . . Thus you see, there being no continuity of environment in their lives, there is no continuity of information, the names, stories, and relics of one place being speedily forgotten under the incoming facts of the next.

One can immediately recognise another significance of the journeying figure in the landscape. Tess, forty miles from Marlott in the Froom Vale, might as well be in another world so far as her mother's horizons are concerned.

'Unwritten folk-lore' plays a large part in Hardy's version of older rural society. Lord David Cecil noted years ago that Hardy's 'tragedy is village tragedy, composed of the drama of broken love and wronged girls, the feuds and the hangings that filled his early memories. And the ballad stories left their mark too. There is always something of the folk-song about Hardy's plots. They are full of true lovers and forlorn maidens and dashing Don Juans. . . . Even *Tess*, considered as so modern and advanced in its day, has a story which, when peeled of its realistic trappings, reveals itself as a regular folk-tale tragedy. Tess, the beautiful innocent maiden, is betrayed by a wicked seducer and ends her life on the gallows-tree.' There is Hardy working in the ballad and folk-story tradition, but, as his letter to Rider Haggard makes clear, there is an integration between the mode and the setting, an apt relation between the kind of tale and the people who take part in it. Thus David Cecil can go on: 'Hardy's stories are full of relics of English popular superstition which played so large a role in the histories he listened to round the fire in the long winter evenings – the witchcraft and the wax images in *The Return of the Native*, the mid-summer rites by which girls sought to divine the name of their future husband in *Tess* and *The Woodlanders*, while country customs and ceremonies and gaieties, carol-singing, harvest-homes, maypoles and mummers' plays are scattered broadcast over his pages.'[6]

There is a whole series of significances in Hardy's use of such material. In the first place, there is the obvious historical enrichment of the fictional world he is creating; but there is also for the reader, because before that it was there for Hardy himself, the enrichment of nostalgia, never more evident than in the early *Under the Greenwood Tree*. There is, as Hardy's own complaint to Rider Haggard demonstrated, the sense of the stable past; but equally there is the view of the more enlightened present, both in character and author. We see this in the relation of Tess and her mother, and yet the better educated Tess can never free herself from the age-old feelings in her blood. Hardy can claim at one moment that 'between the mother, with her fast-perishing lumber of superstitions, folk-lore, dialect and orally transmitted ballads and the daughter, with her trained National teachings and Standard knowledge under an infinitely Revised Code, there was a gap of two-hundred years as ordinarily understood' (Ch. 3); but not much later he can write: 'Tess was steeped in fancies and prefigurative superstitions' (Ch. 6) and can talk of her singing the Benedicite as 'a Fetichistic utterance in a Monotheistic setting', going on to say that 'women whose chief companions are the forms and forces of outdoor Nature retain in their souls far more of the Pagan fantasy of their remote forefathers than of the systematised religion taught their race at later date'. There are no contradictions here. Tess is more sophisticated than her mother, but at bottom she is the same, and the 'Pagan fantasy' does underlie the 'systematised religion'. There is superstition in us all, and Hardy in the two generations conveys the idea that there is both change and changelessness at the same time. More than that, however, this superstition is inextricably related to and one expression of the novel's fatalism. When the cock crows, Farmer Crick may pretend to disbelieve the portent (Ch. 33), but whether he does or not, nobody can do anything about it — and the portent turns out to be correct. Folk-lore in both its influence on and as an expression of man's life is also part of Hardy and rural England.

We may now move on to what I earlier called the more limited socio-economic analysis of the novels. I have already drawn attention to the phenomenon of mobility within Wessex, but this phenomenon was also influential on a larger scale. The railway came to Dorchester in 1847, when Hardy was seven years old. It is a mark of his provincialism that the railway is thought of as an invader; 'Modern life stretched out its steam feeler to this point three or four times a day, touched the native existences, and quickly withdrew its feeler again, as if what it touched had been uncongenial' (Ch. 30). It comes into 'their secluded world'. But Hardy recognises that it has had its effects on the rural social structure. The key passage is the following:

> all the mutations so increasingly discernible in village life did not originate entirely in the agricultural unrest. A depopulation was also

going on. The village had formerly contained, side by side with the agricultural labourers, an interesting and better-informed class, ranking distinctly above the former – the class to which Tess's father and mother had belonged – and including the carpenter, the smith, the shoemaker, the huckster, together with nondescript workers other than farm-labourers; a set of people who owed a certain stability of aim and conduct to the fact of their being life-holders like Tess's father, or copyholders, or, occasionally, small freeholders. But as the long holdings fell in they were seldom again let to similar tenants, and were mostly pulled down, if not absolutely required by the farmer for his hands. Cottagers who were not directly employed on the land were looked upon with disfavour, and the banishment of some starved the trade of others, who were thus obliged to follow. These families, who had formed the backbone of the village life in the past, who were the depositaries of the village traditions, had to seek refuge in the large centres; the process, humorously designated by statisticians as 'the tendency of the rural population towards the large towns', being really the tendency of water to flow uphill when forced by machinery. (Ch. 51)

Of this passage the most intelligent of Hardy's critics from the socio-economic view, Raymond Williams, comments as follows:

Here there is much more than the crude and sentimental version of the rape of the country by the town. The originating pressures within rural society itself are accurately seen, and are given a human and social rather than a mechanical dimension.

Indeed we miss almost all of what Hardy has to show us if we impose on the actual relationships he describes, a neo-pastoral convention of the countryman as an old-age figure, or a vision of a prospering countryside being disintegrated by Corn Law repeal or the railways or agricultural machinery.[7]

That is well said. It warns us against things that were just not historically true. Dorset, a mainly grazing and mixed farming county, did not suffer the worst from the repeal of the Corn Laws and it positively benefited from the London market for milk which the railways opened up. The passage warns us, too, against any simple allegory. The age-old figure of the countryman was really as many different people as there were individuals. What happens to John Durbeyfield does not happen to his fellow-villagers: indeed, Hardy is at pains to point out the singularity of Durbeyfield, even to his attitude to his ancient lineage, for there were other decayed members of ancient families like the Prittles, of whom we hear nothing similar.

Williams is right also to warn us that there is no simple 'country good/town bad' opposition. Indeed, this has often been the equation applied in considering Hardy's strangers, men like Alec d'Urberville and Farfrae. The contrast between d'Urberville and Angel Clare has to recognise that neither really belongs to the instinctive world of rural Wessex: and as for Farfrae, his invasion of Casterbridge does substitute efficiency for more *ad hoc* earlier methods, but then Henchard was also an 'off-comer'. Moreover, though Farfrae's efficiency does mark him as a successful entrepreneur, his economic adventures are no more reprehensible than those of Henchard. He won and Henchard lost, but the big speculation on the weather was not his, but Henchard's. It was Henchard who was out to make a 'killing', but the elements defeated him. Henchard does not, as Douglas Brown would have it, represent the extinction of an older form of the agricultural community: he represents Henchard, a man in a particular situation, for the understanding of which we need some of the necessary background knowledge, but who in no way can be said simply to illustrate that background.

In the same way we need to be careful how we interpret the incident of the threshing machine at Flintcomb-Ash. This era of Tess's life was one of great endurance and great suffering, as the earlier swede-hacking scene makes clear. Hardy tells us of the 'starve-acre place', 'the village uncared for either by itself or by its lord', and Tess's patience as she worked there (Ch. 43).

Much has been made of the invader who controls the threshing machine, and one cannot read away the references to his hellish associations, 'the appearance of a creature from Tophet', who 'served fire and smoke', the 'service of his Plutonic master'. He is the new traveller, who has little to do with the countryside. 'He was in the agricultural world, but not of it . . . his eye on his iron charge, hardly perceiving the scenes around him, and caring for them not at all. . . . The long strap which ran from the driving wheel of his engine to the red thresher under the rick was the sole tie-line between agriculture and him' (Ch. 47).

This machine is then related to Tess's downfall: 'an impersonal agent of destruction', Douglas Brown calls it. As Merryn Williams remarks, 'it is difficult to see how this work is any crueller than reed-drawing, or grubbing up swedes in the pitiless rain. Industrialism can certainly be brutal but then so can nature.' She might have added that no catastrophic inferences are associated with the reaping machine (Ch. 14), or even with the turnip-slicing machine (Ch. 46), also part of Tess's Flintcomb-Ash experience, about which Hardy mentioned that 'for hours nothing relieved the joyless monotony of things'.

What I then find difficult to understand is the way in which Dr Williams continues:

> The machine in *Tess*, which reduces her to a state of near-helplessness ('her knees trembling so wretchedly with the shaking . . . that she could scarcely walk'), is destructive because it is only obliquely related to human needs and to human control. It has been introduced by a farmer in order to get the most out of his labourers; instead of cutting down their working hours it has made them slaves.

and later: 'Tess, as we have seen, only does humanly *meaningful* work at Talbothays, whereas at Flintcomb-Ash she is degraded as a mere wage-slave.'[8] So far as this latter statement is concerned, I do not see how what was done at Flintcomb-Ash was anything less essential or 'humanly *meaningful*' than at Talbothays: it was just more unpleasant. And when Merryn Williams talks about 'a mere wage-slave' and the machine having made them slaves, I do not see anything essentially different in work with the machine and work without it. But what is more important – Hardy does not seem to either, and certainly there is no explicit statement to this effect. Moreover, what Merryn Williams is doing is not literary criticism at all, it is politico-economic comment, and as with a lot of Marxist discussion of the Victorian novel she seems to me to be anachronistically guilty of applying twentieth-century perspectives to distort nineteenth-century literary statement.

In another instance and by another method she appears to leap several necessary stages in her argument when, quoting the passage about the dependence of the Durbeyfield children on their ne'er-do-well parents:

> All these young souls were passengers in the Durbeyfield ship – entirely dependent on the judgment of the two Durbeyfield adults for their pleasures, their necessities, their health, even their existence. If the heads of the Durbeyfield household chose to sail into difficulty, disaster, starvation, disease, degradation, death, thither were these half-dozen little captives under hatches compelled to sail with them – six helpless creatures, who had never been asked if they wished for life on any terms, much less if they wished for it on such hard conditions as were involved in being of the shiftless house of Durbeyfield. (Ch. 3)

she can precede it with the comment that 'Tess's innocence is dependent on her family's circumstances and has to be bartered for a desperately-needed material profit' (Ch. 9). Her vocabulary is coloured and her argument is defective. The socio-economic approach will no better relieve Hardy from those accusations of weighting the scales against his characters than will any other. Indeed, I think it worsens his case, for it blames the system whereas he blames 'the shiftless house of Durbeyfield'. But, beyond that, this comment of Merryn Williams' gives Tess's innocence up for lost, totally, whereas Hardy has Tess suggest that, had her mother enlightened her about the facts of life, things might have been different. After all, for Hardy Tess was a pure woman: she did not go in for seduction knowingly, bartering her innocence for her family's welfare.

Likewise, to return to the threshing machine incident, we should not infer that after her experience Tess had *no* alternative but to succumb to Alec. We must not engulf the individual in the circumstances. Raymond Williams attempts to avoid this. Of the scene in question he writes:

> This is Tess the girl and the worker. The break between her consciousness and her actions is as much a part of her emotional as of her working life. It is while she is working here and elsewhere that her critical emotional decisions are taken; it is through the ache and dust of the threshing machine that she again sees Alec. Hardy thus achieves a fullness which is quite new, at this depth, in all country-writing: the love and the work, the aches of labour and of choice, are in a single dimension.[9]

The critical discrimination is refined and the rhetoric is persuasive, but if you look at the book, the inference about the 'critical emotional decision' regarding Alec will not stand up to scrutiny. Tired as she is with her work, Tess nevertheless spiritedly resists him, and that resistance goes on for weeks and months when Tess is back in Marlott and after she has moved to Kingsbere. The end of the book is, in fact, considerably foreshortened. We are not given details of the circumstances in which Tess reunited herself with Alec d'Urberville, though one must acknowledge that Merryn Williams would be on firmer ground in claiming this as the episode in which Tess bartered herself for her family, making a calculated decision that has nothing emotional about it.

Laurence Lerner has remarked that 'To read through a book like *The Agricultural Revolution 1750–1880* by Chambers and Mingay with Hardy in mind is to notice how little it has to tell us about the concerns of his novels. The upward and downward movement of prices; the relative prosperity of the labourer in corn-growing areas and in pasture; the increase in size of farms – these are not the issues that appear in Hardy, and underlying economic forces of their kind could never be deduced from his fiction.' His example is the decline of the hiring fair in *The Mayor of Casterbridge*, about which he concludes that 'what happened to the fair is not economic but Darwinian: it seems to have lost out in some unexplained struggle for existence'.[10] That is another issue. Suffice it for us to agree that Hardy does not present social or economic history.

It has been my argument also that social and economic forces are not decisive in the lives of his characters. I therefore find myself once more in my frequent state of mingled assent and dissent with Raymond Williams when, nearing the conclusion of his remarks on Hardy, he writes:

> The passion of Marty or of Tess or of Jude is a positive force coming out of a working and relating world, seeking in different ways its living fulfilment. That all are frustrated is the essential action: frustrated by very complicated processes of division, separation and rejection. People choose wrongly but under terrible pressures.[11]

With all that I agree. My disagreement comes in when he strangely limits these preceding remarks with a final group of phrases that confine the responsibility to 'confusions of class, under its misunderstandings, under the calculated rejections of a divided separating world'. The great simplicities of love and hate are not confined within so small a space. The mantle of Marx fits Hardy no better than did that of Schopenhauer.

Those characters, the striking simplicity of whose lives Hardy interprets so profoundly and who flit so tragically across his scene, represent man in his essence. Philosophy too easily reduces the imagination. Wessex is only partly, and not most importantly, the scene of agricultural change in Hardy's own time; it is far more imperative to see it as the vast and ageless setting in which the tragedy of man is acted out, a tragedy terrible in the human perspective, all but insignificant in the cosmic. The conflict of those two viewpoints makes the tragedy all the more bitter from the only angle of vision that is available to us as human beings. That is why the figure in the landscape, isolated, lonely, unprotected, minute, is an apt image to remind ourselves of in concluding an essay on Hardy and rural England.

NOTES

1. Arnold Kettle, Introduction to *Tess of the d'Urbervilles*, written in 1966 and reprinted in *Twentieth-Century Interpretations of 'Tess of the d'Urbervilles'*, ed. Albert J. LaValley (Englewood Cliffs, N.J.: Prentice-Hall, 1969) p. 17.
2. Douglas Brown, *Thomas Hardy* (London: Longman, 1954) p. 65.

3. Arnold Kettle, *Introduction to the English Novel*, vol. II (London: Hutchinson, 1953) p. 54.
4. Raymond Williams, *The Country and the City* (London: Chatto & Windus, 1973) p. 255.
5. J. Caird, *English Agriculture in 1850–1* (London: Frank Cass, 1852) p. 57.
6. David Cecil, *Hardy the Novelist* (London: Constable, 1943) pp. 17–18.
7. Raymond Williams, op. cit., p. 252.
8. Merryn Williams, *Thomas Hardy and Rural England* (London: Macmillan, 1972) p. 177.
9. Raymond Williams, op. cit., p. 257.
10. Laurence Lerner, *Thomas Hardy's 'The Mayor of Casterbridge': Tragedy or Social History* (London: Sussex University Press, 1975) pp. 83–4.
11. Raymond Williams, op. cit., p. 258.

Hardy and 'the Woman Question'

Merryn Williams

Thomas Hardy's career as a novelist coincided with some striking changes in the lives of English women — changes which were mirrored in the novel and which had a deep effect on his last major prose work, *Jude the Obscure*. In the 1912 Postscript to that novel, Hardy said he had been told by a German reviewer

> that Sue Bridehead, the heroine, was the first delineation in fiction of the woman who was coming into notice in her thousands every year — the woman of the feminist movement — the slight, pale 'bachelor' girl — the intellectualized, emancipated bundle of nerves that modern conditions were producing, mainly in cities as yet; who does not recognise the necessity for most of her sex to follow marriage as a profession, and boast themselves as superior people because they are licensed to be loved on the premises. The regret of this critic was that the portrait of the newcomer had been left to be drawn by a man, and was not done by one of her own sex, who would never have allowed her to break down at the end.

The New Women, as feminists were sometimes called (other names were 'wild women' or 'the shrieking sisterhood') were essentially a product of the 1880s, and 1890s, and they are condemned or celebrated in many novels which came out in the few years before *Jude*. (Sue Bridehead definitely was not the first such woman in fiction: we may mention Henry James' Olive Chancellor, Gissing's Mrs Wade and George Moore's Cecilia Cullen, as well as a host of New Women created by less famous novelists.) But throughout Hardy's lifetime there had been enormous improvements in the position of women; the first of many reforming laws, the Infants' Custody Act, was passed the year before he was born. Further reforms in the second half of the century gave married women control of their property and earnings, abolished the husband's right to lock them up, and gave women householders the municipal vote. There was a great growth in secondary and higher education for girls, and this was welcomed by many people who did not want full emancipation because it was recognised that a bad and scrappy education at home, which was all that most women had ever had, did no good to anyone. At the same time, many new jobs for women became available – teaching, professional nursing, work in shops and offices – and these offered some real alternatives to domestic service for the working class and life as a governess or lady's companion for the poorer middle-class girl. It began to be accepted that there was nothing degrading about work before marriage. The young women of the 1890s had much freer lives than their mothers and grandmothers. They could move about as they liked in the cities (Hardy noted in a letter of 1898 how young girls on bicycles 'ride recklessly into the midst of the traffic'), and could leave home to work or study. And as there were many more women than men by the end of the century, they could no longer be told that their chief task was to find husbands.

During these years, too, there was an intense public debate about the role of women, which died down after they finally won the vote and did not resurface for another half century. It started in the 1850s when John Stuart Mill began to argue for full equality between the sexes. Mill's work had a very strong influence on Hardy, although he did not read *The Subjection of Women* (1869) before 1895. Several societies were formed: to campaign for the vote, to improve women's education and work opportunities, to end legal discrimination between women and men. People argued, in and out of novels, about whether woman's place was in the home or whether she might have other aims in life.

The New Woman appeared when the debate had been going on for more than a generation. Early campaigners had asked only for mild reforms, but the New Woman seemed to reject all traditional ideas about modesty, purity and deference. To some she was a woman who wanted the vote, to others a woman who valued her career and her personal development above marriage and children, and to still others a woman who did not believe in marriage at all. All agreed that this was no Angel in the House. The popular view was described in retrospect by Flora Thompson, who grew up in a small Oxfordshire village, in a home not unlike Hardy's, in the last quarter of the century:

> The girl of that day – she then figured as *The Girl of Today* in heavy type newspaper headings – was said to be mannerless, bold in her dress, speech and deportment, without respect for her elders and devoid of feminine charm. Some professed to see in this sad falling-off a sign of the times. A dying century, they said, must naturally be a time of expiring virtues.

Youth also applied to itself the term *fin de siècle* . . . but it signified self-congratulation rather than self-disparagement. New ideas and new ideals were in the air, blowing like a free, fresh wind – as they thought – through the old, stuffy atmosphere of convention, and what to their elders appeared as licence they gloried in as emancipation.

But such ideas had not penetrated to country places. The girls Laura knew at Heatherley were *fin-de-siècle* only in the sense of having been born towards the end of the century. The New Woman, of course, they knew by repute for she was a familiar figure to all newspaper readers, usually depicted as hideous, in semi-masculine garb with hands extended to grab male privileges, while a balloon of print issuing from her mouth demanded 'Votes for Women!'. . . . Mothers and elder sisters described the new women, not one of whom they had seen, as 'a lot of great coarse, ugly creatures who can't get themselves husbands'. 'I'd rather see you in your coffin', parents told their daughters, 'than wearing them bloomers and bawling for votes'.[1]

It is likely that the unsophisticated people among whom Hardy grew up would have felt very much the same. But Hardy himself was aware of a town-based civilisation that offered wider possibilities to women. In 1873, when *Far from the Madding Crowd* was appearing in the *Cornhill*, he was surprised to find that the artist who illustrated it was a young woman, Helen Paterson (later Helen Allingham). Subsequently he called her 'the best illustrator I ever had'. In this novel Bathsheba takes on the masculine role of a farmer, and his next book, *The Hand of Ethelberta*, also shows a heroine behaving unconventionally. Ethelberta is a bossy, manipulating woman who is a great success as a professional story-teller, a role which frees her from 'her hampering and inconvenient sex'. A good many women in his novels do some sort of work; even Elfride writes a book. In this respect they are very different from the old-fashioned heroine who has no occupation and exerts only a moral influence on events.

But while Hardy, like the feminists, believed that women were 'capable of much' (the phrase is Eustacia's), he thought their achievement would always be limited by the fact that they were literally the weaker sex. In a letter of 1897 he suggested that equality between the sexes might never be possible because 'the unalterable laws of nature are based upon a wrong'. 'The woman mostly gets the worst of it in the long run', he wrote in *Jude the Obscure*, and 'The Woman Pays' is the title of a book in *Tess*. Compassion comes over very strongly in his description of the young student teachers at Melchester training school, their tender feminine faces upturned to the flaring gas-jets . . . every face bearing the legend 'The Weaker' upon it, as the penalty of the sex wherein they were moulded, which by no possible exertion of their willing hearts and abilities could be made strong while the inexorable laws of nature remain what they are. They formed a pretty, suggestive, pathetic sight, of whose pathos and beauty they were themselves unconscious, and would not discover till, amid the storms and strains of afteryears, with their injustice, loneliness, child-bearing, and bereavement, their minds would revert to this experience as to something which had been allowed to slip past them insufficiently regarded.

'What are my books but one long plea against "man's inhumanity to man" – to woman – and to the lower animals?' Hardy said to William Archer in 1904. The double standard was an example of man's inhumanity to woman which he attacked forcefully in *Tess of the d'Urbervilles*. Tess, who takes her religious opinions from her husband, is certainly no New Woman, but the book scandalised those who denied that a fallen woman could be pure and those who believed that such subjects should not be mentioned in novels at all. On the other hand it was enormously admired, not only by the public, but also by the small group of novelists who were interested in 'the woman question' and who in many cases wanted to be able to write more freely. George Gissing wrote, 'It is glaringly unconventional, and earns its applause in the very teeth of a great deal of puritanic prejudice. Hardy is a nobly artistic nature.'[2] When his own novel *Denzil Quarrier* came out soon afterwards he noted that 'not a single paper has objected to the theme. Indeed, after Hardy's "Tess", one can scarcely see the limits of artistic freedom.'[3] Grant Allen, then a fairly obscure novelist, wrote a glowing review of *Tess* – 'a holy book, a pure-souled book, the very first book in which Thomas Hardy, a chosen and divinely-inspired teacher of truth, has ventured to speak out for us in his own authentic voice'.[4] His own notorious novel, *The Woman Who Did*, published in the following year, was written 'for the first time in my life wholly and solely to satisfy my own taste and my own conscience'.

From then on most people assumed that Hardy was a friend to women's rights. In 1892 he had to tell the Women's Progressive Society that 'I have not as yet been converted to a belief in the desirability of the Society's first object' (the vote), although he had 'much sympathy with many of your objects'.[5] Over the next ten or fifteen years he became steadily more sympathetic, as we see in this letter of 1906 to the suffragist leader, Millicent Garrett Fawcett:

> I have for a long time been in favour of woman-suffrage. . . . I am in favour of it because I think the tendency of the woman's vote will be to break up the pernicious conventions in respect of women, customs, religion, illegitimacy, the stereotyped household (that it must be the unit of society), the father of a woman's child (that it is anybody's business but the woman's own) . . . and other matters which I got into hot water for touching on many years ago.[6]

It will be seen that Hardy associates women's suffrage with other matters which are not necessarily connected with it. As a matter of fact many of the feminists were religious and only a few were anti-marriage. 'Votes for women and purity for men' was a slogan (from 1913) which sums up their attitude rather better. But one section of feminists, led by Josephine Butler, had passionately attacked organised prostitution and the double standard, as had a famous feminist novelist of the 1890s, Sarah Grand. This certainly gave many people the impression that New Women, unlike the innocent and ignorant mid-Victorian ladies, were extremely frank and knowing about sex.

When we look back at the time of which Hardy speaks – the early 1890s, when he wrote his last two great novels – we find that one reason why he 'got into hot water' was the sharp reaction against 'marriage question' novels, a great number of which came out in the few years before *Jude*. 'I suppose the attitude of these critics is to be accounted for by the accident that during the serial publication of my story, a sheaf of "purpose" novels on the matter appeared,'[7] Hardy wrote at the time. Attacks on the traditional concept of marriage had become quite common. 'It has for some time past', wrote Elizabeth Chapman, a feminist who believed strongly in the marriage tie, 'become difficult to take up a novel in which, openly or covertly, directly or indirectly, the institution of marriage is not either put upon its trial, or at any rate freely discussed and handled with as much or as little ceremony as though it were, say, a moot point in science or a minor question of politics. The once sacred, the once theoretically indissoluble life-tie between husband and wife has become, in short, an open question.'[8]

Divorce was so difficult to obtain in Victorian England that most novelists, including Hardy for the greater part of his career, assumed that a bad marriage could be ended only by death. In 1857 the Matrimonial Causes Act made it legal in certain circumstances; this is the 'new law' referred to in *The Woodlanders*. But the actual number of divorces remained low throughout the nineteenth century, and although many novelists from the 1870s onwards wrote about unhappiness in marriage few of them seem to have thought that this was the answer. What did become acceptable was the idea that people could be married 'in the sight of God' to someone not their legal husband or wife. George Eliot had won a high reputation as a moralist in spite of her unsanctified union with G. H. Lewes. Novels like Wilkie Collins' *No Name* (1862), Meredith's *One of Our Conquerors* (1891) and Gissing's *Denzil Quarrier* (1892) strongly suggest that a person whose marriage has broken down is not blameworthy if he or she forms a faithful union with someone else.

A much more fundamental attack on marriage came from novelists who believed, like Shelley, in 'free unions' as the ideal. Herminia in *The Woman Who Did* says:

> If I love a man at all, I must love him on terms of perfect freedom. I can't bind myself down to live with him to my shame one day longer than I love him; or to love him at all if I find him unworthy of my purest love, or unable to retain it, or if I discover some other more fit to be loved by me.

This argument could have been used by a man, of course, but Herminia, who 'lives for nothing else but the emancipation of women', claims, too, that marriage is 'an assertion of man's supremacy over woman' and that to go through the ceremony would be 'treason to my sex'. It was a fact that throughout most of history married women had been almost completely in their husbands' power. But various legal changes, some of them too recent to have sunk fully into public awareness, made this no longer true by the time Grant Allen wrote. Since 1882 married women had owned their own property, and since 1891 they had had the right to live away from their husbands. They could obtain a divorce in some circumstances, and they could at least try to get custody of their children. On the other hand women who lived in a 'free union' could expect enormous hostility; Elizabeth Chapman described it as the freedom 'to cut their own throats'.

Nevertheless, several novels before *Jude* show the man offering marriage while the woman insists on a free union as a matter of principle. Among them are *Restless Human Hearts* (1875) by Richard Jefferies, *The Story of an African Farm* (1883) by Olive Schreiner, *The New Antigone* (1887) by William Barry, *I Forbid The Banns* (1893) by Frankfort Moore, and in 1895 the famous *The Woman Who Did*. 'It is the women who are the active agents in all this unsavoury imbroglio', Mrs Oliphant wrote in her review of *Jude*; '. . . this is one of the most curious developments of recent fiction'. She noted that the 'astonished men' whom they select for partners 'generally act the part of a startled audience, and, to do them justice, are never the originators of these sentiments'.⁹ The New Woman, then, seemed to be a person who contemptuously rejected what most women had always seen as their principal goal. But all these heroines pay a bitter price for nonconformity; they either change their minds or die.

In the first half of *Jude* Hardy seems to be saying only that people should be allowed to end a marriage that has become miserable and to form a new relationship if they wish. In the fifth book both hero and heroine get their divorces without trouble and a happy, if unconventional, ending looks possible. But at this point Sue begins a new argument – that the legal ceremony itelf kills love – and the book becomes a different kind of anti-marriage novel.

In fact it was not quite an accident that Hardy became associated in the public mind with a group of 'anti-marriage' novelists. He had had some influence on them, through *Tess*, and they in turn had some influence on him. And his correspondence from the 1890s shows that he kept in touch with several other novelists who questioned the traditional roles of women.

One of these novelists was Grant Allen (1848–99), two of whose novels were reviewed along with *Jude* in *Blackwood's* under the heading of 'The Anti-Marriage League'. His *The Woman Who Did* is in many ways a weaker and more dogmatic version of *Tess*. Herminia, who chooses to have a child outside marriage, is beautiful, unselfish and, in the author's eyes, pure, but inevitably she is destroyed by those who see her as a fallen woman. When her daughter turns conventional and rejects her, she commits suicide. It was a shocking book for the Victorians, without being too shocking, and it was also very easy to read. It caused a sensation and went through twenty editions in one year.

Herminia is introduced as 'a free woman', but as Millicent Garrett Fawcett pointed out, 'she has no real individuality or independence' and submits to her lover 'with a woman's meekness' on all points except marriage. 'It is a woman's ancestral part', Allen wrote, 'to look up to the man.' Mrs Fawcett commented, 'It is satisfactory to remember that Mr Grant Allen has never given help by tongue or pen to any practical effort to improve the legal or social status of women. He is not a friend but an enemy, and it is as an enemy that he endeavours to link together the claim of women to citizenship and social and industrial independence, with attacks upon marriage and the family.'¹⁰

On the other hand Hardy seems to have liked the novel; writing to Allen to thank him for his copy he referred to *Jude*, which was still appearing in serial form: 'It touches, in one place, upon the same question of marriage; but my poor heroine learns only by experience what yours knows by instinct.'[11] This was in February 1895, only a month before the manuscript of *Jude* was finished, so Allen's novel came too late to have had much influence on Hardy's. But there is an echo in the penultimate chapter of Allen's idea that people who are ahead of their time must expect to suffer, when the dying Jude says:

> As for Sue and me, when we were at our own best, long ago – when our minds were clear, and our love of truth fearless – the time was not ripe for us! Our ideas were fifty years too soon to be any good to us. And so the resistance they met with brought reaction in her, and recklessness and ruin on me!

The same idea is expressed more crudely by Herminia: 'For whoever sees the truth, whoever strives earnestly with all his soul to be good, must be raised many planes above the common mass of men around him; he must be a moral pioneer, and the moral pioneer is always a martyr. People won't allow others to be wiser and better than themselves unpunished.' Again, towards the end of *Jude* we find: 'Your worldly failure, if you have failed, is to your credit rather than to your blame. Remember that the best and greatest among mankind are those who do themselves no worldly good. Every successful man is more or less a selfish man.' Herminia expresses very similar views: 'To succeed is to fail, and failure is the only success worth aiming at. Every great and good life can but end in a Calvary.'

We know that *Jude* was originally to have been a story about 'a young man who could not go to Oxford'. But at some time in 1893 or 1894 while the novel was being written Hardy became interested in 'the marriage question' and decided that it was going to be a different kind of book from the one he had planned.[12] During these years other novels expressing radical and unconventional ideas about women appeared, and it seems likely, from internal and external evidence, that they had some effect on the final version of *Jude*.

More influential than Allen was Sarah Grand (Frances McFall, 1862–1943), who sent Hardy a copy of her best-selling novel, *The Heavenly Twins*, in 1893, as 'a very inadequate acknowledgement of all she owes to his genius'. His comments suggest that he was not very impressed with it, but some of its ideas seem to have found their way into his own new novel. The heroine, Evadne, is 'a nineteenth-century woman of the higher order with senses so refined that if her moral as well as her physical being were not satisfied in love, both would revolt'. She is an intelligent girl who reads a great number of books, including Mill's, has strong principles and shocks people by her unconventional behaviour; but, inexplicably, she marries an insensitive man twice her age. The relationship breaks down almost at once when she finds out about his past (Sarah Grand shared Hardy's hostility to the double standard), but she finally agrees to live separately under the same roof. 'The man who was liked well enough as a companion, was found to be objectionable in an unendurable degree as soon as he became a husband.' Although he dies and Evadne marries a more congenial man, her nerves have been shattered and she is morbid, sickly and hysterical by the end of the book. There are fairly obvious similarities here to Hardy's Sue Bridehead, and another point in which the two novels resemble each other is the existence of a monster child (in this case produced by a pure young girl whose parents let her marry a man with venereal disease). But it is in basic attitudes, rather than similarities of plot, that Sarah Grand comes closest to Hardy. She believed in legal marriage, but she stressed that it 'should only be entered upon with the greatest care and in the most reverent spirit'. The theme of young people making lifelong commitments without knowing what they are doing is central to *The Heavenly Twins* and to *Jude the Obscure*.

Another 'New Woman' novelist whom Hardy knew was Ménie Muriel Dowie (1867–1945), whose novel *Gallia* came out in the same year as *Jude* and was grouped with it by Mrs Oliphant as an anti-marriage novel. Yet another whom he did not know, but admired, was 'George Egerton' (Mary Chavelita Clairmonte, 1859–1945). Her book of short stories, *Keynotes* (1893), made a deep impression on Hardy, who copied out long passages from her story 'A Cross Line' (about a woman who cannot bear life with her husband) while he was working on the last stages of *Jude the Obscure*.[13] Writing to congratulate Hardy, George Egerton described Sue as 'a marvellously true psychological study of a temperament less rare than the ordinary male observer supposes'.[14]

But it is possible that the most important literary influence on *Jude* was the work of George Gissing, certainly the best of the minor novelists who handled 'the woman question' in the nineties. He and Hardy had met occasionally and exchanged copies of their books since 1886. They never became close friends, but they respected each other's work, Gissing writing to Hardy after reading *The Mayor of Casterbridge* that he had 'constantly found refreshment and onward help'[15] in his books. They shared a dislike of orthodox Christianity and a feeling that it was not possible for a writer to be honest in the England of the 1880s. Another thing they had in common was a reputation for writing morbid and unpleasant books. They were both 'pessimists' in the sense that they did not believe in a Providence which looked after people and therefore many of their novels have unhappy endings. 'The most characteristic, the most important part of my work', Gissing wrote in 1895, 'is that which deals with a class of young men distinctive of our time – well-educated, fairly bred, *but without money.*'[16] This was a type with which Hardy instinctively sympathised too, and he drew it in many of his early novels as well as in *Jude.*

A newspaper of 1895 described Hardy, Gissing and Meredith (who was also sympathetic to feminism) as the 'three most important novelists of the day'.[17] Gissing's biographer speaks of 'a tacit literary alliance between the three men'.[18] Hardy had already spoken of his admiration for Gissing in an interview with William Robertson Nicoll:

> Mr Hardy's gentle urbanity encourages the novice to put questions, and greatly daring, I ventured to ask whether there were any young writers whom he admired. He instantly answered, 'George Gissing', and gave me some account of *The Unclassed.*[19]

The central figure of *The Unclassed* is a prostitute who remains essentially good and becomes 'a pure woman' when she falls in love. 'Thus, the heroine is something like Tess,' wrote a reviewer, 'but the hero is not an Angel Clare.'[20] Hardy may also have taken notice of the sub-plot, about a poor student, Julian Casti, who works through the night and dreams of being a writer. 'The thought of giving pain to any most humble creature was itself a pain unendurable to Julian', Gissing comments, and we are reminded of Hardy's hero who 'could not bear to hurt anything'. Manoeuvred into marriage by a selfish woman, Julian is forced to give up his dreams and dies miserably of tuberculosis.

Two more Gissing novels are significant. The first is *Denzil Quarrier* (1892). Lilian, the heroine, is in many ways Gissing's ideal woman. She is refined, tender-hearted, educates herself in order to share her man's interests and does not want the vote. But as a very young girl she has married a forger who was arrested at the church door, and unable to divorce him she joins her life to Denzil's. When their secret is exposed she commits suicide rather than ruin his career, one of the people who drives her to it being a hard-faced feminist, Mrs Wade. Not only the false marriage but the breakdown of a woman at the climax of the novel is reminiscent of *Jude*. This breakdown is described by a rather foolish clergyman:

> Mrs Quarrier . . . represents a type of woman becoming . . . only too common in our time, women who cultivate the intellect at the expense of the moral nature. . . . Strong-minded women, you will hear them

called; in truth, they are the weakest of their sex. Let their energies be submitted to any unusual strain, let their nerves (they are always morbid) be overwrought, and they snap! . . . Mrs Quarrier was abetted by her husband, by Mrs Wade; they excited her to the point of frenzy, and in the last moment she – snapped!

This reads like a comic description of Hardy's Sue, who is strong-minded in the sense of rejecting convention but who is also morbid and becomes one of the weakest of her sex in the end. Gissing said that his novel was not anti-marriage but 'a strong defence of conventionality'.[21] However, it can just as easily be read as an attack on the 'moral and discreet law which maintains the validity of such a marriage'.

The Odd Women is an uneven, fascinating novel which discusses several aspects of 'the woman question'. It was published in April 1893, about the time when Hardy finished his first outline of *Jude*, and although I have not found evidence that he read it, several passages in the two novels seem to correspond. Gissing, for intensely personal reasons, was obsessed with the problems of intelligent men who married stupid or unsympathetic women. His first novel, *Workers in the Dawn*, has a *Jude*-like situation; the hero marries a woman of a 'somewhat sensual type' and loses the idealistic girl for whom he feels a 'pure devotion of the spirit'; in the end both of them die. In *The Odd Women*, we hear 'how often a woman is a clog upon a man's ambition'. Everard Barfoot, the most important male character, says that 'the mass of women' are 'contemptible', that intelligent men usually 'regard their wives with active disgust', and that some very young men 'are so frantic as to marry girls of the working class – mere lumps of human flesh'. Hardy did not share Gissing's anti-working class bias, but this is still a good description of the fatal marriage with Arabella. Everard also tells the story of a girl who deliberately got pregnant – 'She simply planned to get me into her power – thought I should be forced to marry her. It's the kind of thing that happens far oftener than you would suppose.' 'Lots of girls do it,' says Arabella's friend, 'or do you think they'd get married at all?' Arabella was not quite the first coarse woman in Hardy's fiction, but this was the first time he had shown such a woman deliberately dragging down a more spiritual man.

It will be obvious from what has been quoted that Gissing was hardly a feminist, and in fact he thought that 'more than half the misery of life is due to the ignorance and childishness of women'.[22] He believed, though, that they should be educated and given responsible work, if only because this would make them more suitable companions for men. *The Odd Women* suggests that a historical crisis had been reached and that women could now choose whether to go forward or back. 'Odd' means surplus: in 1891 there were nearly a million more women than men and therefore a high proportion of women did not marry. What to do with these women was a vexed question, since most of them had never thought in terms of careers for themselves. Gissing shows us a family of spinster sisters, getting more demoralised year by year as they work at depressing and badly-paid jobs. Monica, the youngest, feels she cannot bear to live like this and marries an unattractive middle-aged man called Widdowson. Although she tries to make the marriage work she becomes more and more repelled by his possessiveness (Gissing makes the point that a wife is an independent human being and cannot be expected to live only for husband and home). Widdowson himself realises, though only for a moment, that he is being unreasonable:

> Monica's independence of thought is a perpetual irritation to me. I don't know what her thoughts really are, what her intellectual life signifies. And yet I hold her to me with the sternest grasp. If she endeavoured to release herself I should feel capable of killing her. Is not this a strange, a brutal thing?

Monica falls in love with a man in her own age-group, but he gives her no support and she eventually dies bearing Widdowson's child.

Gissing makes Monica affirm 'a woman's right to release herself if she found her marriage was a mistake', and Everard Barfoot says, 'If my wife should declare that she must be released, I might suffer grievously, but being a man of some intelligence, I should admit that the suffering couldn't be helped; the brutality of enforced marriage doesn't seem to me worth considering.' Hardy, too, felt strongly that the man's wish to possess and dominate the woman was 'a strange, a brutal thing'. In *Jude the Obscure* he reworked Gissing's conception of the middle-aged husband to show him behaving by a different standard. Phillotson, like Widdowson (even the names are similar), is obviously unsuited to the girl he has married, but after this becomes clear he decides with much pain that he cannot force her to stay with him. (It has to be remembered that most people at this time believed that a husband had the right to lock up his wife if she misbehaved.) Hardy reinforces the argument by making Phillotson lose his job because he lets her go, while almost everyone praises him when he takes possession of her again at the end.

The other plot of *The Odd Women* centres on Rhoda Nunn, literally a nun-like woman in that she decides consciously to do without men. 'Before the female sex can be raised from its low level', she says, 'there will have to be a widespread revolt against sexual instinct.' Rhoda helps to run a bureau which trains young girls for clerical work, and believes in 'the education of women in self-respect and self-restraint'. Most unusually for a heroine, she is neither beautiful nor charming; Gissing calls her an 'unfamiliar sexual type, remote indeed from the voluptuous'. Any relationship with a man must 'permit her to remain an intellectual being', and although she considers marriage, or alternatively a 'free union' with the misogynist hero, Everard, she finally decides to remain as she is.

Hardy did not discuss the position of single women in *Jude*, although he was quite aware of what he called 'the present man-famine' (*Ethelberta*, Ch. 34), and assumed that the ordinary commonplace woman would do anything to get a husband. But the language and ideas of *The Odd Women* are often paralleled in his last novel. Sue is both Monica and Rhoda – the charming girl trapped and at last destroyed by the wrong marriage and the emancipated, almost sexless New Woman – 'a distinct type, a refined creature, intended by Nature to be left intact'. Rhoda is described at one point as an 'ascetic who has arrived at a morbid delight in self-torture', which is a fair description of Sue at the end of her novel. Each of them is partly responsible for a death Sue is blamed for killing the undergraduate whom she refused to live with, and Rhoda causes a girl to commit suicide by refusing to have her back at the training school after she has had an affair with a married man. There is a certain coldness about both which suggests that the new type of woman is incapable of meeting a man's needs.

There is a note of hope, rather rare for a Gissing novel, at the end of *The Odd Women* when Rhoda feels an instinctive pity and tenderness for Monica's child. 'Make a brave woman of her', she says to Alice, the baby's aunt who has found her vocation in bringing her up. Looking after children, one's own or other people's, is certainly one kind of work for women (and it is noteworthy that this generation of feminists showed very little hostility to children). There are no children left alive at the end of *Jude the Obscure*, but Hardy did not forget their importance. His poem, 'To an Unborn Pauper Child', written some time in the next few years, suggests that in spite of the pervasive tragedy in the world, an individual child might still be happy.

The feminist movement, and some of the novels associated with it, certainly had their effect on Hardy, but it is too simple to call Sue 'the woman of the feminist movement'. She joins no pressure groups, she does not even mention the vote, and she shows very little awareness of the total situation of women. The most 'feminist' remark she ever makes is thrown off fairly casually: 'I have been looking at the marriage service in the Prayer-book, and it seems to me very humiliating that a giver-away should be required at all. According to the ceremony as there printed, the bridegroom chooses me of his own will and pleasure; but I don't choose him.

Somebody *gives* me to him, like a she-ass or she-goat, or any other domestic animal.' At the same time she is quite willing to go through this ceremony with a man she is not in love with anyway, so she hardly acts on her principles. Hardy's reluctance to get too involved in political or quasi-political issues made him strangely silent on 'the woman question'.

However, Sue's life-style and her basic assumptions put her a world away from the sheltered Victorian heroine. Her father is alive, but she never sees him – something which would have been almost inconceivable twenty or thirty years earlier. In this novel families no longer enclose people; when Drusilla is 'put into the new ground, quite away from her ancestors', we are witnessing the end of a way of life in which a woman was never allowed to go very far from her group. Sue takes it for granted that she should work, even when she has children, but on the other hand the question of what kind of work she does is never very important. She drifts from religious art-work to teaching and then to motherhood combined with various odd jobs. There is no serious commitment to a purpose, such as we find in Helen Allingham, or Tryphena Sparks (a headmistress at twenty-one), or the many other women of that generation who struggled to be doctors, scholars or reformers. The contrast between her relaxed attitude to her work and Jude's undying commitment to Christminster is very sharp.

There remains the question of why Hardy 'allowed her to break down at the end'. What the German reviewer may not have known was that there was a very long tradition in English literature of making women break down. Shakespeare's Ophelia, Richardson's Clarissa, Scott's Bride of Lammermoor, Catherine in *Wuthering Heights*, Lucy in *The Ordeal of Richard Feverel*, George Eliot's Caterina Sarti, Mary Braddon's Lady Audley and Gissing's Lilian Quarrier are all heroines who go mad or die. And even when a heroine does not die, her outraged emotions may drive her into a serious illness or a dose of brain fever (Caroline Helstone, Lucy Snowe, Laura Fairlie, Mrs Gaskell's Cousin Phillis, Sarah Grand's Evadne). Hardy fully shared the popular belief that a woman's mind was more delicately balanced than a man's and was therefore more likely to give way. The death of the children is presumably just as agonising for Jude, but he does not break down, and Sue does. Like Gissing's refined women, she cannot give the hero the support he needs and is ultimately no more use to him than Arabella. 'Strange difference of sex,' Jude (or Hardy?) says, 'that time and circumstance, which enlarge the views of most men, narrow the views of women almost invariably.' This cheerless conclusion is one which Hardy had thought about for some time.

Sue is not the first woman in his fiction to break down: Tess is apparently not quite sane when she murders Alec (the tortured woman in *The Bride of Lammermoor* also stabs her false husband), and it is worth looking carefully at a short story written around 1890, *Barbara of the House of Grebe*. Barbara is a 'tender but somewhat shallow lady' whose first husband dies partly because she recoils from him when he has been mutilated in an accident. Her new husband, finding that she still loves his rival, subjects her, in the privacy of their bedroom, to a long course of mental cruelty – 'till the nerves of the poor lady were quivering in agony under the virtuous tortures inflicted by her lord, to bring her truant heart back to faithfulness'. She ends up 'scared and enervated . . . completely worn out in mind and body', and dies.

The power of a husband over his wife, supported as it was by public opinion, religion and the law, seemed to Hardy the cruellest case of man's inhumanity to woman. In his poem, 'A Conversation at Dawn', a woman pleads with her husband to let her go to her lover, but, unlike Phillotson, he refuses:

> 'Even should you fly to his arms, I'll damn
> Opinion and fetch you; treat as sham
> Your mutinous kicks,
> And whip you home. That's the sort I am.'

'I daresay it happens to lots of women,' says Sue, 'only they submit, and I kick.' But Hardy suggests strongly that however much a woman 'kicks' the man can always break her spirit, if he is determined to do so. Arabella says to Phillotson, 'She'd have come round in time. We all do! . . . I shouldn't have let her go! I should have kept her chained on – her spirit for kicking would have been broke soon enough! There's nothing like bondage and a stone-deaf taskmaster for taming us women. Besides, you've got the laws on your side.' When Phillotson finally decides to take his wife back he is likely to be 'more orthodoxly cruel to her than he had erstwhile been informally and perversely kind'. 'A little judicious severity, perhaps . . .', he muses; and his friend Gillingham, continuing the horse-breaking imagery, says, 'Yes, but you must tighten the reins by degrees only. Don't be too strenuous at first. She'll come to any terms in time.'

Sue is last seen as 'a staid, worn woman', forcing herself to do the housework which she dislikes 'to discipline myself' and assuring her husband that, in the words of the once-despised marriage service, she wants to honour and obey him. Neither she nor he is likely to be happy, any more than Barbara and Lord Uplandtowers. Men and women, and even children, are damaged by female weakness and male power.

Hardy and 'the Woman Question'

Hardy sympathised with any moves which were likely to improve the status of women, but ultimately he could not believe that legal or social changes would help them, seeing that 'the unalterable laws of nature are based upon a wrong'.[23] He created no tough New Women, like Gissing's Rhoda, who could survive without men. The positive developments around the end of the century found no echo in his fiction. Women, for him, remained victims, because they had been born 'the Weaker'.

NOTES

1. Flora Thompson, 'Heatherley', *Observer Magazine*, 21 October 1979.
2. Quoted by Adrian Poole, *Gissing in Context* (London: Macmillan, 1975) p. 121.
3. Pierre Coustillas and Colin Partridge (eds), *Gissing: The Critical Heritage* (London: Routledge & Kegan Paul, 1972) p. 192.
4. Grant Allen, 'Fiction and Mrs. Grundy', *Novel Review*, July 1892.
5. Richard Little Purdy and Michael Millgate (eds), *The Collected Letters of Thomas Hardy*, I (Oxford: Clarendon Press, 1978) p. 266.
6. Letter of 30 November 1906 (in the Fawcett Library).
7. Richard Little Purdy and Michael Millgate (eds), *The Collected Letters of Thomas Hardy*, II (Oxford: Clarendon Press, 1980) p. 93.
8. E. R. Chapman, *Marriage Questions in Modern Fiction* (London: Lane, 1897) p. 10.
9. Margaret Oliphant, 'The Anti-Marriage League', *Blackwood's Magazine*, January 1896; reprinted in *Thomas Hardy: The Critical Heritage*, ed. R. G. Cox (London: Routledge & Kegan Paul, 1970) p. 260.
10. Millicent Garrett Fawcett, 'The Woman Who Did', *Contemporary Review*, May 1895.
11. *Collected Letters of Thomas Hardy*, II, p. 69.
12. See John Paterson, 'The genesis of *Jude the Obscure*', *Studies in Philology*, LVII (1960).
13. I am indebted for this point to Gail Cunningham's *The New Woman and the Victorian Novel* (London: Macmillan, 1978) p. 105.
14. *Collected Letters of Thomas Hardy*, II, p. 102n.
15. *Life*, p. 182.
16. Jacob Korg, *George Gissing: A Critical Biography* (Seattle: University of Washington Press, 1963) p. 263.
17. Quoted by Michael Collie, *George Gissing: A Biography* (Folkestone: Dawson, 1977) p. 10.
18. ibid., p. 11.
19. W. Robertson Nicoll, *People and Books* (London, 1926) p. 190.
20. *Gissing: The Critical Heritage*, p. 77.
21. ibid., p. 188.
22. Korg, op. cit., p. 185.
23. *Collected Letters of Thomas Hardy*, II, p. 153.

The Love Story in *Two on a Tower*

John Bayley

Hardy's modesty hid a secret conceit; his diffidence was of the sort that goes its own way in private, and is amazed and upset to encounter public incomprehension and disapproval. Intent on his plot in *Two on a Tower*, he had no perception of the fact that the novel-reading public might regard as improper, disturbing, even scandalous, the ingenious twist by which an amorous Bishop of Melchester might be induced to marry a lady already pregnant by another man.

In his essay 'Candour in English Fiction' (1890) he remarked on 'the fearful price' which a novelist in England had to pay for the privilege of enjoying an audience. As his pleasure in being a member of the Rabelais dining club shows, he was always glad to assume the role of manly frankness, that of the writer who calls a spade a spade and scorns concealment and hypocrisy. It is an unlikely and incongruous persona for Hardy, whose sense of refinement was really as strong as his instinct for privacy: any offence he might give would not be because he was being deliberately bold and coarse, but because things that seemed quite normal and acceptable to that inner sense could shock the public susceptibilities of conditioned readers.

Hardy would never have written a deliberate *fabliau*, a *conte drolatique* which would advertise itself as being only for those of robust tastes. Had he done so he would not have received the kind of criticism he did, and which put him out so much. The real truth of the matter is that in his earlier novels Hardy was probably not conscious of the ways in which he inadvertently upset a novel-reader's preconceived notions. His own intentness, both on the working out of the story and on the kind of inner dream it expressed for him, made him unaware of the different conventions in and out of which he slipped, and the changing perspectives on characters and tale which resulted from this.

Both the vitality and the oddity of *Two on a Tower* proceed from the way it disconnects mode and convention. One can hardly say that these are incongruous with each other, because that implies the kind of deliberate relation of the two which in Hardy's earlier work seems notably lacking. This absence of relation is typical of the atmosphere of his novels – the earlier ones particularly. I commented on it in my book on Hardy,[1] when I compared the relation of the different aspects of a Hardy novel to that of the cows, grass, and trees in a landscape. Their relation is one of tones and themes and conventions juxtaposed but seeming in their context naturally affiliated, each being absorbed in its own independent life and its own way of doing business.

In the later novels this seemingly artless indifference of one feature of the work to another is distinctly modified. It never disappears; rather it seems as if exploited deliberately. The relational aspect of things in the novel becomes more challenging and more self-consciously systematic. In his introduction to *The Woodlanders* David Lodge has noticed the way in which Hardy combines a Darwinian statement of nature as impersonally and inimically competitive – the crowded trees in a plantation wound and kill each other as they strive for survival – with a pastoral and almost traditionally idyllic view of nature as harmonious and responsive to 'the heart that loves her' and is in tune with her, that of the woodman Giles Winterborne. His death is lamented, through the rustic muse medium of Marty South. The point is made even more explicit in a review by John Carey, who writes of 'the delicate balance Hardy holds between these conflicting value-systems'.[2]

The idea of Hardy holding 'a delicate balance' between the 'value-systems' in his fictions may strike most readers as rather an unreal one. Such terms hardly seem apposite to the stories he tells and the way he tells them. None the less one must admit that their general tenor would be endorsed by Hardy himself, who in any discussion of his writing would certainly have taken the line that the artist was fastidiously aware of every effect he had put in. All his projections and effects are never less than consciously ambitious; he invokes the biggest ideas in the service of his fiction, as well as the most august of literary precedents – epical, tragical, and pastoral. And the juxtapositions in the later novels, if far from delicate, are certainly by intention boldly arresting. Tess the milkmaid lies like Iphigenia on the altar of Stonehenge. Henchard, the former mayor of a small provincial town, the fool Whittle his only follower, goes out on to the heath like King Lear into the storm. Such conjunctions, invoked or implied, show not so much the way Hardy's imagination naturally worked as the ways in which he came to make systematic use, for the novel, of a formula based on the originally free associations of his wide reading and pondering.

For there is a difference, and an important one, between these meaningful – sometimes all too meaningful – conjunctions, and the more indeterminate ways in which different modes of creation and narration cohabit together, nurtured without distinction in the singularity of Hardy's mind. Tess as country girl, as scion of an ancient house, as Pure Woman and exemplary victim – these roles underline all the coincidences of the ironic in which the novel abounds. Lady Constantine in *Two on a Tower* is also created in various manifestations, but in her case they are imminent in the text more subtly and more vivaciously.

She has the soft and loving temperament suited both to a Christian devotee and a woman made for earthly love: she unites in her person the maternal and the erotic, the image of Mary and the image of Venus. The former is stressed inconographically in the brief idyll after the Bath wedding, when she and Swithin are together in their hut at the base of the tower. Since they are without anything to eat on this first evening the young lover endeavours to catch young rabbits to feed his mistress, and does actually contrive to secure four sparrows and a thrush for their supper. The erotic charm of the scene is very great, and the mythological suggestions do all that is necessary, as Hardy no doubt intended. They are in a sense daring enough for the time and the audience, though no doubt most of the audience would have apprehended them rather vaguely and not taken in their specific literary and pictorial associations. But there is an unexpected change to narrative of a quite different sort, and with quite a different mode of suggestion. Chapter 20, which succeeds the night of the lovers' mythological supper, opens with the words: 'When Lady Constantine awoke next morning Swithin was nowhere to be seen.' He returns 'before she was quite ready for breakfast'. The juxtaposition of this plain but significant touch with the more grandiose amatory mythology is clearly not in any degree intentional: it happens, in fact, because Hardy is so much involved in his story in the way that came most obviously, and therefore from our point of view most inspirationally, to him.

Nor is there any touch of irony in the fact that the lovers are, as they now suppose themselves to be, man and wife, who have slept together and awoken. The erotic charge which the narrative gets into the phrase 'When Lady Constantine awoke next morning' is extremely complex, but its complexity depends upon its separate elements being indifferent to each other, as they are to the other narrational aspects of the situation. The slight shock, perhaps a pleasurable one, which a Mudie reader would experience at the beginning of this chapter, comes from the quotidian reality of married people waking up being superimposed upon the image of the lovers, more specifically the young lover as Cupid, and the older

Venus. What have they been doing in the night? The reader knows, but doesn't know, in the same sense that one side of the narrative ignores the other, and so the nature of romance and that of physical reality each have their place in the erotic pattern and in the reader's reception of it.

'Lady Constantine' is itself a name from elsewhere, from a related but different style of narrative or novelette, and though she is – or supposes she is – now a married woman – Mrs St Cleeve – the continuance of the former name signifies romance and adultery, which are alluringly present not only in spite of but because of the fervency with which the two lovers have recently celebrated their marriage vows. Hardy contrives to make marriage seem more shocking, or more romantic, than living in sin: or rather his peculiar narrational sandwich does it for him. It is just because of his love for ironies and incongruities – as of 'big' effects – that their absence in this sort of context is so striking. We have had them in plenty at the Bath wedding – Hardy always rejoices in the irony of weddings or attempted weddings – where the dotty old deputy clergyman had got it into his head that he was supposed to be officiating at a funeral, and was found by his clerk waiting among the graves.

'Lady Constantine', in the hut at the foot of the great tower, has also the status of captive maiden, as well as that of maternal Venus and married woman getting ready for breakfast. 'Before she was quite ready for breakfast she heard the key turn in the door, and felt startled, till she remembered that the comer could hardly be anybody but he.' She has been locked in for fear of a possible intruder, and after the accident at the railway station the previous evening Swithin had announced his plan to 'keep you a captive in the cabin till the scar has disappeared.' The bruise was inadvertently caused by the riding whip of her brother, who had not recognised her or been aware of the accident, but the maiden in story receives such blows, like the Arthurian Enid struck by the dwarf, and is rescued and guarded by a knight-errant. That evening in the tower the lovers watch the Aurora Borealis, 'like the form of the Spirit-maiden in the shades of Glenfinlas', a reference to a romantic poem by Sir Walter Scott.

All these elements in the composition give it a peculiar fascination, characteristic of Hardy at his most fictionally creative but seldom found in such concentration as here. They concentrate on the tower itself and the ways in which it is perceived and taken pleasure in – literal, romantic, and symbolic. The astronomical observatory is of course Hardy's 'big idea', and nothing illustrates better the difference between such an idea and the way it is actually implemented in the processes of the novel. A contrast between the 'ghastliness' of the infinite spaces, as visited through an astronomer's telescope, and the human and earthbound emotions of that same astronomer: this is a good Victorian notion for poets and thinkers. It is not the notion but the treatment of it that is so peculiar to Hardy. For a start the starry heavens are not important except as a separate element in the composition. It is the tower that is in the imaginative foreground, and the tower is only incidentally an observatory. In one aspect it is a strange man-made object, in its natural setting: in another, a symbol of marriage itself.

Or at least of a love-relation involving marriage. The fact that marriage itself does not legally take place suits a 'novel', and also – much more importantly – it suits Hardy's imagination. Nowhere else does he give such an effective and in an involuntary sense such a complete picture of a love-relation. It is no sense a self-conscious study, like the relation of Jude and Sue in *Jude the Obscure*; indeed there is a quite singular gaiety about it, as if the relation had been ambushed into its peculiar kind of truth by the contrivances necessary to the tale. Hardy is never without pretension, but in this case pretension is monopolised by the wish (as he tells us in the 1895 Preface) 'to set the emotional history of two infinitesimal lives against the stupendous background of the stellar universe'. The stupendous background is certainly there, but in no more significant a relation to the progress of the love-story than a waterfall would be to a cow grazing in the field in front of it.

The same is true of the tower itself, a sense of whose natural being permeates the novel as the heath does in *The Return of the Native*. Like the heath it is clearly something that Hardy knew – there are two follies like it in the Wimborne vicinity – and which his imagination could work on and elaborate, as he expanded the size and primitiveness of the heath. But again there is no conflict or meaningful interaction of systems: the story of Swithin and Viviette is in quite arbitrary association with the tower, however important it is as a physical embodiment of that story. If the tower is marriage, then Swithin's occupation as astronomer is the masculine life, selfish and self-absorbed; and fondly overseen, taken pride in, and encouraged by the feminine principle.

The fact that Swithin is looking through his telescope is merely Hardy's way of indicating that a man absorbed in his pursuits forgets about the business of love. Hardy would be capable of saying that outright but he does not need to: the juxtaposition of elements in the story does it much more subtly as well as more comprehensively. Love is fervid and sincere, romantic, delectable, even faithful; but love is not the real interest of a man's life, nor for the woman can it be more important than her social position – or rather her psychological position vis-à-vis society – and the necessity of preserving it.

Such a statement would in itself be banal, but the gaiety with which the lovers' instincts and attractions are presented, and the lack of any seeming attempt – a rather rare thing in Hardy – to draw a conclusion, give lightness as well as truth to the elements that compose the picture. Hardy moves with the greatest naturalness from the day-dream and the romance, the pastoral and mythological, to the motives and contrivances of fabliau, and the calculations that go with it. When Viviette discovers her pregnancy nothing matters but the solution of her problem. 'I would marry a tinker for that matter; I have physical reasons for being any man's wife.' The situation of Viviette and her lover is not unlike that of Vronsky and Anna Karenina at the crisis of their relations. The sense of being trapped which violently oppresses Anna releases in her lover a deep sense of personal, almost solipsistic satisfaction; he cannot help enjoying the crisis which to her is so nerve-wracking and destroying. Hardy here draws straight on country reminiscence and country lore, dressing it up for a romantic and higher social role. The pregnant girl must persuade her lover to marry her, which it is taken from granted he will be extremely reluctant to do. Hardy plays a grim little variation on this theme in *Jude the Obscure*, when Arabella persuades Jude to marry her by pretending she is pregnant.

In *Two on a Tower* Hardy makes the growing separateness of the lovers depend on contrivance and coincidence, but in the background it presents itself with a natural equanimity. The variation here is the maternal forbearance and self-sacrifice of Viviette Constantine, anxious as she is not to stand in the way of her lover's career. But her pregnancy changes all that.

> A horrid apprehension possessed her. . . . suppose . . . he were to inform her that, having fully acquiesced in her original decision, he found the life he was leading so profitable as to be unable to abandon it, even to please her; that he was very sorry, but having embarked on this course by her advice he meant to adhere to it by his own.

Should she, now that her lover has gone off on his astronomical travels at her own insistence, bear his child alone and wait for him to return and claim her? But would he return, and would he claim her? At the tower 'there was not a star to suggest to her in which direction Swithin had gone'. Her predicament is extremely moving, no less so for the various kinds of artifice which have produced it and created her. Hardy feels for it and for her, as for Miss Aldclyffe in *Desperate Remedies*, seduced by a dissolute cousin, Tess who would have scorned to marry her seducer, and Jude compelled, as he thinks, to marry the girl who has tricked him. The country situation is repeated by Hardy in all sorts of literary contexts without losing its primal sense of pathos, nor – as the reviewers' reaction testified – its capacity to shock the reader. The *Spectator* slated *Desperate Remedies* for the same reason that the reviews tut-tutted at the marriage of the pregnant Viviette to a bishop. The rural theme so natural to Hardy was unmentioned in polite society, though, or perhaps because, it must have occurred there just as often.

And so Viviette acquires a new role. To transpose thus the roles of his heroine is a part of Hardy's tender fantasy about her, as noticeable in its simpler way in his treatment of Cytherea Graye in *Desperate Remedies* as it is in that of *Tess of the d'Urbervilles*. The persecuted maiden appeals to Hardy all the way to her darkest and most potent appearance as the Woman who was Hanged. Actual memories and literary fancies combined here in Hardy's mind, and, as so often happens with him, combined without seeming to recognise each other's provenance. This may account for the striking difference between his two kinds of heroine. On the one hand there are Bathsheba Everdene, and Arabella and Sue Bridehead in *Jude* – figures perceived with great sympathy and curiosity but also with detachment, a detachment which recognises their native strength and independence. Bathsheba, 'feared at tea-parties and loved in crises', is the sort 'of whom heroes' mothers are made'; her emotional vulnerability contrasts with but does not impair this kind of strength. Arabella is both tough and shrewd, and Sue has her own kind of will and determination, a will, indeed, which constitutes the chief phenomenon of her nervous being.

But on the other hand there are the heroines of whom Hardy can make what he wishes, and Viviette is among the most memorable of these and certainly the most moving. Physically she has much in common with Eustacia Vye in *The Return of the Native*, a bolder but also a cruder projection. The conception of Viviette Constantine is both more subtle and more effortless, her nature and background to be inferred, like those of a Shakespeare character, with nothing evidently manufactured about them – her unhappy marriage and the probability that it was her brother's work are not given to the reader but accessible to him. In this sense she has a more continuous kind of reality than that of the more famous heroines; her lonely life has its succession of days tellingly conveyed in the opening paragraphs, when she is driven past the tower on two occasions, enquires about it, but does not visit it, and then eventually does so when spring weather has dried out the ploughed land around it. This continuity gets into the progress of the love affair, leading its own life, so to speak, beside the carefully contrived pattern of events which determines its outcome.

But even more important to the unique status of the book in Hardy's work is its simultaneous relation to his own early experience of marriage, and to his childhood friendship with Mrs Martin, wife of the owner of Kingston Maurward, the house that frequently appears in his early fiction. The importance of this dual influence hardly needs to be enlarged upon. Hardy had known, though at an age much younger than that of St Cleeve, affectionate female patronage; on his side, and probably on hers, there was a kind of erotic attraction. For him too the magic of a higher class, with its physical luxuries and spiritual refinements. Mrs Martin, like Lady Constantine, was a devoted Anglican, and Hardy must have responded to the same sort of sentiments in her which Lady Constantine feels at Swithin's confirmation, when she regards him 'with all the rapt mingling of religion, love, fervour, and hope which women feel at such times, and which men know nothing of'. The episode of Swithin's confirmation is necessary to bring the bishop into play, but it also brings out, with all Hardy's tranquil oddness of relation, an alternative status of Swithin as a child indeed. She wonders what the bishop will say, in laying hands on her lover's head – whether 'this thy servant' or 'this thy *child*', and when it is the latter she feels both a prick of conscience that she might be thought to have 'trapped an innocent youth into marriage', and the more comforting thought 'that she had raised his social position thereby'. The literalness embodied in this reflection is again leading its own life beside the romantic and novelistic story of the lovers.

As a young man fresh to London Hardy went to call on Mrs Martin at her house in Bruton Street. After the butler had let him in and gone to inform his mistress Hardy suddenly panicked, recollecting that the benefactor and friend of his early youth must now be quite advanced in years; and this was confirmed by his brief meeting with her. Although invited to call again he never did. The incident has obvious affinities with its grand fictional counterpart at the end of *Two on a Tower*, when Swithin returns to Viviette and his child, and sees his former love as an old woman. Playing an equally lively part beside these potent memories are both Hardy's perhaps unconscious feelings about marriage, and – a rather different thing – his early experiences of it. We notice two aspects of this in *Two on a Tower*; a sense of the lovers' isolation from each other, even in the midst of their devotion; and an assumption, somewhere at the heart of the novel, that Swithin's ambitions and powers as an astronomer are largely responsible. Hardy shows his usual equanimity on this point, the text taking it for granted that Swithin is rightly selfish in his ambitions and desires, and Viviette devoted in hers for him. Her role is only reversed when she becomes pregnant, biological exigency overriding the normal preponderance of masculine requirement. Swithin wants to marry her in order to be at peace to continue his work, and does not reflect on the possible consequences.

Something in Hardy was well aware of his own relation to Swithin, of the fact that his genius as novelist and poet cut him off from a full domestic intimacy; but in the created medium of *Two on a Tower* he seems aware of this genially, almost tenderly, and with none of the bitterness that his own later years would bring into his novels. At the time of *Two on a Tower* he and Emma, comparatively happy together, were living at Wimborne, years before the grimly estranged respectability of Max Gate, and still regarded themselves as a footloose and comradely couple, she assisting with making fair copies of his work rather as Viviette helped copy down Swithin's calculations. Within such an arrangement coldness and exclusion are none the less on the cards, even natural and inevitable, as were the love feelings which had suddenly burst upon Swithin, and caused him to lean against the concave wall of the tower staircase, 'quite tremulous with strange incipient sentiments'.

F. B. Pinion is surely right in suggesting that the germ of the idea may come from George Eliot's *The Mill on the Floss*, where Maggie Tulliver learns of the astronomer in the Latin grammar who hated women. 'You know, they live up in high towers, and if the women came there, they might talk and hinder them from looking at the stars.' Wholly characteristic of Hardy's creative cast at this period is the way in which he makes this idea cohabit naturally with all the tenderness of romance, in the same way that Viviette's terror at the social consequences of her pregnancy is as instinctive and natural to her as her love for Swithin and her readiness to sacrifice her interests to his. These are not ironies but facts which have all the dignity, the necessity and the pathos of life about them. They give the particular note of deadpan blandness to Hardy's comment at the beginning of Chapter 14 about 'the alchemy which transmuted an abstracted astronomer into an eager lover – and, must it be said? spoilt a promising young physicist to produce a commonplace inamorato'. The tone of that, and the lightness of touch on the three adjectives – 'abstracted,' 'promising', and 'commonplace' – show an unexpected, almost Shakespearian mixture of distancing, sympathy and toleration. It is also very close to Hardy's sense of himself at this time, the day-dreams and creations of encounters that might have been that fill his actual poems, and the consciousness in which they grew. All his life, we know, Hardy day-dreamed of the 'love passages' which might have taken place between himself and Mrs Martin, had he gone back and renewed their friendship; and such '*rêves d'escalier*', in which desire and reality both understand and ignore one another, are the most fruitful source of imagination in both his novels and his poems.

Let us return, in conclusion, to my earlier reference to *The Woodlanders*, and to David Lodge's suggestive comments on it in his introduction. At that time in his novel-writing career the characteristic elements of Hardy's outlook and imagination declared themselves in a much more positive, even portentous, way than they did at the time of *Two on a Tower*. The method is more graphic, more earnest and habituated, and makes a more powerful impact on the reader: but the adjective 'powerful', so frequently applied to Hardy, fits him only with a kind of impersonal oddness. The latent power moving in such incongruous harmonies in *Two on a Tower* has congealed in the later novel into elements disparate and over-emphatic. Hardyan incongruity is most itself when most spontaneous and natural, as in our novel it appears to be.

A version of pastoral is the effective mechanism in both novels, filling out and carrying forward the love interest. David Lodge suggests its workings in *The Woodlanders*: nature simultaneously shown both in a Darwinian light – a ruthless struggle for survival which extends to the trees and plants themselves – and in the context of classical mythology, lamenting Giles Winterborne and his sad fate in the manner of Theocritus and Bion. Such a tradition of lament extends, Lodge claims, to death and rebirth also; and even to the salvation of Grace Fitzpiers from the mantrap, greeted ecstatically by her estranged husband, as if she were Adonis miraculously saved from the fangs of the boar.

This is to make *The Woodlanders* sound like a critics' novel, such as are written today; and one must admit that there is something purposeful and unspontaneous in it, something designed specifically for the analytic intelligence. As in most such novels, conceptions of things are more prominent than the things and people themselves. The pastoral scenes and settings in *Two on a Tower* are by contrast not only more lively but more essentially real; we do not consider their artifice as we become engrossed in their story. Hardy's natural traffic in oddity makes his characters more convincing, whereas Grace and Marty South and Giles Winterborne, Fitzpiers and Felice Charmond, lose credibility from the very emphasis with which their roles are determined. Meanings are more important there than characters. I myself find that whereas *The Woodlanders* loses life with re-reading, *Two on a Tower* gains it. Bishop and all, there is in its closing scenes more of the true Hardyan pathos, that goes with peculiarity, than in the set pieces of the later and more famous novel.

NOTES

1. *An Essay on Hardy* (Cambridge: Cambridge University Press, 1977).

2. Introduction to the New Wessex Edition of *The Woodlanders* (London: Macmillan, 1975); reprinted in *Working with Structuralism* (London: Routledge & Kegan Paul, 1981), reviewed by John Carey in *The Sunday Times*, 14 June 1981.

The Experimental and the Absurd in *Two on a Tower*

Rosemary Sumner

Though usually and rightly classified as a minor novel, *Two on a Tower* contains some of Hardy's most original and adventurous experiments. His use of "the stupendous background of the stellar universe" has come in for a good deal of criticism, on the grounds that it is not integral to the novel, that it does dwarf the characters in spite of Hardy's claim to the contrary in the Preface, and that it is too remote from human concerns to function effectively in a novel. This dismissive attitude is strange since it is generally accepted that the way the background is used is one of the distinctive features of Hardy's major novels. As Lawrence says in his 'Study of Thomas Hardy': ". . . this is the quality Hardy shares with the great writers, Shakespeare or Sophocles or Tolstoi, this setting behind the small action of his protagonists the terrific action of unfathomed nature."[1] In Hardy's exploration of this theme in *Two on a Tower* he arrives at a vision of the universe which is fundamentally different from that presented in his earlier novels and is more akin to the view of "the relation between man and his circumambient universe"[2] found in many twentieth-century works.

The heath in *The Return of the Native* (published four years before *Two on a Tower*) at first sight seems to function in a similar way to the "stellar universe" in that it provides "the terrific action of unfathomed nature". But, even in the first chapter, in which no characters appear, Hardy stresses the heath's affinity with humanity; it is "like man, slighted and enduring", it is "the hitherto unrecognised original" of unconscious terrors but at the same time a stabilising influence, giving "ballast to the mind adrift on change, and harassed by the irrepressible New" (1.1). Hardy is, of course, far from suggesting that it is benevolent, but he does emphasise the closeness of the tie between the heath and the people. Even Eustacia's stormy relationship with it is a kind of harmony: "Never was harmony more perfect than that between the chaos of her mind and the chaos of the world without'' (5.7). The sky above the heath shares in this intimacy with the human beings; Clym looks at the moon which "depicted a small image of herself in each of his eyes" and feels himself "voyaging bodily through its wild scenes, standing on its hollow hills, traversing its deserts, descending its vales . . ." (3.4). Hardy brings it down to almost manageable proportions by making the lovers use the eclipse, that "remote celestial phenomenon", as a signal for meeting.

Two on a Tower suggests a more extreme attitude and feeling about humanity's position in the cosmos which Hardy did not express so fully or so clearly again until his later poetry, and even then not quite with the combination of the horrifying and the absurd which gives this novel from time to time its odd, modern flavour. The "stellar universe" in *Two on a Tower* offers no "ballast" to the mind. It may indeed, like the heath, "reduce to insignificance . . . the turmoil of a single man" (*The Return of the Native* 5.2), but instead of inducing a sense of balance, it is shattering, reducing "everything terrestrial to atomic proportions" (Ch. 34). Lady Constantine's (and the reader's) first look through Swithin's telescope reveals the sun as "a whirling mass, in the centre of which the blazing globe itself seemed to be laid bare to its core. It was a peep into a maelstrom of fire, taking place where nobody had ever been or ever would be" (Ch. 1). This immediate emphasis on the alien nature of the universe seen through the telescope highlights the difference between *Two on a Tower* and *The Return of the Native*, where the indifferent heath has its affinity with man. The remote moon is reflected in Clym's eyes, but in *Two on a Tower* the connection is much more tenuous and "the ghastly chasm" is "bridged by the fragile line of sight" (Ch. 4). Instead of identifiable shapes of mountains and valleys on the moon, we confront "monsters of magnitude without known shape. Such monsters are the voids and waste places of the sky" (Ch. 4). Using his astronomer as his vehicle, Hardy creates a sense of the size and formlessness of the universe, and of its decay. Swithin points out dying stars: "Imagine them all extinguished, and your mind feeling its way through a heaven of total darkness, occasionally striking against the black, invisible cinders of those stars" (Ch. 4). The characters are facing an experience that "reduces the importance of everything" (Ch. 4) and makes them aware of "the presence of a vastness they could not cope with, even as an idea" (Ch. 8). In the other novels, Hardy is usually concerned with the closeness of the relationship between people and their surroundings. The laws of nature are not made for humanity, but Hardy usually shows that people can, if they will, adapt themselves to the nature of things, cover their stacks, bend a spout or allow for the changeableness of the English summer.

Just occasionally we are reminded that though we are "part of the great web of human doings", the great web itself is, from some views, insignificant. This is the effect of the birds from beyond the North Pole in *Tess of the d'Urbervilles*: "gaunt spectral creatures with tragical eyes – eyes which had witnessed scenes of cataclysmal horror in inaccessible polar regions of a magnitude such as no human being had ever conceived, in curdling temperatures no man could endure . . . but of all they had seen which humanity would never see, they brought no account . . . they dismissed experiences they did not value for the immediate incidents of this homely upland – the trivial movements of the two girls" (Ch. 4.3).

Here, as in *Two on a Tower*, Hardy is creating the sense of a universe not made for man, extending infinitely beyond human comprehension. The idea that "beyond the knowable there must always be the unknown" underlies all his writing and is particularly emphatic in *Two on a Tower*, where the possibility that the universe is infinite and meaningless is contemplated. His use of "the voids and waste places of the sky" to suggest this resembles the use of "the void", "the abyss" in twentieth-century novels. The experience in the gulf in Conrad's *Nostromo* (1904) is akin to that evoked by the infinity of space in *Two on a Tower*. Decoud "beheld the universe as a succession of incomprehensible images . . . the solitude appeared like a great void and the silence of the gulf like a tense thin cord to which he hung suspended . . ." (*Nostromo*, Pt 3, Ch. 10). This is similar to Hardy's "monsters without known shape" and the thin cord linking Decoud to the universe is like the "fragile line of sight" which connects Swithin and Viviette to it. Conrad's account of the "crushing, paralyzing sense of human littleness" (*Nostromo*, Pt 3, Ch. 8) corresponds to Hardy's account of "the blow with which the infinitely great, the stellar universe, strikes down upon the infinitely little, the mind of the beholder" (Ch. 8) and Conrad's "abyss of waters without earth or sky" (*Nostromo*, Pt 3, Ch. 8) to Hardy's "deep wells for the human mind to let itself down into . . . and side caverns and secondary abysses to right and left" (Ch. 4). Both writers create for the reader the nightmarish imaginative experience of physically entering these abysses while simultaneously suggesting the inexplicable nature of the universe and our position in it.

The Marabar Caves in *A Passage to India* function in a similar way. Forster places them in time and space: "the sun who has watched them for countless aeons may still discern in their outlines forms that were his before our globe was torn from his bosom" (*A Passage to India*, Ch. 12). The emptiness of the caves ("Nothing is inside them . . . if mankind grew envious and excavated, nothing, nothing would be added to the sum of good or evil" (Ch. 12)) corresponds to the "voids and waste places" of

Two on a Tower. The overwhelming of Mrs Moore by the echo with its message that "Everything exists. Nothing has value", is essentially the same kind of experience as that of Viviette and Swithin as "they more and more felt the contrast between their own tiny magnitudes and those among which they had recklessly plunged till they were oppressed with the presence of a vastness they could not cope with even as an idea" (Ch. 8). Forster, however, makes this vision of the possible total meaninglessness of existence central to the novel; for Hardy, it is just one of "a series of seemings". But all three are tentative about the implications of their vision. Hardy perhaps sums it up for all of them in saying "I am utterly bewildered to understand how the doctrine that, beyond the knowable, there must always be an unknown, can be displaced".[3]

I think these comparisons with Conrad and Forster throw some light on Hardy's position as a nineteenth-century novelist and on the relation of *Two on a Tower* to his other novels. His Preface indicates that he saw "the stellar universe" as one of the two main concerns of the novel, though the lesser of the two. Yet even though he calls it "a slightly-built romance", he embodies in this novel a way of seeing existence which was for many of his contemporary readers either shattering or outrageous. It was not, of course, a totally new conception, though because of the work of Darwin it was being more widely discussed in the 1880s than before. In nineteenth-century literature it tended to find expression in poetry rather than in the novel, perhaps because it is easier, as Hardy suggested, to get away with "ideas and emotions which run counter to the inert crystallised opinion"[4] in verse than in prose. Hardy's notion that to make an impact a writer must be "five and twenty years ahead of his time"[5] applies even to works he regarded as slight. *Nostromo* and *A Passage to India* can certainly be regarded as major twentieth-century novels. The reasons for the "minor" quality of *Two on a Tower* are not to be found in the elements it shares with them, though it could be argued that it is the way these elements are related to the rest of the novel that is responsible for its relatively slight stature.

I think that to take the comparisons even further into the twentieth century is helpful here. A critic writing on a group of post-war writers states that

> for many intelligent and sensitive human beings the world of the mid-twentieth century has lost its meaning and has simply ceased to make sense. . . . Suddenly man sees himself faced with a universe that is both frightening and illogical – in a word, absurd.

He claims that in spite of "extravagant fantasies" these writers are essentially realistic, and their work is a challenge to accept the human condition as it is, in all its mystery and absurdity, and to bear it with dignity, nobly, responsibly; precisely *because* there are no easy solutions to the mysteries of existence, because man is ultimately alone in a meaningless world.⁶

Much of this, by Martin Esslin on the Theatre of the Absurd, could be applied to the bulk of Hardy's work; but what is particularly interesting in relation to *Two on a Tower* is the association of man "ultimately alone in a meaningless world" with the idea of the absurd, for it is probably the absurdities in the novel which have been responsible for its relegation to the second class among Hardy's works. This is an experiment that does not wholly succeed; yet in setting "the emotional history of two infinitesimal lives against the stupendous background of the stellar universe" and adding a third element of farcical human behaviour embodied in absurd intricacies of plot Hardy is being just as daringly experimental as he was when he explored Sue Bridehead's psychological complexities twelve years later.

Hardy's perception of the nature of existence as it is expressed in *Two on a Tower* has much in common with Beckett's, whom Esslin described as the most poetic of the absurdist dramatists. In *Lessness*, everything is pared away except the tiny human figures and the void: "All sides endlessness earth sky as one no sound no stir. Grey face two pale blue little body heart beating only upright." By focusing exclusively, as I have been doing, on the universe revealed by the telescope in *Two on a Tower* we get something of the same effect of tiny human beings facing a formless vastness. As Lance St John Butler says in an essay aptly entitled "How it is for Thomas Hardy", for both Hardy and Beckett, "On the ultimate level, there is nothing".⁷ But, as Butler emphasises, "the world is only *finally* empty, not immediately". Though the world outside the window in *Endgame* is "corpsed", like Swithin's cinders of stars, we can be only intermittently conscious of our place in space. Critics who complain that "the stellar universe" is merely episodic (and therefore insignificant) have not seen that its intermittent recurrence is a way of using the structure of the novel to correspond to our capacity for exposure to it. Though Swithin welcomes his "emancipation from the trammelling body" he also knows that it is "impossible to think at all adequately of the sky – of what the sky substantially is, without feeling it as a juxtaposed nightmare. It is better – far better – for men to forget the universe than to bear it clearly in mind" (Ch. 4). Hardy, like Eliot in *Burnt Norton*, realises that "human kind / Cannot bear very much reality", and that "the changing body / Protects mankind from heaven and damnation / Which flesh cannot endure".

Hardy uses various means in the novel to blot out, from time to time, the nightmare of the universe. A spell of continuous rain makes it seem "as if the whole science of astronomy had never been real, and the heavenly bodies, with their motions, were as theoretical as the lines and circles of a bygone mathematical problem" (Ch. 9). But a function of his art in *Two on a Tower* is to ensure that we do, at least intermittently, "think adequately of the universe", while ironically drawing attention to the ways in which we try to shield ourselves from these thoughts. Though he exposes us less harshly and continuously than Beckett does in, for instance, *Happy Days*, some aspects of his treatment of Viviette are similar in their impact. Winnie's desperate efforts to sustain "the old style" and to structure her day with trivia so as to hide from the horror she is faced with are in their absurdity similar to Viviette's frenzied efforts to keep up the conventions. The concealment of her marriage to Swithin in case her county neighbours won't ask her to tea, the secret meetings, the repeated escapes from imminent discovery function in the same way as Winnie's use of her bag. An inexorable bell governs Winnie's sleeping and waking, just as a rigid social law drives Viviette to marry the Bishop.

It is usually argued that the absurd complications of the plot in *Two on a Tower* are entirely due to Hardy's tendency in the lesser novels to get knotted up in pointless complications. It is true that this happens here, as it does in *Desperate Remedies* and *A Laodicean*, but I think there is also a realisation in *Two on a Tower* that the very absurdity of such complications has its function in the novel. It is significant that most of these complications arise from conflicts in Viviette's personality, on the one hand sensitive and passionate, both in her love for Swithin and in her perception of the universe ("it annihilates me") and on the other, ludicrously concerned to conform to the social conventions of her day. Hardy explores with compassion, as Beckett does, the absurd and sometimes heroic ways in which the characters try to stave off the recognition of possible ultimate nothingness.

One of the difficulties of bringing together these incongruous elements is the use of language which (unless disintegration of syntax and other experimental devices are employed) tends to impose a form and structure which implies a sense of order, however little the author wishes to create this effect. Hardy draws attention to this when he contrasts the sky in the northern hemisphere, with its named constellations and accretions of legend "without which it had almost seemed that a polar sky could not exist", with "the limitless vacancy . . . of an even more unknown tract of the unknown. Space here, being less the historic haunt of human thought than overhead at home, seemed to be pervaded with a more lonely loneliness" (Ch. 41). He makes a similar point about the stars in the northern sky which are not visible to the naked eye and which had "for infinite ages spent their beams without calling forth from a single earthly poet a single line" (Ch. 8). This juxtaposition of a universe given shape by language with one that recedes infinitely, unknowable and unnamed, is for Camus the essence of the absurd. In *The Myth of Sisyphus* he says: "A world that can be explained by reasoning, however faulty, is a reasonable world. But in a universe suddenly deprived of illusions and of light, man feels a stranger. . . . This divorce between man and his life, the actor and his setting, truly constitutes the feeling of Absurdity."

Swithin's comment that the inept name of "Coal-sack" for one of the "voids and waste places of the sky" has "a farcical force from its very inadequacy" (Ch. 4) makes explicit Hardy's sympathy with the concept of the absurd. It is an acknowledgement that any attempt to render the universe familiar is futile, whether by rational, explanatory or farcical means; yet the farcical method is more powerful than any conceptual approach. The incongruity of the name has the same kind of effect as Winnie up to her waist in the earth cleaning her teeth and doing her hair. The use of the word "burlesque" when Swithin is rebuked by the Bishop is another indication that Hardy is consciously using this element in the novel. Swithin feels it incongruous that "he who had soared amid the remotest grandeurs of nature" should have his "tender and refined passion . . . debased to burlesque lines" (Ch. 29).

Seen in the light of these burlesque, farcical and absurd qualities in the novel, the final sentence, perhaps Hardy's most startling ending, begins to make sense, as a final jolt to the reader's sense of order and congruity. The shock of jumping abruptly from the genuinely moving death of Viviette to the savage irony of the last sentence might have worked if the last two chapters had not led us right away from the absurd mode. But the Bishop has fulfilled his function and disappeared from the novel. Viviette has made use of him, but not, in Hardy's view, in an immoral way. There are later indications of his views on the subject in Jude's attitude to "the beggarly question of parentage. . . . What does it matter?" (*Jude the Obscure*, V, 3) and in Hardy's unpublished letter of 1906 to the Fawcett Society, in which he suggests that the father of a woman's child is nobody's business but her own. One final example of an idiotic sexual convention diminishes instead of enhancing our response to the "infinitesimal lives against the stupendous background".

We have long ago abandoned the idea of a naive, unconscious Hardy whose stories "started up in his head"[8] of their own volition, yet many people have felt that the incongruities of *Two on a Tower* are accidental. I do not think so. In a letter to Gosse,[9] he referred to critics who had privately praised *Two on a Tower* as his most original novel so far. This suggests he was aware of making some kind of experiment. His delight in incongruity shows itself frequently in his work, and it is more than a humorous chuckle at "Life's Little Ironies". In the Apology to *Late Lyrics and Earlier* he makes an elaborate, tongue-in-cheek defence of "the juxtaposition of unrelated, even discordant effusions", which, he says, caused the poems "to be read as misfires because they raise the smile that they were intended to raise". Though he half-apologises for not foreseeing that "people might not perceive when the tone altered", he concludes by saying that he must trust to "those whose intuition is proof against accidents of inconsequence". This is characteristic of Hardy's convoluted manner when he is on the defensive, but it is none the less evident that he sees the inconsequential as a vital element in his work.

Beckett said "the chaos is all around us . . . the only chance is to let it in . . . to find a form that accommodates the mess – that is the task of the artist now". In both drama and prose works, he has combined a sense of chaos with a highly patterned structure – with, for instance, the correspondence of the two acts of *Waiting for Godot* and *Happy Days* and the intricate plotting of the sentences in *Lessness*. Hardy is tentatively doing something similar in *Two on a Tower*. The incongruities are combined with a tight pattern of correspondences and contrasts – stars and human beings, passion and science, youth and maturity, two unhappy marriages, two nearly illegitimate children (Viviette solves both her maid's problem and her own by marriage), two characters disappearing into Africa, and so on. Such structuring is Hardy's common practice, but here, as in many of the minor novels, he piles on top of this so many complications of plot, with various trivial problems being set up and solved (as with the bracelets) that this diverts attention from the central image of two little figures against the stars. Unlike Beckett's, Hardy's patterning does not intensify the concentration on the centre. In *Two on a Tower* he is groping towards the kind of technique which uses the grotesque (two characters in dustbins, a woman up to her waist in the earth) as a way of jolting us into an imaginative apprehension of the human condition. He is only partly successful.

But in the treatment of Viviette, he wholly succeeds in his aim. She is, perhaps, Hardy's most heroic character. In combining in her intensity of feeling, psychological complexity and a capacity for altruism, he makes her embody an idea of human potential which, even though set against a "stupendous background", does indeed make the reader feel "that of these contrasting magnitudes the smaller might be the greater". He creates a sense of the "magnitude" of her emotional life from the beginning.

When Swithin is ill, she is "in that state of anguish in which the heart is no longer under the control of the judgement, and self-abandonment, even to error, verges on heroism" (Ch. 9). This high value placed on the human heart and even the capacity for "self-abandonment" is central to Hardy's conception. The sheer ability to feel is for him what gives human life a grandeur to match "the stellar universe". On the night when Swithin suggests marriage, "human life at its highest excitement was beating within the dark and isolated tower" (Ch. 15). In "Candour in English Fiction" (1890) Hardy pleaded for "fiction dealing with human emotion on a comprehensive scale", and for long before that he had himself embodied in both his major and his minor fiction "the strongest passion known to humanity";[10] in *Two on a Tower*, in proposing a high evaluation of spontaneity, he was being as challenging as he was in *Tess* and *Jude*.

Viviette's conflicting impulses between what is conventionally regarded as right and what she feels with such intensity is vividly presented in numerous scenes where "her intention wheeled this way and that like the balance of a watch" (Ch. 15), and where she contradicts herself from moment to moment – "I cannot . . . yes, I'll come" (Ch. 8) and "Yes, go! No, – I cannot bear it" (Ch. 15). This is very like the behaviour of Sue Bridehead, and even the dialogue is almost identical, with Sue saying "Go" and "I can't – bear – ", when she simultaneously spurns and kisses Jude; but Sue is masochistically indulging herself emotionally, whereas Viviette is as vividly aware of Swithin's problems as her own. Though "unstable of mood", she is not at all unstable psychologically. She has none of the neurotic self-absorption of characters like Sue or Boldwood.

Hardy has an almost Lawrentian delight in Viviette's sensuality. An amusing example occurs when she is entertaining the Bishop at dinner and "recently gratified affection lent to her manner just now a sweet serenity, a truly Christian contentment" (Ch. 25). The sensual and spontaneous nature of her love is an essential starting point for a great step forward in her development – her attainment of the kind of love which puts the needs of the loved one far above the self. Viviette's struggle to control her powerful instincts and feelings in order to reach something even better is unusual in Hardy's novels and probably in life. He more often shows characters behaving like Eustacia, who "let things fall out as they may rather than wrestle hard to direct them". Years later, in "Thoughts at Midnight", he wrote:

> Mankind, you dismay me
> When shadows waylay me! . . .

> Acting like puppets
> Under Time's buffets.

But Viviette does not act like a puppet. "Her life during that morning and afternoon was wholly introspective" (Ch. 35). This is reminiscent of Isabel Archer's night of meditation in *The Portrait of a Lady*, published in the previous year. Both characters' fluctuations of thought and feeling are minutely explored. The striking difference between them is that Isabel's meditation is wholly retrospective, directed towards understanding her own past behaviour, but with little suggestion that she can actively take steps to make a better future, though she will understand it better; Viviette does take a new look at the past, but the essence of the passage is concerned with her struggle to change herself. She gradually comes to recognise that "true benevolence" lies in freeing Swithin, and that "it could be done", however painful it would be to herself. The impressiveness of her struggle is partly due to the success and sympathy with which Hardy has created her as a passionately emotional woman. James is interested in how Isabel comes to a retrospective understanding of the choices she has made in the past. Viviette is involved in the process of making a better self. In his *Thomas Hardy: the Will and the Way*, Roy Morrell illustrates Hardy's "basic Existential concern with choice", and shows how in the novels " 'being' is essentially meaningless. What counts is the way man is oriented to the future, to what can be done." [11] Viviette is like the little body in *Lessness*: "One step in the ruins in the sand on his back in the endlessness he will make it." Viviette gains no reward for her step except "a sweet sense of rising above self-love", but it makes her one of Hardy's most admirable characters.

The scientific half of the contrast between the scientific and the intuitive interests Hardy less, precisely because the scientific mind, as he conceives it, offers little scope for the exploration of inner struggles. Away from Viviette, Swithin's life narrows down to his one interest, astronomy. He does not even notice "the novel forms of human and vegetable life" in the new countries he visits. An account of his year after leaving her would not give "a single additional glimpse . . . of Swithin in his relations with his old emotions". The reason, Hardy says, is that in science there is "little food for the sympathetic instincts which create the changes in a life" (Ch. 41). Thus Swithin is detached from what for Hardy, as for Lawrence, is the essence of existence: "it is the way our sympathy flows and recoils that really determines our lives." [12]

Though Swithin can feel pity for dying stars, and he recognises that what has happened to Viviette is "fearful, catastrophic . . . instead of musing over it, he shunned the subject". He first appears in the novel gazing in amazement at the strangeness of outer space. At the end he is gazing at human beings with equal detachment: "He was as one who suddenly finds the world a stranger place than he thought; but is excluded by age, temperament and situation from being much more than an astonished spectator of its strangeness" (Ch. 40). Making Swithin a character who is "too literal, direct and uncompromising" to understand the "customary complication of feeling" of Viviette has perhaps resulted in an oversimplified idea of "the scientist"; but in shaping the book so that Swithin first introduces the grandeurs of space which are then overshadowed by the greater grandeur of Viviette's human capacities, Hardy has created a form which effectively embodies his conception.

Yet *Two on a Tower* remains a minor novel. The trouble lies in the interesting but not wholly successful experiment with "the Absurd". Where twentieth-century writers succeed with extravagant fantasies and bizarre poetic symbolism, Hardy allows his imaginative perception to be swamped by excessive plotting: brother, Bishop, bequest, bracelets diminish the stark image of the little, struggling valiant figures set against "the stupendous background".

NOTES

1. D. H. Lawrence, *Phoenix* (London: Heinemann, 1936) p. 419.
2. ibid., p. 527.
3. *Life*, p. 370.
4. ibid., p. 284.
5. Letter to Mrs Henniker, in *One Rare Fair Woman*, ed. Evelyn Hardy and F. B. Pinion (London: Macmillan, 1972) p. 26.
6. Martin Esslin, *Absurd Drama* (Harmondsworth: Penguin, 1965) p. 23.
7. Lance St John Butler, *Thomas Hardy After Fifty Years* (London: Macmillan, 1977) p. 119.
8. Donald Davidson, 'The traditional basis of Hardy's fiction', *Southern Review*, VI (1940).
9. Letter to Edmund Gosse, quoted in R. L. Purdy, *Thomas Hardy; A Bibliographical Study* (Oxford: Clarendon Press, 1954) p. 44.
10. Preface to *Jude the Obscure*.
11. Roy Morrell, *Thomas Hardy; the Will and the Way* (Kuala Lumpur: University of Malaya Press, 1965) pp. 144, 155.
12. D. H. Lawrence, *Lady Chatterley's Lover*, Ch. 9.

Fifty Years On

Christopher Wiseman

The camera caught it. 1909 and you
With Florence on the beach at Aldeburgh,
Sitting in your suit and hat, looking
Not out to sea, but slightly downwards,
Your eyes unfocused, as if it were all over
And nothing mattered. Or were you travelling time?

It was time, wasn't it, time that hollowed you?
Twist as you did it held and taunted you,
Sharp memories tearing at the worn heart
Until you hung ruined in the mindless jaws.

A fierce winter. As I write, Dorset is under snow,
Black spectral trees rearing like gibbets
Over blank and neutral widenesses.
Drifting snow. Drifts of time. An altered place
With Egdon shrunk, the furze and woodsmoke gone.
Grandchildren of rustics sit in council houses
And watch the world explode to fragments
On rented colour television sets.
The churches are empty, rotting in the weather.
Tick, tock. The years. Nobody there. Ah no . . .

Fifty years on and time has not been kind.
You told us, Hardy; you knew and told us
Something had turned the wrong way.
Nations are broken. Our poetry doesn't rhyme.
Stone crumbles, wood decays, people are diminished.
And instead of finding grey and green felicities,
We live with rancour, betrayal and loss,
With all the sour appalling coincidences.

Fifty Years On

We falter forward. Time cackles and grins.
A rictus wide as the mocking sky.

(Reprinted by kind permission of the author from
The Upper Hand, published in 1981 by the
Enitharmon Press.)

'Words, in all their intimate accents'

Tom Paulin

Recently I was looking through a handbook or reader's guide to Yeats's poetry — it was full of useful facts, sources and so on — when I came across a curious footnote: 'For the meaning of this poem see below, page 80.' Not, 'for an interpretation', but 'for the meaning'. There was something naive, vulnerable, terribly earnest and very dim about that little signpost which directed the reader towards a place called Meaning, and it reminded me of an essay I once read where a critical theorist suggested that it was possible, providing the right critical tools were employed, to discover the 'actual meaning' of a poem. Somewhere, he suggested, there was a lost city called Actual Meaning where the structuralist, the Leavisite, the phenomenologist walked hand in hand: they knew the truth, and that truth was single and definite.

The problem here is that much criticism of poetry, like much teaching of poetry, is a very moral, very puritanical, activity which insists that a poem makes a statement and that we ought to concern ourselves with the nature of that statement — with its meaning — rather than with Art, which is self-delighting, a joy-in-itself, and not a sermon, or a lecture. Together with this stress on meaning — the idea, to put it crudely, that a poem is *about* something outside itself — goes an insistence on visual imagery, and I think it would be a very healthy thing if we stopped reflecting on the word 'image' and considered the obvious fact that poems are not primarily patterns of images, but patterns of sounds. Before picture-thinking, before words, there was a voice; and so I propose to consider the voice, or voices, of Hardy's poetry. Here I'm following what I think is one of the greatest statements ever made about the essential nature of poetry: Robert Frost's remark in a letter to John Bartlett that a sentence is 'a sound in itself on which other sounds called words may be strung'.

There is a little-known poem of Hardy's called 'On a Midsummer Eve' which locates his inspiration, his Muse, in a strange ghostly voice, that intimate speaking voice which he shares with Robert Frost:

I idly cut a parsley stalk,
And blew therein towards the moon;
I had not thought what ghosts would walk
With shivering footsteps to my tune.

I went, and knelt, and scooped my hand
As if to drink, into the brook,
And a faint figure seemed to stand
Above me, with the bygone look.

I lipped rough rhymes of chance, not choice
I thought not what my words might be;
There came into my ear a voice
That turned a tenderer verse for me.

It is that tender voice which we hear in all Hardy's greatest poems. And in order to be visited by that voice he had to rid his poetry of certain received voices. In his earliest poems (there are many of them in *Wessex Poems*) there is a struggle between two different vocal tones. One is a high melodious public Parnassian voice; the other is an intimate tender Gothic speaking voice. And here I am using the terms 'Parnassian' and 'Gothic' to describe the two traditions of English poetry. Parnassian poetry is melodious, and sometimes plummy (it is the sort of poetry that is mellifluously recited between concerts on Radio Three), but its tradition comprises some of the greatest poets: Spenser, Milton, Wordsworth, Tennyson. The Gothic tradition is perhaps less recognised: it has a thorny fricative texture, lacks sonority, smoothness, and obviously regular metre, and is intimately keyed to all the shifts and changes in the speaking voice. Wyatt, Donne, Browning, Hopkins, Hardy and Frost belong to this Gothic tradition.

Hardy began by writing poems in the Parnassian manner of Shakespeare's sonnets:

> For winning love we win the risk of losing,
> And losing love is as one's life were riven;
> It cuts like contumely and keen ill-using
> To cede what was superfluously given.

And then he began to hear the Gothic voice and his verse changed. Here, the two strongest influences were the Dorset dialect (like Hopkins, he greatly admired the fine dialect poetry of William Barnes) and Browning's poetry. Browning speaks always in the voice of an invented character, and his poems are filled with direct speech. So, too, are Hardy's poems packed with conversations; there are two voices in the last line of his Browning-like poem, 'The Two Burghers': ' – "Not mortal?" said he. "Lingering – worse," said I.' The line is an iambic pentameter whose form has been stretched to accommodate the voice of the shocked questioner and the terse, sinister and cynical answer of the jealous husband.

This relishing of the cadences of actual living speech is felt in the first and the last stanza of 'Standing by the Mantelpiece':

> This candle-wax is shaping to a shroud
> To-night. (They call it that, as you may know) –
> By touching it the claimant is avowed,
> And hence I press it with my finger – so. . . .
>
> And let the candle-wax thus mould a shape
> Whose meaning now, if hid before, you know,
> And how by touch one present claims its drape,
> And that it's I who press my finger – so.

The lines are freaked and syncopated by the use of commas, dashes, brackets, and these catch the unique whispering voice of the speaker. Then, unfortunately, the entire register of the poem changes and the speaker becomes a sort of ventriloquist's dummy, a medium taken over by a dead familiar voice:

> To-night. To me twice night, that should have been
> The radiance of the midmost tick of noon,
> And close around me wintertime is seen
> That might have shone the veriest day of June!

This is a sub-Tennysonian, sub-Shakespearian voice: plangent, plummy, rolling out full vowels like marbles. It is the voice of verse-speaking competitions, the voice of a Gielgud reciting Shakespeare. It is a voice we may associate with John of Gaunt's 'This England' speech, with *The Times* crossword and a deathly hush in the close tonight. It is a voice barren of individual accent – the voice, I suppose, of a ruling class. Had Hardy written often in that voice I don't think his poetry would have been much ettended to.

The lines I have just quoted have a regular and monotonous metre, but Hardy's real poetic identity emerges in his manner of shifting accent and stress within a line so that the vocal patterns change line by line within a poem. Take the first stanza of 'The Self-Unseeing':

> Here is | the anc|ient floor,
> Footworn | and hol|lowed and thin,
> Here was | the for|mer door
> Where the | dead feet | walked in.

The first line consists of a trochee and two iambs; the second line of a spondee, an iamb, and an anapaest; the third has the same pattern as the first line, a trochee followed by two iambs, but with an internal rhyme ('for' and 'door'); while the fourth line is a most marvellous and surprising line – a trochee followed by two spondees. Unless we read these lines with the ear, not the eye, then the poem is a flat descriptive statement. Behind the lines, too – and this is felt in Hardy's sharp sudden trochees – there is the rhythm of a fiddler's reel (he mentions his father playing the fiddle in the next stanza). And these rhythms, the rhythms of old folk-tunes, glimmer sharply along the lines of many of Hardy's poems. Take, for example, the opening of his ballad, 'The Alarm':

> In a ferny byway
> Near the great South-Wessex Highway,
> A homestead raised its breakfast-smoke aloft;
> The dew-damps still lay steamless, for the sun had made no skyway,
> And twilight cloaked the croft.

This is similar to another poem, 'To My Father's Violin', which contains the lines: 'In the gallery west the nave / But a few yards from his grave.' And what one can notice here is the extreme disparity between the lugubrious content of the lines (as in 'Where the dead feet walked in') and the underlying wild dancing tune (perhaps the best example of this is the Irish ballad, 'Finnegan's Wake'). The folk imagination combines death and resurrection in the self-delighting wildness of sheer rhythm, and this resembles Yeats's remark that passionate rhythm preserves and transforms personal emotion by lifting it out of history into the realm of 'impersonal meditation'.

According to Yeats, Robert Bridges was able to make commonplace words magnificent by 'some trick of speeding and slowing' in these lines:

> A glitter of pleasure
> And a dark tomb.

And Hardy again and again employs this deft technique of changing the cadencing line by line. This is what happens in 'Lying Awake':

> You, Meadow, are white with your counterpane cover of dew,
>   I see it as if I were there;
> You, Churchyard, are lightening faint from the shade of the yew,
>   The names creeping out everywhere.

The first three lines become progressively lilting and anapaestic, and then the last line, true to that Gothic principle of surprise Hardy insists on, springs a different rhythm upon the ear. Its five strong stresses (there are only eight syllables in the line) build a feeling of awe and still movement; the resurrection is vocal as well as visual.

Here again I am pointing to a connection, or an identity, between rhythm and mystical experience, and this is the connection Yeats makes in his essay, 'The Symbolism of Poetry', when he says:

> The purpose of rhythm, it has always seemed to me, is to prolong the moment of contemplation, the moment when we are both asleep and awake, which is the one moment of creation, by hushing us with an alluring monotony, while it holds us waking by variety, to keep us in that state of perhaps real trance, in which the mind liberated from the pressure of the will is unfolded in symbols.

This rhythm of contemplation can be heard in a very minor poem of Hardy's called 'Spectres that Grieve'. Here he imagines the hell of the unjustly libelled: all those historical figures like, say, Richard III, who may have been better than their historical reputations give them credit for. The poem contains visual imagery – 'phosphor dye', ghostly light – but its best stanza is this one:

> And much surprised was I that, spent and dead,
> They should not, like the many, be at rest,
> But stray as apparitions; hence I said,
> 'Why, having slipped life, hark you back distressed?'

The syntax of these lines is keenly deliberate, even self-conscious, and the backward push and fall in the voice which the subordinate clauses register create a strange questioning tone, a kind of dry searching puzzled whisper. We can hear that tone through the Miltonic music of these lines:

> But thou, say wherefore to such perils past
> Return'st thou? wherefore not this pleasant mount
> Ascendest, cause and source of all delight?

These lines are from Cary's translation of Dante (the translation Hardy read), and it is curious to notice how there is a similar vocal tone in many translations of Dante. For Hardy's poem, Cary's lines, Shelley's 'The Triumph of Life' and Eliot's spectral colloquy in 'Little Gidding', all share that dry mysterious whispering tone, that ghostly authoritative voice which is both wistful and certain.

The voice, personal identity and immortality are all connected for Hardy. This is clearly apparent in 'Voices from Things Growing in a Churchyard' where the meek voice of Fanny Hurd and the no-nonsense briskness of Bachelor Bowring mingle with the rustic accent of Thomas Voss and the chill snobbish accent of Lady Gertrude. There are two other immortal voices in this poem: the warm erotic voice of Eve Greensleeves, a rich dusky accent, and the gruff bitterness of Squire Audeley Grey's tone. Hardy calls them 'murmurous accents', and when he says that they afford 'an interpreter much to teach' he means that we must register their individual accents in all their various uniqueness: their personalities survive in their voices.

Hardy locates survival or immortality in vocal cadence, and we can catch this especially in his great elegy, 'At Castle Boterel':

> As I drive to the junction of lane and highway,
>   And the drizzle bedrenches the waggonette,
> I look behind at the fading byway,
>   And see on its slope, now glistening wet,
>   Distinctly yet
>
> Myself and a girlish form benighted
>   In dry March weather. We climb the road
> Beside a chaise. We had just alighted
>   To ease the sturdy pony's load
>   When he sighed and slowed.

There is that still perfect phrase, 'In dry March weather', whose three strong stresses temporarily arrest the movement of the line; they give it that permanence and freedom from historical movement which is essential to Yeats's definition of rhythm. Also there is a pattern of end and internal rhymes on 'i' – 'benighted', 'dry', 'climb', 'beside', 'alighted' – and this pattern connects with the rhymes on 'road' – 'climb the road', 'alighted/load', 'sighed and slowed'. It is this patterning of sounds around the central hub of the stanza – 'dry March weather' – which both creates and makes permanent the personal emotion.

There is a similar effect in the fourth stanza:

> It filled but a minute. But was there ever
>   A time of such quality, since or before,
> In that hill's story? To one mind never,
>   Though it has been climbed, foot-swift, foot-sore,
>   By thousands more.

The stanza begins with that terse half-line – 'It filled but a minute' – which has the quality of arrested movement, of still permanence, that is created by 'In dry March weather'. Around this is a pattern of end and internal rhymes – 'before', 'story', 'sore', 'more' – which is partly a deliberately dragging weary temporal movement, as in 'foot-swift, foot-sore'. And so the poem sets the permanent rhythm of eternity against the more laborious rhythms of time:

> I look and see it there, shrinking, shrinking,
>   I look back at it amid the rain
> For the very last time; for my sand is sinking,
>   And I shall traverse old love's domain
>   Never again.

The phrase 'shrinking, shrinking', like 'foot-swift, foot-sore', is the impermanent temporal movement, but the last phrase, 'Never again', does not possess a decaying sentimental cadence, a dying fall. It is not an example of what Yeats termed 'passive suffering' because it has a quality of tragic joy: the words are cut clear like an epitaph.

This is present also in 'The Phantom Horseman', which is properly the last poem of Hardy's sequence, 'Poems of 1912–13', where the poem ends with a vision of his wife as she was when young, a 'ghost-girl rider' who 'Draws rein and sings to the swing of the tide'. The anapaestic tendency of this line is tensed by the opening spondee – 'Draws rein' – and the internal rhyme of 'sings' and 'swings'. There is movement and stillness, as in Eliot's Chinese jar or Florizel's speech on Perdita's dancing; and there is also a rhythmic echo of another poem in the sequence, 'I Found Her out there':

> Yet her shade, maybe,
> Will creep underground
> Till it catch the sound
> Of that western sea
> As it swells and sobs
> Where she once domiciled,
> And joy in its throbs
> With the heart of a child.

Put the last two lines together, so that they make one line – 'And joy in its throbs with the heart of a child' – and you have a line similar to 'Draws rein and sings to the swing of the tide'. Here the personal emotion which is felt in the word 'sobs' is transformed by 'joy' and 'throbs' so that it becomes impersonal, permanent – a wild, eager or tragic joy. Here the temporal movement of the waves is transfigured through rhythm into something very similar to Yeats's identification of passionate rhythm, speech rhythm, with ice and salt.

The connections between poetic rhythm and the religious instinct must lie at the very roots of any culture: out of the first chant, the most primitive liturgy, worship and society began; and here children possess the wisest knowledge of poetry: they care only about the rhythms and sounds of a poem, not about what it says, or means. In the first Hardy poem quoted above, 'On a Midsummer Eve', voice and vision are identified; and this connection is clearly made in other poems. In a slight poem, 'In the British Museum', a labourer looks at the Elgin Marbles and muses on how these inanimate objects once echoed the voice of St Paul: 'Words . . . in all their intimate accents' – a line that goes beyond its context to become a kind of symbolist, self-referring phrase. Hardy is describing his own poetry, his intimately vocal aesthetic. And when he says 'accent', he means not simply stress and emphasis, but a provincial accent; and this is apparent in the poem which immediately follows it, 'In the Servants' Quarters', where a constable says to the apostle Peter, 'Why, man, you speak the dialect / He uses in his answers. . . . / There he's speaking now! / His syllables / Are those you sound yourself when you are talking unawares.'

Here, I do not mean that the Word is voiced only by those who are blessed or cursed with a provincial accent, but that the 'provincialism of feeling' which Hardy set against Matthew Arnold's concept of culture does embrace very importantly the poetic voice. I am not going to offer a barbarian aesthetic, only point to the fact that Hardy's extraordinary sensitivity to the speaking voice must have been nurtured in the depths of a rural folk culture, and that he discovered and made his poetic voice by trusting and receiving the voices of the people around him.

His poem, 'In a Whispering Gallery', which is set in St Paul's Cathedral, shows a mingled trust and doubt:

> That whisper takes the voice
> Of a Spirit's compassionings,
> Close, but invisible,
> And throws me under a spell
> At the kindling vision it brings . . .

And then, as in 'The Shadow on the Stone', he wonders if there is a natural solution to the mystery: 'Or if the voice so near / Be a soul's voice floating here.' Although this poem does not employ direct speech, many of Hardy's poems are colloquies in which wistful bodiless voices answer each other, or where different cadences playfully engage with each other.

This playfulness and subtlety of vocal tone is present in 'Transformations', which begins with a definite and assertive trochaic rhythm:

> Pórtion óf this yéw
> Ís a mán my grándsire knéw,
> Bósomed hére at its fóot.

The anapaest which concludes the third line – 'at its foot' – moves the lines towards a gentler, exploratory iambic rhythm:

> This bránch may bé his wífe,
> A rúddy húman lífe
> Now túrned to a gréen shóot.

This ruminative iambic rhythm crosses the trochaic rhythms of the poem, and in the last stanza is triumphant and trochaic. This extraordinary skill which counterpoints the trochaic with the iambic is best heard in 'Beeny Cliff' and in 'Friends Beyond' (a poem which has as its vocal inspiration that marvellous poem of Browning's, 'A Toccata of Galuppi's').

Hardy's poem begins with a sprightly and formal list of the dead friends who lie in the churchyard: 'William Dewy, Tranter Reuben, Farmer Ledlow late at plough.' This, technically, is a 'trochaic octameter', as are these lines of Brownings': 'Oh Galuppi Baldassaro, this is very sad to find! / I can hardly misconceive you; it would prove me deaf and blind.' Browning's poem has a tantalising rhythm – it is most subtly and fantastically cadenced – and Hardy's danger in using it as a model for his poem is that his own voice might be submerged by Browning's. This does not happen because Hardy alters the triplet form by making it into terza rima and introducing a short second line.

Thus his first line, 'William Dewy, Tranter Reuben, Farmer Ledlow late at plough', is followed by 'Robert's kin, and John's, and Ned's', before the full trochaic line is reasserted by 'And the Squire, and lady Susan, lie in Mellstock churchyard now'. What most strangely happens is that the short second line begins with a confidently trochaic push ('Róbert's kín') before easing into iambic metre ('and Jóhn's, and Néd's'). Now, iambic metre is the metre which is closest to the speaking voice and so what Hardy is doing here is freshening the heightened trochaic metre with a more natural and flexible rhythm, and this prevents the sound-pattern of the poem from becoming too definite and monotonous. And throughout the poem he plays the intimate accents of various speaking voices against the insistent demands of the metre.

'Friends Beyond' is a paradigm of Hardy's poetic technique; it is a warm, witty, beautifully cadenced poem which pays many graceful compliments to 'A Toccata of Galuppi's'; it is in fact a form of 'reply poem'.

Here, my position is possibly an extreme aesthetic one: the aesthete and the nihilist are alike in their refusal to stoop to the trammelling practicalities of meanings, opinions, and definite statements. And yet too much literary criticism ignorantly espouses the opposite extreme, and many literary critics, I suspect, are eye readers avid for actual meaning and visual imagery. The great Russian poet, Osip Mandelstam, called such critics 'enemies of the word' and he identified them with bureaucrats, party functionaries, literary and political commissars. In his essay, 'About the Nature of the Word', he questions what he calls the 'bondage' of the word to its denotative signficance, and concludes: 'the word is not a thing. Its significance is not the equivalent of a translation of itself.' In certain historical periods the cry goes up that art must be 'relevant', 'committed', 'socially and politically conscious' – that a poem exists to serve an opinion, an idea, or an ideology. Even a tough card-carrying liberal, like Lionel Trilling, views poetry as existing in the service of an idea; and the result of this terrible explicatory pressure which is everywhere applied to art is that a poem becomes a merely useful object, like an old radio set, and so is never valued for what it is, but for what it does. But the cruel philistinism of certain forms of critical interpretation is set aside whenever we listen to a poem and are taken by its rhythms, its cadences.

To be taken by a rhythm is to know a kind of triumph, and the great refrains in 'During Wind and Rain' have a quality of tragic joy, of pure self-delighting skill, which spits into the face of time:

> Hów the sićk leáves reél dowń in thróngs . . .
>
> Dowń their carvéd naḿes the raíndrop ploúghs.

The packed stresses build a rhythm which contradicts, or plays against, the content of the lines, and so the poem wears the mask of style, the words move together in a graceful ritual and we attend their ceremony.

Hardy's Use of the Hair Motif

Peter W. Coxon

> Kissing her hair I sat against her feet,
> Wove and unwove it, wound and found it sweet;
> Made fast therewith her hands, drew down her eyes,
> Deep as deep flowers and dreamy like dim skies,
> With her own tresses bound and found her fair,
>   Kissing her hair.
>   (Swinburne)

Harold Orel in his short study of Hardy's drama *The Famous Tragedy of the Queen of Cornwall* regards a particular description of Iseult the White-handed as a 'significant detail'[1] (she has 'corn-brown hair'). With wistful regret Hardy recalls here the experience fifty years earlier when he entered the Royal Duchy of Cornwall and encountered his own fair Iseult in the person of Emma Gifford. The romance of that meeting is amply recorded in numerous poems that flowed from Hardy's pen in the years following Emma's death in 1912, and not a few of them allude to the impressive beauty of her hair. He mused nostalgically on the idyllic summer of 1870:

> Divine things done and said
> Illumined it,
> Whose rays crept into corn brown curls . . .
>   ('This Summer and Last')

Emma presaged the later drama as she

> . . . would sigh at the tale
> Of sunk Lyonnesse,
> As a wind-tugged tress
> Flapped her cheek like a flail;
>   ('I found her out there')

A number of poems exhibit a vivid sense of place-association. A visit to St Juliot in 1913 recalls '. . . a maiden abiding / Thereat as in hiding; / Fair-eyed and white-shouldered, broad-browed and brown-tressed' ('A Dream or No') and

> Where you will next be there's no knowing,
>   Facing round about me everywhere,
>   With your nut-coloured hair,
>   And gray eyes, and rose-flush coming and going.
>   ('After a Journey')

Emma was a skilled horse-woman and Hardy recalls '. . . the woman riding high above with bright hair flapping free – / The woman whom I loved so, and who loyally loved me' ('Beeny Cliff').

The force of Hardy's memories of Emma was undoubtedly stimulated when he read her diary after her death.[2] One section in particular is cited at length in *The Life of Thomas Hardy*, in which Emma remembered her Cornish residence: 'scampering up and down the hills on my beloved mare alone, wanting no protection, the rain going down my back often and my hair floating in the wind . . .'. Immediately following this passage Hardy added his comments on Emma as she then was: 'Though her features were not regular her complexion at this date was perfect in hue, her figure and movement graceful, and her corn-coloured hair abundant in its coils.'

Earlier in the diary Emma recounted the gaiety of her youth in Plymouth. She attended numerous parties: 'Splendid sashes and stockings and shoes also adorned us, and our hair floated about in the rush of air made by our whirlings – Never to be forgotten parties!'[3] As a child Emma was the 'only fair child of her father with bright hair, which he would stroke with sighings occasionally'.[4] Emma does not admit to preferential treatment. She points out that of Gifford's children she alone inherited the fair complexion of her mother's side of the family.[5] And when the young Hardy revisited St Juliot in the summer of 1870 it was Emma's complexion that attracted his attention. He found 'a young lady in summer blue, which suited her fair complexion far better . . .'.[6] Emma's recollections undoubtedly stirred Hardy's memory and made their own contribution to the remarkable poems written when she died. Curiously, one of these does not evince the same spirit of untrammelled affection. In *The Wind's Prophecy* the poet vacillates between two women who are rivals for his love, one who has 'ebon loops of hair' and lives in a city home, the other residing on the coast and having 'tresses flashing fair'. The latter is certainly Emma but the identification of the 'dark She' of the poem remains a mystery.[7]

It is not unreasonable to enquire whether the striking effects of Emma's features and in particular the fine head of hair which are evident in the poems contributed to the portrayal of female characters in the early novels. Hardy the novelist made a point of guarding jealously the personal experiences which were the sources of his inspiration, and it would be wrong to select one source as a strand of evidence and follow it willy-nilly through the novels. However, Hardy admitted that the character and 'appearance' of Elfride in *A Pair of Blue Eyes* (1873) had 'points in common' with Emma in young womanhood.[8] Permissibly one can envisage the reflection of actual experience in Stephen's first encounter with Elfride: 'with plenty of loose curly hair tumbling down about her shoulders' (Ch. 2). When Elfride plays the piano to him, the glow of a candle shapes her 'accidentally frizzled hair into a nebulous haze of light, surrounding her crown like an aureola' (Ch. 3). When she sets off at a gallop on her pony, she is described with '. . . her light figure contracting to the dimensions of a bird as she sank into the distance − her hair flowing' (Ch. 7). Elsewhere in the novel Elfride's relationship with Knight draws further accounts of her 'plenteous twines of beautiful hair' (Ch. 25), her 'luxuriant head of hair' (Ch. 28), and her 'great abundance of hair' (Ch. 28). Elfride's hair was the hallmark of female sexuality: 'You saw her hair as far as you could see her sex, and knew that it was the palest brown' (Ch. 18), and Knight's love for her is born when he begins to notice her person. In the late afternoon he walks with her on the lawn, and 'the ends of her hanging hair softly dragged themselves backwards and forwards upon her shoulder as each faint breeze thrust against or relinquished it' (Ch. 17).

Manifold descriptions of the colour, texture, shape and luxuriance of women's hair are scattered throughout the rest of Hardy's novels and it would be hazardous to argue that the impact of the novelist's early rapture with Emma formed the stimulus of later descriptions. In the early novels it is possible that an occasional sentence echoes the Cornish experience, as when the delectable Fancy Day in *Under the Greenwood Tree* looks out of the window of her cottage and the carollers receive the vision of a young woman wrapped in a night-robe 'whilst down her shoulders fell a twining profusion of marvellously rich hair . . .' (I, Ch. 5).[9] The portrait of Emma comes through strongly in the nostalgic poems of a much later period and the few allusions to her tresses are limited to the earliest novels. For the increasingly subtle symbolism of the major novels one must look elsewhere for potential sources of influence. One of these may well be found in the artistic movements of the mid-Victorian period. I refer here to the Pre-Raphaelite movement and in particular to the publication in 1866 of Swinburne's *Poems and Ballads*. The fresh and original vigour of Swinburne's poetry opened up for would-be poets and writers of the 1860s and 1870s what seemed to be endless vistas of beauty. Hardy himself recalled the impact which the First Series of love lyrics made on him when he worked in London as a young man:

> O that far morning of a summer day
> When, down a terraced street whose pavements lay
> Glassing the sunshine into my bent eyes,
> I walked and read with a quick glad surprise
>   New words, in classic guise . . .
>
> ('A Singer Asleep')

A cursory glance through Swinburne's lyrics reveals the treatment of romantic themes in full-blooded and sensuous terms. Noticeable among recurrent images are descriptions of a woman's head of hair as an expression of female sexuality. The colour, shape, gloss and perfume of the physical object haunt the poems and are used as symbols of female beauty, close physical intimacy, dominance and fatal allure.[10]

A number of Hardy's portraits are touched by the Pre-Raphaelite ideal of the beautiful woman with the 'curled golden hair', and he actually mentions the school and its young poet in *Two on a Tower* ('that youth with the "corn-coloured" hair, as a poet of the new school would call it . . .' (Ch. 25)). Again, in the short story entitled 'Fellow Townsmen' (published in *Wessex Tales*), the face of Lucy Savile had 'a beautiful outline; the Raphaelesque oval of its contour was remarkable for an English countenance . . . (Ch. 2). The heroine once had 'dark brown hair . . . the parting down the middle . . . a thin white line, a narrow crevice between two banks of shade . . .' (Ch. 9).

It is an interesting fact that the brunettes of Hardy's fiction integrate most successfully with nature and the physical world. The world is acceptable to them; it is regarded as an ally and the stresses and strains which are an inevitable part of the whole of life are ameliorated in coming to terms with it. In the main theirs is a satisfactory existence and seldom do they emerge as tragic figures on account of their own precipitate action. Among the brown-haired women there are some who are fair: Cytherea Gray ('shining corn-yellow'), Elfride Swancourt ('the palest brown'), Fanny Robin ('real golden hair', 'yellow hair'), Ethelberta Petherwin ('squirrel-coloured hair'), Thomasin Yeobright ('wavy chestnut hair', 'brown hair'), Anne Garland ('round brown curls', 'Anne the fair'), Paula Power ('good English brown', 'fair curly hair'), Elizabeth-Jane Henchard ('brown – rather light'), Marty South ('a rare and beautiful approximation to chestnut'). Others are dark: Fancy Day ('plentiful knots of dark brown hair'), Tess Durbeyfield ('earth-coloured hair', 'dark brown hair', 'twisted dark hair'), the first Avice Caro ('brown tresses of hair'), the second Avice ('her dark hair braided up') and the third Avice ('the colour of the thick tresses being obviously repeated in the irises of her large deep eyes'). Major characters with black hair are fewer but they constitute a distinct group among Hardy's women. Highly-sexed, passionate and discontented with the world as they find it, theirs are volatile dispositions. They struggle constantly to impose their idealised view of how to live upon reality. With these women there is sometimes the suggestion of inherited Latin temperament which serves to emphasise their alienation from the natural environment of Wessex.

The black-haired women number at least four. Bathsheba Everdene ('dark-haired maiden', 'knots of black hair'), Eustacia Vye ('the luxuriance of her shady hair', 'a mane as black as night'), Viviette, Lady Constantine ('her hair was black as midnight', 'masses of hair once darkness visible'), and Lucetta Templeman ('dark-haired'). It seems probable that Sue Fawley had 'dark' if not black hair, but Hardy is not explicit on this point, although he does describe her 'vivacious dark eyes and hair'. Arabella Donn is a 'fine dark-eyed girl' but no details are given of her particular hair colour.

Before examining more closely the symbolic aspects of women's hair in the major novels, comment is necessary on the remarkable attentiveness to detail which characterises Hardy's descriptions. The multifarious changes of coiffure which attended the mid-Victorian period are handsomely documented in the novels. The year 1865 marked the advent of flexuous *chignon* styles which were calculated to emulate Greco-Roman modes (under Pre-Raphaelite influence?). The severer style which had the hair parted in the centre, waved on the temples and gathered to a bun on the nape of the neck was rejected, and the emphasis was put on the hair being dressed higher on the head 'with the main mass of the *chignon* lifted . . . and placed on the back of the head. Coils, braids, switches, curls, *water falls*, frizettes and false pieces of every description were now being used.'[11] The next decade saw a more elaborate coiffure: 'curls were worn on the forehead; the hair was swept up at the sides, showing the ears once more – to curls on the top, and the back hair was dressed in plaits, curls, ringlets, or coils, all cascading down from a high bun or coil, to low in the nape.'[12] Interest centred at the back as with dresses. The so-called 'drooping *chignon*' was retained, but the coils of hair were looser and the hair was built high with *frizzles* on the forehead. Combs held the back hair which was dressed in plaits or large rolls.

Illustrations of the varying hair styles – *chignon*, coils, braids and curls – are found throughout the Hardy novels. In *Under the Greenwood Tree*, Fancy Day has 'plentiful knots' (I, Ch. 6) and 'wavy bundles' (III, Ch. 1) of dark brown hair; in *Far from the Madding Crowd*, Bathsheba is described variously as having 'ropes of black hair' (Ch. 2) and 'knots of black hair' (Ch. 33); in *The Hand of Ethelberta*, the heroine has her hair 'fastened in a sort of Venus-knot behind' (Ch. 4), further described by Faith Julian as a 'shining bunch of hair' (Ch. 4).

In *A Laodicean* Somerset recalls the face of Paula, '. . . the breadth of that clear-complexioned forehead – almost concealed by the masses of brown hair bundled up around it . . .' (Ch. 12); and later, when he encounters her in the garden, her 'hair hung under her hat in great knots so well compacted that the sun gilded the convexity of each knot like a ball' (Ch. 15).

In *Tess of the d'Urbervilles*, Tess's imposing figure is enhanced by the 'thick cable of twisted dark hair hanging straight down her back to her waist' (Ch. 14), which in the daytime becomes a 'coiled-up cable' (Ch. 27), 'twisted up in a large round mass at the back of her head' (Ch. 36). Arabella's head-piece is 'twisted up' in an enormous knob at the back of the head (*Jude the Obscure*, I, Ch. 9).[13]

Cascading curls and ringlets are also much in evidence in the early novels. Cytherea's hair 'rested gaily on her shoulders in curls' (*Desperate Remedies*, Ch. 1). Fancy is jealous of her rival who has long curls 'without being put in paper' (*Under the Greenwood Tree*, III, Ch. 3) and outrages the congregation in church at Mellstock with her fashionable display 'of hat, feather and curls trailing down her back' (IV, Ch. 5). Elfride has 'loose, curly hair tumbling about her shoulders' (*A Pair of Blue Eyes*, Ch. 2; cf. also Chs. 25, 28).

The hair dressed high with waves or frizzles over the forehead receives mention,[14] as does the attractive effect of braided locks.[15] Hair adorned with flowers or jewelry is also noted,[16] together with the popular mode of fastening hair with buckles or back-combs.[17] The Victorian technique of brushing or teasing the hair to obtain a 'blown' effect is mentioned in a minor incident in Ethelberta's adventures (*The Hand of Ethelberta*, Chs. 9 and 28) but has tragic import in the career of Tess (*Tess of the d'Urbervilles*, Ch. 7).

The dictates of mid-Victorian coiffures led to the demand for large quantities of false hair. Up to 1867, dark hair was fashionable and quantities of false hair were imported from France and Italy. In that year, however, golden and light-tinted hair began to be favoured. 'Artificial hair was imported chiefly from Northern France, Belgium and Germany.

German hair, being lighter in colour, was the most valuable and the wholesale price varied from 30 to 60 shillings a pound. The peasent girls from whom the hair was obtained were given trinkets or articles of dress in exchange for their tresses, which might weigh from three-quarters to one and a half pounds.'[18] The enormous boom in the hair trade was not without its bizarre elements. It was reported in *The Times* (3 April 1869):

> An American paper states that in consequence of the demand for hair of peculiar colours and shades a new branch of 'Kleptic industry' has sprung up in New York. It appears that the hair thief abounds in the horse cars of the city, where the excuse of putting his elbow on the window enables him to operate with greater ease; but he is also to be found in every place of public gathering, the church included. The tresses dangling behind the head are his easy prey.

Early the following year a letter to *The Times* (20 January 1870) warned ladies

> . . . against the scoundrels (male and female) who are now infesting the thoroughfares and omnibuses of London and stealing hair.
> A young friend of ours has just had the whole of her hair cut off in broad daylight in Westbourne Grove, one of the most crowded streets in London, and the theft was so cleverly performed that she was quite unconscious of it until her return home, although her bonnet string was cut through and her net divided into three pieces.
> It is to be hoped that the police will really endeavour to put a stop to this serious nuisance, otherwise ladies will be afraid to walk in the streets.
> I am at a loss to suggest any precaution that the ladies themselves may take. A more sensible shape of bonnet than the present might do something, but fashion, I fear, will not change in time to be of much use.

A fitting background is thus provided for those instances in the novels where false hair is mentioned. In Hardy's first published novel (*Desperate Remedies*, 1870), people assembled in Hocbridge Town Hall observe the entrance of newcomers 'silently criticising their dress – questioning the genuineness of their teeth and hair . . .' (Ch. 1). Cytherea attends to Miss Aldclyffe's toilette and lets her 'hair fall about her shoulders, and began to arrange it. It proved to be all real . . .' (Ch. 4). In the altercation that follows Miss Aldclyffe orders Cytherea to 'make more show of my hair than that or I shall have to buy some, which God forbid!' (Ch. 4). In the interests of the Gothic plot in the same novel Manston's mistress is made to wear false hair (Ch. 18). The repertoire of Mrs Menlove's feminine artifices includes false hair (*The Hand of Ethelberta*, Ch. 28). The wearing of false hair assumes symbolic signficance in two of the major novels. In *The Woodlanders* Marty parts with her chestnut tresses (Ch. 2), which are then braided and transformed into an impressive feature in Mrs Charmond's *tournure* (Ch. 13); and in *Jude the Obscure* the hero is taken aback on his wedding night when Arabella removes the false tail of hair which had been formed into a glamorous chignon at the back of her head (I, Ch. 9).

Hair as a chief love-token is common to all ages, and the appropriation of a severed tress has associated sexual overtones. Pope's poem, 'The Rape of the Lock', fuses a number of elements in the mystique of hair and the incident which the poem celebrates; and Lord Petre's rash impulse in snipping off one of Miss Arabella Fermor's locks may have influenced a scene in *Two on a Tower*. On this occasion the roles are reversed and Lady Constantine has designs on Swithin:

> What whim, agitation, or attraction prompted the impulse, nobody knows; but she took the scissors and, bending over the sleeping youth, cut off one of the curls, or rather crooks, – for they hardly reached a curl, – into which each lock of his hair chose to twist itself in the last inch of its length. The hair fell on the rug. (Ch. 5)

Elfride, in *A Pair of Blue Eyes*, was unhappy at the thought of parting with a lock of her hair as a souvenir for Knight ('Hair is unlucky, she murmured, when he took his leave' (Ch. 30)). In *The Trumpet-Major* the lock of hair given by Anne to Bob when they were juveniles is also an innocent keepsake (Chs. 14 and 15), but stronger sexual implications are to be reckoned with when Bob passes on Matilida's black hair-lock to John (Ch. 33). Likewise in *The Mayor of Casterbridge* the passionate affair between Henchard and Lucetta is deliberately recalled when Henchard surrenders his watch and chain at the bankruptcy proceedings after removing 'the hair-guard made and given him by Lucetta' (Ch. 21). The amorous conquests of Troy in *Far From the Madding Crowd* are symbolised by his possession of love-locks from Fanny and Bathsheba. The act of cutting-off which precedes the possession of Bathsheba's hair is a significant detail in a scene which is charged with sexual symbolism. The momentous 'rite' is solemnised by Troy's marital promise to 'keep this (i.e. the lock) in remembrance of you (Bathsheba)' (Ch. 28).

In addition to the use of the hair-motif in the development of plot,[19] the physical appearance of head hair is handled to express sexual jealousy and enhanced sexual feeling. In *Under the Greenwood Tree*, Fancy Day becomes jealous of her rival's fair hair, which seems to her, in the first flush of her courtship by Dick Dewy, infinitely preferable to her own dark-brown curls (III, Ch. 3); and a similar scene is enacted in *The Trumpet-Major* when the light-haired Caroline, Bob Loveday's sweetheart, attracts Anne Garland's jealousy (Ch. 35). Troy's petty quarrelling with Bathsheba is exacerbated by the discovery of a coil of fair hair in Troy's possession. Bathsheba's response is one of jealous outrage (*Far from the Madding Crowd*, Ch. 41). Surprisingly, Victorian censorship ignored or overlooked two melodramatic incidents in *Desperate Remedies* which employ women's hair as a powerful sex symbol. Miss Aldclyffe soothes the distressed Cytherea in bed with the words 'put your hair around your mother's neck, and give me one good long kiss' (Ch. 6), and Manston at the end of the story attempts to rape her, 'overturning the table, springing over it, seizing one of the long brown tresses, pulling her towards him and clasping her round' (Ch. 20).

In the major novels the hair-motif makes an important contribution in the portrayal of the female character. It is a motif which can be subjected to scrutiny and appreciated for its precise contribution in the composition of the love story. Its recurrence in the Hardy novels is impressive and invites a special but unexaggerated assessment. In my view it is a stable symbol of female sexuality and is employed with supreme sensitivity by Hardy in the presentation of his people.

Of the major characters in *Far from the Madding Crowd* Bathsheba is presented as a full-blooded and passionate woman whose beauty is commensurate with her sexuality. When we first meet her she is surrounded by bright colours, and in the sunlight the jet of her hair is fittingly complemented by her vivid clothes: 'It was a fine spring morning, and the sun lighted up to a scarlet glow the crimson jacket she wore, and painted a red lustre upon her bright face and black hair' (Ch. 1). That her physical beauty might induce delusions of grandeur is suggested as she observes herself in her looking-glass as a 'fair product of nature' (Ch. 1). The same chapter marks her again as 'the red-jacketed and dark-haired maiden', and when Gabriel Oak realises her identity the imagery is sustained: 'the girl now dropped the cloak, and forth tumbled ropes of black hair over a red jacket' (Ch. 2).

Boldwood's attention is directed to Bathsheba when 'he saw her black hair' (Ch. 17) in the Casterbridge market-house; and later when he turns up at the shearing supper he sees Bathsheba presiding over the rustic scene: 'unusually excited, her red cheeks and lips contrasting lustrously with the mazy skeins of her shadowy hair' (Ch. 23). The third man in the story who responds to Bathsheba's beauty is Sergeant Troy, and the scene of his dazzling sword-display and appropriation of a lock of her hair in the hollow has obvious sexual undercurrents. Troy's scarlet form moves towards her through the ferns and his dexterous performance bewilders and captivates her. When he severs one of her tresses his sexual domination and her submission are complete. What he had done

> brought the blood beating into her face, set her stinging as if aflame . . . and enlarged emotion to a compass which quite swamped thought. It had brought upon her a stroke resulting, as did that of Moses in Horeb, in a liquid stream – here a stream of tears. She felt like one who has sinned a great sin. (Ch. 28)

In the first flush of their love the couple meet clandestinely and marry in Bath. Cain Ball recounts to Oak how he found them: 'her hair was brushed splendid. And when the sun shone upon the bright gown and his red coat – my! how handsome they looked' (Ch. 33). At this point Jan Coggan attempts to restrain the vulgar comments of some of the farmhands that Bathsheba was acting 'over-intimate' with Troy, but his defence is lined with irony: 'Our mistress has too much sense under they knots of black hair to do such a mad thing' (Ch. 33). The smouldering discontent in the subsequent relationship between Troy and Bathsheba eventually erupts when she discovers a coil of yellow hair in Troy's watch case. Her jealousy is roused and Troy perversely feeds it maintaining that 'her [i.e. Fanny Robin's] hair has been acclaimed by everybody who has seen her since she has worn it loose, which has not been long. It is beautiful hair . . .' (Ch. 41). Troy reminisces on Fanny Robin's beauty, which we learn from Joseph Poorgrass's description later in the novel was veritably Pre-Raphaelite: 'It was light . . . but she wore it rather short, and packed away under her cap. . . . But I have seen her let it down when she was going to bed, and it looked beautiful then. Real golden hair' (Ch. 41). The two passages in conjunction suggest Troy's physical intimacy with Fanny, and his possession of her hair-lock confirms the association. At this stage Bathsheba does not know about Fanny, but her outburst has an intuitive accuracy: 'You won't burn that curl. You like the woman who owns that pretty hair – yes, it is pretty – more beautiful than my miserable black mane!' (Ch. 41).

Bathsheba's eventual discovery is brutal, when, realising her worst suspicions, she opens the lid of Fanny's coffin: 'Fanny's face was framed by that yellow hair of hers, and there was no longer much room for doubt as to the origin of the curl owned by Troy' (Ch. 43). The fatality of facial beauty reaches its nadir here, and not even the jealous Bathsheba can bring herself to destroy Fanny's lock of hair. It is kept in her memory and is the first token gesture of the harsh path of self-control which Bathsheba learns to follow despite her instinctual impulsiveness and perversity. That there is hope for her may be indicated in the last of Hardy's subtle descriptions of hair as a symbol. When she goes to Boldwood's party Bathsheba asks Liddy, 'Can't my hair be brushed a little flatter?' (Ch. 52).

In *The Return of the Native*, the characters of Eustacia Vye and Thomasin Yeobright are set in opposition. The latter is drawn integrated with the world about her; she is a child of nature. Seen first in Diggory Venn's van, she reveals 'A fair, sweet, honest country face . . . reposing in a nest of wavy chestnut hair' (I, Ch. 4). The vacillations of Wildeve distress her but do not disturb her repose and quiet resignation to the turn of events. Her native Egdon is no enemy to her and her physical appearance is at one with it. She muses in the loft of Mrs Yeobright's cottage:

> 'Dear Clym, I wonder how your face looks now?' she said, gazing abstractedly at the pigeon-hole, which admitted the sunlight so directly upon her brown hair and transparent tissues that it almost seemed to shine through her. (II, Ch. 2)

and is in complete harmony with the seasons of the year:

> Thomasin came out of the tree, shook from her hair and dress the loose berries which had fallen thereon, and went down the hill with her aunt, each woman bearing half the gathered boughs. (II, Ch. 2)

She captures the spirit of the 'golden-haired' Pre-Raphaelite beauty:

> The sun, where it could catch it, made a mirror of Thomasin's hair, which she always wore braided. It was braided according to a calendric system: the more important the day the more numerous the strands in the braid. . . . Years ago she had said that when she married she would braid it in sevens. She had braided it in sevens to-day. (II, Ch. 8)

If Thomasin's hair betokens satisfaction with existence, that of Eustacia tells a different story: of her wild passion, sensuality and utter refusal to accept life as it is. She regards her condition as unfortunate and rebels against it to her own destruction. Her proud and vibrant nature is vividly portrayed in a description of her appearance:

> She was in person full-limbed and somewhat heavy; without ruddiness, as without pallor; and soft to the touch as a cloud. To see her hair was to

fancy that a whole winter did not contain darkness enough to form its shadow; it closed over her forehead like nightfall extinguishing the western glow.

Her nerves extended into those tresses, and her temper could always be softened by stroking them down. When her hair was brushed she would instantly sink into stillness and look like the Sphinx. If, in passing under one of the Egdon banks, any of its thick skeins were caught, as they sometimes were, by a prickly tuft of the large *Ulex Europoeus* – which will act as a sort of hairbrush – she would go back a few steps, and pass against it a second time. (I, Ch. 7)

Exposed to nature, she fights it and regards it with scornful antagonism. Further descriptions reinforce the impression of her powerful and alluring sexuality: 'Across the upper part of her head she wore a thin fillet of black velvet, restraining the luxuriance of her shady hair . . .' (I, Ch. 7) and 'A beauty, with a white face and a mane as black as night . . .' (IV, Ch. 3).

The tension of Clym's encounter with Eustacia at the close of the novel is set against a precise account of Eustacia's toilette operations. Her response to his accusation is eloquently conveyed in her silent ritual:

When he opened the door she was standing before the looking-glass in her night-dress, the ends of her hair gathered into one hand, with which she was coiling the whole mass around her head.

Her hand relinquished the rope of hair and dropped to her side, and the pile of tresses, no longer supported, fell from the crown of her head about her shoulders and over the white night-gown. She made no reply (V, Ch. 3).

A little later, distraught and caught up in a maelstrom not entirely of her own making, she is exposed to the harsh elements of the heath and 'appeared to be utterly indifferent to the circumstance that her bonnet, hair and garment were becoming wet and disarranged by the moisture of her cold, harsh pillow' (V, Ch. 4). The final description of Eustacia conveys a feeling of tranquillity and harmony with the forces of nature tht she never knew when she was alive: 'Her black hair was looser now than either of them had ever seen it before, and surrounded her brow like a forest' (V, Ch. 9).

Descriptions of women's hair have no significant symbolism in *The Mayor of Casterbridge*, and this is not surprising when one considers that the novel's over-arching concern is with a man's character and actions.[20] The women in his life are sketched as foils enlarging the dimension of his complex character. First, Susan Henchard, reappearing on Weydon-Priors highroad as Mrs Newson, is a pale reflection of the dignified victim betrayed by Henchard in the opening pages of the novel: 'Her hair had not lost colour' but 'it was considerably thinner than heretofore' (Ch. 3). Her daughter, Elizabeth-Jane, avoids the impulsiveness and perversity of other Hardy heroines and, like Thomasin, overcomes numerous vicissitudes by her prudent and unpretentious behaviour. Only once is her hair given detached notice:

> Indoors she appeared with her hair divided by a parting that arched like a white rainbow from ear to ear. All in front of this line was covered with an encampment of curls, all behind was dressed smoothly, and drawn to a knob (Ch. 14).

She thus fits a thoroughly domestic context. Henchard does, however, touch a sensitive nerve in the plot when he presages the fact that Elizabeth-Jane is not his daughter on the basis of her brown hair (Ch. 14). Lucetta Templeman is Henchard's counterpart. She fits the mould of Hardy's other passion-driven heroines whose history is marred by submission to the fleshly instinct. When Elizabeth-Jane calls at High Place Hall she receives her first impression of Lucetta: 'on the sofa with two cylindrical pillows reclined a dark-haired, large-eyed pretty woman of unmistakably French extraction . . .' (Ch. 22). Henchard's original claim on her is symbolised by his possession of a hair-guard given him by her. Lucetta's pride in her beauty takes a bitter blow when she witnesses the skimmington-ride mummery. The pilloried victim had 'her neck uncovered and her hair in bands, and her back-comb in place' (Ch. 39). Her reputation for neat coiffure had preceded her and led to the accuracy of the vulgar display.

In *The Woodlanders* female sexuality is vividly portrayed in the symbolic treatment of a woman's head hair. The first chapter introduces the peasant girl, Marty South, actively engaged in the harsh labour of making spars. Physical labour of this sort had brought a 'premature finality' to the 'provisional curves of her childhood's face', but she had been blessed with an exceptional feature – 'her hair':

> Its abundance made it almost unmanageable; its colour was, roughly speaking, and as seen here by firelight, brown; but careful notice, or an observation by day, would have revealed that its true shade was a rare and beautiful approximation to chestnut (Ch. 2).

It was upon these glorious tresses that the visitor to her cottage had designs. Mr Percomb, on behalf of Mrs Felice Charmond, lady of the manor, was about to propose to Marty that she part with her hair for a sum of money. The insidious Mr Percomb is particularly persuasive in his arguments and resorts to male domination ('he touched her hair with his cane'), cajolery ('No, no, no! she cried. . . . You are tempting me. You go on like the Devil to Doctor Faustus in the penny book . . .'), and blackmail ("Twill be bad for you if you don't') in his errand. Marty eventually cuts her hair when she hears that Giles Winterbourne is betrothed to Grace Melbury, but we are left in no doubt about the pain caused by her decision. As she sees the two sovereigns on the mantel-piece she strokes her tresses, and when she severs them exclaims 'I've made myself ugly – and hateful – that's what I've done!' (Ch. 3).

It has already been mentioned that peasant girls in Italy and Germany parted with their hair in the mid-nineteenth century, and some of them were probably not unhappy to exploit their natural resources. But the incident involving Marty's hair is on a different level to hair manufacture. It is designed to set a sinister tone at the outset of the novel. It is symbolic of the violation of Marty's physical integrity and suggests the authoritarianism and fading beauty of the dark lady of the manor house. The powerful influence which Mrs Charmond exerts first on Grace Melbury and then on Fitzpiers is conditioned by the initial attraction of her facial beauty – complete with Marty's tresses. Marty is a sullen witness as she and Grace watch the carriage pass:

> Mrs. Charmond did not see them, but there was sufficient light for them to discern her outline between the carriage windows. A noticeable feature in her *tournure* was a magnificent mass of braided locks.
>
> 'How well she looks this morning,' said Grace. . . . 'Her hair so becomes her worn that way. I have never seen any more beautiful!' (Ch. 13)

On Fitzpiers' first visit to Hintock House he finds Mrs Charmond in her boudoir:

> reclining on a couch in such a position as not to disturb a pile of magnificent hair on the crown of her head. A deep purple dressing-gown formed an admirable foil to the peculiarly rich brown of her hair-plaits (Ch. 26).

Both Grace and Fitzpiers are made to suffer at her hands and Fitzpiers, who resembles Troy in his powerful response to women, barely escapes complete humiliation. Eventually he does question the authority and authenticity of Felice Charmond's sexual power, and in that lies his redemption. Fitzpiers had cherished the memory of Felice Charmond's beauty from the days of an adolescent encounter in Heidelberg when she 'wore a long tail of rare-coloured hair' (Ch. 26). Marty's letter had disclosed the artificiality of Mrs Charmond's crowning glory. The disclosure brought Fitzpiers to an awareness of the triviality of his relationship with her, based as it was solely on sexual gratification:

> Marty had not effected it by word of mouth; the charge about the locks of hair was made simply by Fitzpiers reading her letter to him aloud to Felice in the playfully ironical tones of one who had become a little weary of his situation. . . . He had stroked those false tresses with his hand many a time without knowing them to be transplanted, and it was impossible when the discovery was so abruptly made, to avoid being finely satirical, despite his generous disposition. (Ch. 43)

Thus Marty had the last word in Mrs Charmond's fate. Her untimely missive led to the quarrel with Fitzpiers and subsequently to her murder; Hardy describes the letter ominously as 'the tiny instrument of a cause deep in nature'[21] (Ch. 45).

The hair-motif is used with superb artistry in *Tess of the d'Urbervilles*. The unified beauty of Tess permeates the story and yet in the description of her facial perfection carries overtones of the dangers of sensual attraction. There are at least sixteen allusions to Tess's hair, and they are clustered around five focal points in the novel where Tess is exposed to the attention of the two men in her life. The earliest descriptions are found when Tess is first introduced during the local Cerealia at Marlott. She appears in a group of village dancers (a veritable band of vestal virgins) and is singled out as a female divinity:

> The young girls formed, indeed, the majority of the band, and their heads of luxuriant hair reflected in the sunshine every tone of gold, and black, and brown. . . .
> She was a fine and handsome girl . . . her mobile peony mouth and large innocent eyes added eloquence to colour and shape. She wore a red ribbon in her hair. . . . (Ch. 2)

She is seen on this occasion by Angel Clare, who is on a country ramble with his brothers. She is portrayed at this period in her life as a fine peasant girl attuned to the secrets of nature:

> Tess . . . marching on upon long stalky legs, in tight stockings which had little ladder-like holes at the knees, torn by kneeling in the roads and

banks in search of vegetable and mineral treasures, her then earth-coloured hair hanging like pot-hooks. . . . (Ch. 5)

The second focal point provides evidence that hair imagery is being used as a powerful symbol of the snares of female sexuality. Mrs Durbeyfield decks out Tess with a view to catching Alec d'Urberville's eye:

> she fetched a great basin, and washed Tess's hair with such thoroughness that when dried and brushed it looked twice as much as at other times. She tied it with a broader pink ribbon than usual. Then she put upon her the white frock that Tess had worn at the club-walking, the airy fulness of which, supplementing her enlarged *coiffure*, imparted to her developing figure an amplitude which belied her age, and might cause her to be estimated as a woman when she was not much more than a child. (Ch. 7)

The degradation felt by Tess after Alec had seduced her is delicately conveyed in the harvesting scene:

> the eye returns involuntarily to the girl in the pink cotton jacket, she being the most flexuous and finely-drawn figure of them all. But her bonnet is pulled so far over her brow that none of her face is disclosed while she binds, though her complexion may be guessed from a stray twine or two of dark brown hair which extends below the curtain of her bonnet. (Ch. 14)

Her fine tresses are now tightly concealed beneath her bonnet. Only when disarranged in the course of her work are they exposed to view, and then they become an extension of her distraught personality:

> At intervals she stands up to rest, and to retie her disarranged apron, or to pull her bonnet straight. Then one can see the oval face of a handsome young woman with deep dark eyes and long heavy clinging tresses, which seem to clasp in a beseeching way anything they fall against. The cheeks are paler . . . the red lips thinner than is usual in a country-bred girl. (Ch. 14)

When her baby is baptised her personal dignity is encapsulated in a nocturnal scene:

> Her figure looked singuarly tall and imposing as she stood in her long white night-gown, a thick cable of twisted dark hair hanging straight down her back to her waist. (Ch. 14)

Another focal point is fixed in Tess's new life at Talbothays dairy. The effects of her physical violation have been slowly repaired and the farm life sees her emerge into mature womanhood. A new and tender relationship starts to take shape between her and Angel Clare, who soon becomes aware of Tess's sexual magnetism. The effect she has on him is expressed in symbolically sensual terms. On one occasion he catches sight of Tess just risen from bed

> yawning, and he saw the red interior of her mouth as if it had been a snake's. She had stretched one arm so high above her coiled-up cable of hair that he could see its satin delicacy above the sunburn . . . (Ch. 27)

and at the beginning of their love-play:

> Tess's excitable heart beat against his by way of reply, and there they stood upon the red-brick floor of the entry, the sun slanting in by the window upon his back, as he held her tightly to his breast; upon her inclining face, upon the blue veins of her temple, upon her naked arm, and her neck, and into the depths of her hair. (Ch. 27)

Curiously, a number of the passages which are devoted to Tess's facial beauty also mention the colour red (or pink). She has a 'mobile peony mouth', her hair is decorated with red or pink ribbons, she wears a pink cotton jacket, the couple embrace upon a red-brick floor, and Angel reports to his mother that Tess has 'deep red lips'. There are certainly sexual overtones here.[22]

Within the space of two chapters Tess's hair is mentioned four times as she comes within the orbit of Angel's fascinated gaze. Two of these may be mentioned.[23] He cannot resist making love to her, putting

> his arm lightly round her waist . . . beneath her hanging tail of hair. (The younger dairymaids, including Tess, breakfasted with their hair loose on Sunday mornings before building it up extra high for attending church.) (Ch. 29)

On another occasion:

> Clare had resolved never to kiss her . . . but somehow, as Tess stood there in her prettily tucked-up milking gown, her hair carelessly heaped upon her head till there should be leisure to arrange it when skimming and milking were done, he broke his resolve, and brought his lips to her cheek for one moment. (Ch. 29)

The pathetic scenes at Wellbridge mark the fourth focal point. Tess's confession is delivered as she nestles close to the man who will push her over the brink of despair.

The ashes under the grate were lit by the fire vertically, like a torrid waste. Imagination might have beheld a Last Day luridness in this red-coaled glow, which fell on his face and hand, and on hers, peering into the loose hair about her brow, and firing the delicate skin underneath. (Ch. 34)

She assumes a more formal posture and experiences the loneliness of Angel's rejection of her, with 'her hair twisted up in a large round mass at the back of her head' (Ch. 36), but even in Angel's arid imagination Tess's beauty and dignity are clearly adumbrated. His mother reminds him: 'You said the other day that she was fine in figure; roundly built; had deep red lips like Cupid's bow; dark eyelashes and brows, an immense rope of hair like a ship's cable . . .' (Ch. 39).

Tess's capitulation to Alec in the closing drama of the novel is prefigured in the final focal point at Flintcomb-Ash. As Alec watches Tess working on the threshing machine: 'She hardly knew where she was, and did not hear Izz Huett tell her from below that her hair was tumbling down' . . . (Ch. 48).

In the last of the major novels, *Jude the Obscure*, Arabella's 'super-numerary hair-coil' (v, Ch. 5) symbolises the artificiality of a relationship based solely on sensual appeal. For Jude it came to represent the fatality of the flesh. His capitulation to Arabella's wiles is ironically illustrated again in terms of the hair-motif when he gets drunk in the very tap-room he had visited with Arabella some months before and which sported a picture of Samson and Delilah on its wall.[24] Later in the story, when Sue finds herself in Arabella's bedroom, she sees 'the detached tail of Arabella's hair hanging on the looking-glass, just as it had done in Jude's time' (IV, Ch. 2). Sue gazes at it and at the same time perceives the snares of sexual attractiveness which it represents and which disgust her. She rejects giving herself to Jude and violating her integrity by consenting to an early marriage. Arabella is the full-blooded passionate woman who knew well how to make use of her artful accessories. Jude was astonished when he saw her undress on their wedding night: 'A long tail of hair, which Arabella wore twisted up in an enormous knob at the back of her head, was deliberately unfastened, stroked out, and hung upon the looking-glass which he had bought her' (I, Ch. 9).

The sudden break-up of the marriage is given a comic twist as Arabella's hair becomes dislodged during one of their altercations; and as the quarrel is carried on in the garden, Arábella's vulgarity goes on public display as she yells at Jude 'perversely pulling her hair into a worse disorder . . . her bonnetless, dishevelled hair blowing in the wind' (I, Ch. 11).

Sue's hair does not receive the same attention but two passages where it is mentioned do have symbolic force. The stage in Sue's life when she prescribes to form finds 'her hair which formerly she had worn according to the custom of the day . . . now twisted up tightly, and she had altogether the air of a woman clipped and pruned by severe discipline' (III, Ch. 1); and the section of the novel (Bk VI) which deals with the total disintegration of her family life is prefaced by the curious quotation from the Apocalypse of Esther: 'And she humbled her body greatly and all the places of her joy she filled with her torn hair.'[25] Her life thereafter was to be a sorrowful penance, devoid of natural pleasure and joy in beautiful things.

Our study of the hair-motif has taken us from Hardy's own youthful love for Emma with her 'curled golden hair', perpetuated in the wistful outpourings of 1912 and 1913, the clear lines of her portrait in *A Pair of Blue Eyes*, the artistic (Pre-Raphaelite, Swinburne) and social (fashions, hair-styles) influences of the mid-Victorian period, to Hardy's primary and idiosyncratic treatment in the six major novels. In the earlier novels his descriptions of hair may be just part of the total picture of female sexuality to which he gives lyrical expression. It is in the major work that we can descry a symbolic dimension which merits analysis and identification.

NOTES

1. H. Orel, *The Final Years of Thomas Hardy, 1912–1928* (London: Macmillan, 1976) p. 106.
2. The diary has been published under the title *Some Recollections*, ed. E. Hardy and R. Gittings (London: Macmillan, 1961).
3. ibid., p. 11.
4. ibid., p. 16.
5. In the previous paragraph Emma notes that her mother's sister, to whom Gifford was originally engaged, was a 'lovely golden-haired girl'.
6. *Life*, p. 78.
7. She has been identified as Tryphena Sparks by L. Deacon and T. Coleman in *Providence and Mr Hardy* (London: Hutchinson, 1966) pp. 84–5, but this is highly questionable; see F. B. Pinion, *A Commentary on the Poems of Thomas Hardy* (London: Macmillan, 1976) p. 144.
8. *Life*, p. 74.
9. See also *Desperate Remedies* (Ch. 1) and *The Laodicean* (I, Ch. 7; II, Ch. 5).
10. A whole clutch of Swinburne's poems are worth noting. They include 'A Ballad of Life', 'A Ballad of Death', 'Laus Veneris', 'Anactoria', 'Hymn to Prosperine',

'Hermaphroditus', 'Fragoletta', 'Faustine', 'The Leper','Rondel', 'Erotion', 'Félise' and 'An Interlude', to mention but a few. Other poems are permeated with descriptions of 'woven tresses' ('Sapphics'), 'hair's pure purple' ('The Masque of Queen Barsabe'), 'the flower that Venus's hair is woven of' ('St Dorothy'). 'Gold hair she had . . .', 'coloured hair, tender hair' ('The Two Dreams'), 'the hair's painted curve and fall' ('Aholibah'), 'hair smelling of the south' ('Love and Sleep') and 'curled golden hair' ('Madonna Mia').

11. G. de Courtais, *Women's Headdress and Hairstyles in England from* AD *600 to the Present Day* (London: Batsford, 1973) p. 124.
12. D. Yarwood, *English Costume from the Second Century* BC *to 1950* (London: Batsford, 1952) p. 23.
13. Cf. also *Two on a Tower*,Ch. 24, and *The Well-Beloved*, I, Ch. 7.
14. Cf. *A Pair of Blue Eyes*, Ch. 3; *The Hand of Ethelberta*, Ch. 33; and *The Mayor of Casterbridge*, Ch. 14.
15. Cf. *The Return of the Native*, II, Ch. 8; IV, Ch. 3; *The Woodlanders*, Ch. 13; and *The Well-Beloved*, II, Ch. 7.
16. Cf. *The Hand of Ethelberta*, Ch. 1, and *The Mayor of Casterbridge*, Chs. 5 and 39.
17. Cf. *The Mayor of Casterbridge*, Ch. 39, and *The Well-Beloved*, II, Ch. 1.
18. Cf. G. de Courtais, op. cit., p. 124.
19. Shades of the Gothic novel beset Hardy's use of hair as a clue in the unravelling of the plot in *Desperate Remedies*. Doubts about the fate of Manston's wife are raised when Mrs Crickett examines the colour of strands of hair left on his pillow (Ch. 9). In *The Mayor of Casterbridge*, Henchard's fleeting observation of the colour of Elizabeth-Jane's hair presages the disastrous revelation that is to follow (Ch. 14), and the plot of *The Woodlanders* hinges on the fate of Marty's hair (Chs. 2, 8, 43).
20. Henchard's demonic impulsiveness is expressed by his 'flashing black eye, and dark, bushy brows and hair' (Ch. 5).
21. The phraseology appears to be an adaptation of Lear's tirade against Regan ('Is there any cause in nature that makes these hard hearts?': *King Lear*, Act III, Sc. 6).
22. The same colour has sexual connotations where Alec d'Urberville is concerned. He will be the 'blood-red ray in the spectrum of her young life' (Ch. 5), his house is red, so too are his lips described and the gifts with which he plies Tess (roses and strawberries). An ominous omen of Tess's loss of virginity may be seen when a thorn from one of Alec's roses 'accidentally pricks her chin' (Ch. 6). The final dénouement is Alec's murder resulting in the 'scarlet blot' on Mrs Brooks' ceiling (Ch. 56). From first to last Alec's life is conditioned by sexual aggressiveness and Tess's relationship with him highlights the unfairness of the human situation. Her only fault is her beauty, and pressures beyond her control shape her destiny. See Tony Tanner's excellent article 'Colour and movement in Hardy's *Tess of the d'Urbervilles*', *Critical Quarterly*, X (Autumn 1968), pp. 219–39.
23. Cf. also Ch. 30.
24. At the end of the novel, after Jude has been cajoled into a second marriage to Arabella, he lies in her bedroom, a 'shorn Samson' (VI Ch. 7).
25. Hardy cites the Authorised Version, which does not contain a correct translation of the original Greek. 'All the places of her joy' is ambiguous and should be rendered 'all the places of the ornaments of her joy' (Revised Version). The passage in the Apocalypse (14:2) describes a ritual act of sorrow and penance in which the queen strips herself of her royal attire, dons sackcloth and mourns with her long hair strewn over her face.

Hardy and His 'Literary Notes'

Lennart A. Björk

I

The myth that Hardy was an untutored, poorly read, unconscious craftsman is now no longer believed in. As we have studied his work and his intellectual background more closely he has emerged as a well-read and highly conscious literary artist. It is strange, in fact, that *The Life of Thomas Hardy* alone did not change the persistent image of him as a primitive, unlettered provincial much earlier, for the autobiography – no doubt intentionally – reveals him to be a widely read man by any standards. The *Life* includes a vast number of references to, quotations from, and comments on books, periodicals and articles in all fields of human interest. Most of these passages, so it was claimed, were extracted from Hardy's diaries and notebooks by the second Mrs Hardy, after which the manuscript materials were destroyed. We now know, of course, that part of this is pure fiction – Hardy extracted these passages himself. My emphasis here is rather on the great number of notebooks once in existence. There is abundant evidence to suggest that Hardy was a compulsive note-taker and that these notebooks would have given us as detailed a picture of a man's intellectual background as it is possible to get from any written source.

The "Literary Notes" constitute only a fraction of Hardy's note-taking. It is an important fraction, however, for it is to some extent a carefully preserved selection of his notebook material. This is obvious not only from the first notes, copied from earlier notebooks under Hardy's supervision into his "Literary Notes" by the first Mrs Hardy, but also from much later entries. In late 1886 or early 1887, for instance, Hardy started extracting passages from von Hartmann's *Philosophy of the Unconscious*. He stopped after only one entry, however, with the notation "(continued in P.B.33)".[1] Then, some fifteen years later, he again copied from the same work into the "Literary Notes", but now several passages. Whether he re-read the original source or whether he copied from his pocket-book cannot now be established. There are also examples of Hardy dividing his notes from a source between the "Literary Notes" and a preserved notebook entitled "Facts".[2] My points here are simply that, first, Hardy kept separate notebooks for different purposes; secondly, that the "Literary Notes" contain material extracted from other notebooks; and, thirdly, that by calling them his "Literary Notes" Hardy here collected and preserved material which he considered particularly relevant to, and useful for, his more strictly literary pursuits.

The "Literary Notes" cover some sixty years of note-taking; the earliest entry is dated July 1865, the last, October 1927. Their overall span is no less impressive whether considered in its purely chronological or broadly intellectual dimensions. They range from the Greek dramatists to George Bernard Shaw and from *The Milliner and Dressmaker and Warehouseman's Gazette* to Einstein. What I propose to do here with this vast material is to single out a few chips from Hardy's workshop; that is, to give a few examples of the different uses Hardy put his notes to. Then I shall also comment in a more general way on some of Hardy's marked preoccupations, especially in religion and aesthetics, as they are revealed in the "Literary Notes".

A convenient way of arriving at a manageable, although rough, categorization of the notes is to relate them to Hardy's distinction in his "The Profitable Reading of Fiction" between two kinds of literary elements. The reader, Hardy there says, may indeed profit from what he labels the "accidents and appendages" of fiction, including, for instance, "trifles of useful knowledge, statistics, queer historical fact"; but, he continues, the "true object" of fiction – "a lesson in life, mental enlargement" – can be derived only from "elements essential to the narratives themselves and from the reflections they engender".[3] The "Literary Notes" contain both kinds, serving, as we shall later see, different functions in Hardy's texts: the "accidents and appendages" lend themselves primarily to direct and rather obtrusive references, whereas the "essential" elements – the more ideologically oriented notes – come to support, for the most part unobtrusively, the thematic structures of his writing.

Hardy started keeping the "Literary Notes" in the spring of 1876, in time, that is, to use them in *The Return of the Native*.[4] The material incorporated in this novel suggests that at the time he probably thought he would rely more closely on the notes for his fiction than later proved to be the case, for in no other novel are the traces of the "Literary Notes" as numerous. But the overwhelming predominance of the "accidents and appendages" category in the early notes also indicates that his concept of the function of the "Literary Notes" gradually changed. Let us consider a few examples.

Among the notes which Emma Hardy re-copied for her husband we find the following entry from Macaulay's essay on Warren Hastings: "*The Speech of Sheridan* on the Oude Charge – The finest delivered within the memory of man. Not reported – lost to us" (entry 22). When Hardy later came to give his account of Grandfer Cantle's over-enthusiastic description of a musical performance by Clym's father, Hardy detected a similarity between the two orations:

> As with . . . Sheridan's renowned Begum Speech, and other such examples, the fortunate condition of its being for ever lost to the world invested the deceased Mr Yeobright's *tour de force* on that memorable afternoon with a cumulative glory which comparative criticism, had that been possible, might considerably have shorn down. (I, v)

Hardy obviously read Macaulay with a sense of humour and some scepticism; but more significantly the passage is, as we shall see again later, a typical example of Hardy's use of reference as a stylistic device for creating, within his peculiar ironic mode, authorial distance from his characters and for establishing a confidential understanding with the reader. By lifting Cantle into the realm of historic rhetoric the narrator invites the reader to join him in a sophisticated, though good-humoured, smile at Cantle's zestful yarn. The reference to Macaulay's Sheridan was also, no doubt, intended to raise the novel from the level of pastoral romance, with which Hardy, much to his annoyance, had been so closely, and as at times he thought so exclusively, associated in the reviews of his earlier fiction.

Macaulay is of course eminently quotable for "accidents and appendages" material of this kind, and Hardy helped himself generously. In "Frederick the Great", for instance, he noted Macaulay's gentlemanly criticism of the Prussian king for his war against the fair Maria Theresa and copied into his "Literary Notes": "A great want of gallantry. Frederick the Great making war upon the beautiful Maria Theresa" (entry 35). Hardy associated this observation with Diggory Venn's manoeuvres against Eustacia:

> He had determined upon the bold stroke of asking for an interview with Miss Vye – to attack her position as Thomasin's rival either by art or by storm, showing therein, somewhat too conspicuously, the want of gallantry characteristic of a certain astute sort of men, from clowns to kings. The great Frederick making war on the beautiful Archduchess . . . [was]

not more dead to difference of sex than the reddleman was, in his peculiar way in planning the displacement of Eustacia. (I. x)

Here, as well, the reference is slightly ironic and gently humorous and helps to maintain the detached authorial point of view. In addition, from what we know of Hardy's lack of self-confidence and his well-documented educational and social insecurity, we cannot disregard the possibility that he felt that such references conferred a certain learnedness and respectability on his prose.

This seems equally true about his use of the following entry, copied from Clarendon's *History of the Rebellion*: "*Good done by illegitimate means* [The impeachment of Ld Strafford was a triumph of justice, but a mockery of law] (entry 161)." Hardy fell back on this for his comment on Diggory Venn's methods of scaring Wildeve away from Eustacia:

The doubtful legitimacy of such rough coercion did not disturb the mind of Venn. It troubles few such minds in such cases, and sometimes this is not to be regretted. From the impeachment of Strafford . . . there have been many triumphs of justice which are mockeries of law. (IV. iv)

The reference is not all ostentation, of course. Hardy inserted it no doubt to help maintain, as in the previous example, the detached narrative point of view and, perhaps more importantly, to guide reader response to Diggory Venn in a positive direction. After all, the reddleman's tactics needed some justification, and reference or allusion is with Hardy an important stylistic device in ennobling, or undercutting, his characters.[5]

As such it is a device which is primarily used for the major characters. Eustacia is no exception. For instance, in the "Queen of Night" chapter she is subjected to no fewer than thirty-four allusions in some twenty pages.[6] We can safely assume that she was a challenge for Hardy's imagination. For example, on one of the occasions when he tried to capture her beauty he turned to the animal world for comparison:

There was a certain obscurity in Eustacia's beauty. . . . In her winter dress . . . she was like the tiger-beetle, which, when observed in dull situations, seems to be of the quietest neutral colour, but under a full illumination blazes with dazzling splendour. (I. x)

Hardy was indeed a close observer of nature; but this simile is based on a second-hand impression, for he here resorted to an excerpt he had made from J. G. Wood's *Insects at Home*: "The head of this beetle seems <when

casually observed,> to be merely dull green, but under a powerful light, & lens, it blazes with gem-like hues, almost dazzling in their splendour" (entry 322).

There are some twenty examples of such applications of the "Literary Notes" in *The Return of the Native*. Many of them are of doubtful artistic quality. Often, in fact, they quite simply give the impression of an author who feels obliged to sprinkle his pages with learned allusions, an accusation which was raised by Hardy reviewers early on in his career. However, let me take one final example from the novel, but now of a more fortunate artistic use of a note. From a magazine review in January 1877 Hardy copied:

> This vegetation [of the Carboniferous period] was luxuriant, but very uniform . . . few forms of plants . . . no flowers . . . monotony. There were none of the higher animals: no birds rested on the branches of the trees: no mammal in the forests. The air was sultry & full of vapour, the soil hot & steaming: & the stillness was profound, broken only by the plashing of the rain, or the whistling of the wind as it passed by the leaves of the trees! The earth was probably covered by a dense envelope of clouds. (entry 880)

From this rather unlikely source Hardy drew inspiration as he worked on a description of a harrowing day in Clym's life. It is the day when he has broken with his mother. We find him waiting for Eustacia on the heath:

> He was in a nest of vivid green. The ferny vegetation round him, though so abundant, was quite uniform: it was a grove of machine-made foliage, a world of green triangles with saw-edges; and not a single flower. The air was warm with a vaporous warmth, and the stillness was unbroken. Lizards, grasshoppers, and ants were the only living things to be beheld. The scene seemed to belong to the ancient world of the carboniferous period, when the forms of plants were few, and of the fern kind; when there was neither bud nor blossom, nothing but a monotonous extent of leafage, amid which no bird sang. (III. v)

This is, to my mind at least, a less obtrusive incorporation of notebook material than the earlier examples. By associating Egdon with the carboniferous period Hardy puts the heath in an endless time perspective, and the timelessness of Egdon – in contrast to the temporary concerns of human beings – is a major theme in the novel. So, although most of the early "Literary Notes" are of the less significant "Accidents and appendages" kind, serving direct and fairly superficial allusive functions, there are also instances of material which Hardy considered profitable from a "mental enlargement" point of view and which seem more organically incorporated into his novel. They are all, I think, of interest as they show the maturing novelist trying out his laboriously compiled notebook material for stylistic effects in his fiction.

II

For better examples of the "mental enlargement" category of notes, however, let us proceed to Hardy's last novels. Late in 1887 or early 1888 Hardy read *The Service of Man* by Cotter Morrison, one of the leading Positivist writers in England at the time. He copied a long passage from it, including Morrison's observation that "Primitive religion had little or no connection with morals" (entry 1464). Hardy remembered the point when, about a year later, he described a quarrel about Angel Clare's religion between Tess and Alec: "She tried to argue, and tell him that he had mixed in his dull brain two matters, theology and morals, which in the primitive days of mankind had been quite distinct" (xlvii). As with most of his later use of the "Literary Notes", Hardy here incorporated notebook material to serve a thematic function. Morrison provided Hardy with an argument in support of his criticism of modern Christianity in the novel. Consequently, we can suspect, Hardy thought the note just the kind of stuff likely to be instrumental in bringing about "mental enlargement".

Another passage from *Tess* exemplifies the same technique and the same category of notebook material: the scene is the bedroom of the four dairymaids at Talbothays. The girls all feel attracted to Angel Clare, and that the attraction is of an instinctual, sexual kind is clear from Hardy's vocabulary:

> The air of the sleeping-chamber seemed to palpitate with the hopeless passion of the girls. They writhed feverishly under the oppressiveness of an emotion thrust on them by cruel Nature's law – *an emotion which they had neither expected nor desired.* [my italics] (Ch. 23)

A few months before writing this Hardy had made the following entry into his "Literary Notes":

> The life of the animal creation is at the mercy of *an instinct wh. they can neither comprehend nor disobey.* . . . Happiness must be subordinated to the

supreme purpose of leaving a progeny wh. can successfully prolong the endless struggle. [entry 1630; my italics]

It is true that Hardy departed from the wording of his note, although the "neither-nor" structure suggests a textual affinity as well; but, more significantly, the point made – the unfair gift of man's sexual instinct – is identical in the two passages. Again the example testifies to the extent to which, but also the relative ease with which, Hardy could rely on his notes for ideological matters.

Often when Hardy came to describe something of which his first-hand experience was not extensive, he drew support, naturally enough, from his note-taking. This is the case, for instance, in his rendering of Jude's first night in Christminster. Hardy's personal knowledge of Christminster/Oxford was limited.[7] But his celebrated description of Jude's responses, particularly his vision of the spectres of past poets, scholars and philosphers haunting the venerable quadrangles, seems almost rooted in personal experience. However, I am convinced that – without underestimating Hardy's imagination – his very conception of Jude's first encounter with Christminster owes a great deal to the following excerpt he made from John Morley in 1887:

> The indefinable charm that haunted the grey & venerable quadrangles of Oxf^d & Camb^g ^{e}, those associations of saints & sages, of scholars & poets, that lingered around the halls & libraries, the solemn chapels, & old-world gardens, of those two cities, & made of them a dream of music for the inward ear, & of delight for the contemplative eye. (entry 1400)

If the similarity of concept between this entry and Hardy's description should not be convincing enough, there is another piece of undeniable proof of his use of the "Literary Notes" for the same scene. This is the quotation from Newman's *Apologia*, which is quoted verbatim in the novel, including the ellipses, from one of Hardy's very first entries in the "Literary Notes":

> My argument was . . . that absolute certitude as to the truths of natural theology was the result of an assemblage of concurring and converging probabilities . . . that probabilities which did not reach to logical certainty might create a mental certitude. (II. i)[8]

I am not suggesting that this rather pretentious quotation enhances Hardy's description, but only that it shows his use of the "Literary Notes" for his dramatization of Jude's first experiences in Christminster.

III

It was for his fiction that Hardy first started compiling his "Literary Notes", and it is in his novels – as I have tried to show with my previous examples – that we find the most easily traceable use and impact of them in the form of quotations or references. This does not mean that I attribute the most profound influence of the notes to such occurrences. The manifold forces at work in a writer's complex intellectual background are hardly decipherable on the basis of a few quotations. But neither in the novels nor in his other work can I here consider the more time- and space-demanding relationship between Hardy's writing and the broader and more pervasive influences of nineteenth- and early twentieth-century thought in the "Literary Notes". I shall continue therefore with my more limited aim of looking into Hardy's workshop to comment on his direct appropriation of individual entries in his non-fictional works; for there are tangible instances also in his poetry, autobiography and critical prefaces and essays, to show that he resorted to his notes whenever he felt the need for their immediate and concrete support.

The clearest and most striking example from his poetry is found in his tribute to Gibbon, in the well-known "Lausanne, In Gibbon's Old Garden: 11–12 p.m.". In the penultimate stanza Gibbon asks the speaker of the poem:

> How fares the Truth now? – Ill?
> – Do pens but slily further her advance?
> May one not speed her but in phrase askance?
> Do scribes aver the Comic to be Reverend still?
>
> Still rule those minds on earth
> At whom sage Milton's wormwood words were hurled:
> *"Truth like a bastard comes into the world*
> *Never without ill-fame to him who gives her birth"*?

Hardy had copied the relevant text from Milton as a separate entry in his "Literary Notes" in 1894 (entry 1924) – at a time, that is, when he was still smarting from the reviews of *Tess* and when he was at work on *Jude the Obscure*. He found, of course, moral and ideological support from Milton's *The Doctrine and Discipline of Divorce* in *Jude* as well – in the epigraph to Part IV.[9] The lines to honour Gibbon's intrepid search for truth are, however, an unusually direct use of the notebook material in his poetry.

It is equally difficult to trace direct applications of the "Literary Notes" in the *Life*, though there are, as I said earlier, many excerpts from other notebooks which were later destroyed. Yet, for his account of the opening of the year 1899, Hardy consulted his "Literary Notes" for suitable matter. He was looking for something to support his argument against those critics who had been hostile to his having turned from prose to poetry. Having found what he searched for, he wrote:

> It may be observed that in the art-history of the century there was an example staring them in the face of a similar modulation from one style into another by a great artist. Verdi was the instance, "that amazing old man" as he was called. Someone of insight wrote concerning him: "From the ashes of his early popularity, from *Il Trovatore* and its kind, there arose on a sudden a sort of phoenix Verdi. Had he died at Mozart's death-age he would now be practically unknown." And another: "With long life enough Verdi might have done almost anything; but the trouble with him was that he had only just arrived at maturity at the age of threescore and ten or thereabouts, so that to complete his life he ought to have lived a hundred and fifty years." (p. 300)

The quotations about Verdi, which Hardy obviously found relevant to his own situation, he lifted from two entries he had made in 1908, that is, some ten years after the year he was writing about in the *Life*.

If we return briefly to the theory that Hardy's reliance on his notebooks is to a marked extent an expression of his basic educational and social insecurity, this seems a particularly plausible explanation for his appeal to authority in his critical essays. For they contain an unusually high number of references to, and quotations from, established critics including, among others, Aristotle, Horace, Addison, Arnold, Symonds, Taine, Pascal and Wordsworth. Hardy's reliance on authorities and his notebooks is, however, still greater than the directly acknowledged quotations and references indicate.[10] This is true also about the most personal of his main essays, "Candour in English Fiction". In this forceful essay Hardy issues a call for "original treatment", which he defines as follows:

> treatment which seeks to show Nature's unconsciousness not of essential laws, but of those laws framed merely as social expedients by humanity, without a basis in the heart of things; treatment which expresses the triumph of the crowd over the hero, of the commonplace majority over the exceptional few. (Orel, p. 27)

Everything here *could* be original with Hardy, but it is not. For, in an article in *Revue des deux Mondes* for May 1886, called "De la Littérature Réaliste", Hardy had read and copied:

> The new art seeks to imitate nature in her unconsciousness, her moral indifference, her absence of choice: it expresses the triumph of collectivity over the individual, of the crowd over the hero . . . (entry 1632)

Of course, neither here nor elsewhere is it my aim to prove any undue borrowing on Hardy's part. I am only trying to offer a glimpse into his workshop to show that − whether he was making a point of limited or far-reaching implications − Hardy did not hesitate to lean on proved authorities, copied into his "Literary Notes"; he used them to back up his own views, even in circumstances where we might have expected him to be completely independent. This is perhaps the place to emphasize that it is all too easy to be unfair to Hardy with the available notebook material; to deduce, which I most emphatically do not, that he is more derivative and less original than other authors whose study notes have not been subjected to this kind of detailed inquiry.

IV

Let me go beyond the mere chips from Hardy's workshop to comment, though briefly, on the notes as more substantial blocks in the whole structure of Hardy's intellectual background. Recent scholarship has already shown that Hardy's notebooks extend considerably our knowledge of his religious, philosophical, psychological and aesthetic interests and beliefs.[11] All I propose to do here is to call attention to, and give a few examples of, the remarkable *consistency* in the point of view of Hardy the note-taker. He copied, that is, in some important areas, the same opinions after the turn of the century as he had done in the 1870s. And, what is more to the point, he kept copying them in the meantime as well. It is not much of an exaggeration to maintain that Hardy became obsessed with certain religious, philosophical and aesthetic opinions. Let me exemplify with some of his notes on God and on aesthetics.

I do not wish to get into the well-explored subject of Hardy's religious beliefs except to note the phenomenon that Hardy seems to have been unable to come across a striking piece of criticism of the Christian God without copying it down. Thus in 1881 he noted that "*Voltaire* . . . dwelt upon the folly of supposing that the Creator of men had "drowned the fathers & died for the children" without having reclaimed the race from wickedness by either method" (entry 1240). Some twenty years later he was captivated by the concept of a "non-active & passionless God" (entry 2039). A decade later still the statement "If God is omnipotent it is impossible that he should be good at all" (entry 2382) found its way into his notes. And he had seen the same point implied in an entry he made some forty years earlier when he copied from George Henry Lewes's *The Story of Goethe's Life* that "Goethe's religion was all taken out of him by the Lisbon earthquake" (entry 105). My point is that for someone who was a proclaimed agnostic – with, I suspect, a leaning towards atheism – Hardy showed an unusual interest in the Christian God. I should add perhaps that there is no doubt about the meaning of the word "God" in these notes. Yet it may be helpful to recall Hardy's own definition in the following well-known admission in the *Life*, for this is also the meaning of the word in the "Literary Notes": "I have been looking for God 50 years, and I think that if he had existed I should have discovered him. As an external personality, of course – the only true meaning of the word" (p. 224). In the light of this piece of autobiographical information the basic repetitiveness of the notes suggests that Hardy felt the need to brace himself repeatedly against the temptations of Christian belief and to convince himself repeatedly, with the aid of such *per se* rather crude intellectual assurances, of the impossibility of believing in a Christian God. That Hardy did not believe in God is indeed a commonplace observation, but my emphasis is on the repetitiveness of his collection of anti-Christian statements.[12]

We find a similar pattern in his aesthetic notes, especially in his extracts on realism and art. As Penelope Vigar, among others, has shown, there is a non-realistic tendency in Hardy's art from the very beginning.[13] That his theory kept abreast, perhaps even preceded, his practice seems likely from his cautious step of prefixing his own non-realistic practice in *Desperate Remedies* with the following well-known observation by Sir Walter Scott: "Though an unconnected course of adventure is what most frequently occurs in nature, yet the province of the romance-writer being artificial, there is more required from him than a mere compliance with the simplicity of reality." As we know, Hardy availed himself of the freedom from reality – as he seems to have interpreted it – which Scott here granted. And Hardy had already in 1862 read Walter Bagehot's staunch advocacy and defence of the idiosyncratic vision of an artist – an important element in any anti-realistic belief.[14] Hardy's own earliest preserved statement on realism seems to be from 1883 when in his dairy he wrote that "All art is only approximative" (*Life*, p. 163). From then onwards he copied a great number of repetitively anti-realistic statements of which I need quote only a few. On the matter of idiosyncrasy, for instance, he gleaned De Quincey's observation that an author "gives us not fact, but his peculiar sense of fact" (entry 1718); from Pater he quoted the almost identical notion of an artist's "transcript of his sense of fact rather than the fact" (entry 1721). In relation to more general aspects of art and realism he entered in 1891 that "Art is a method of expression or presentation" (entry 1815); later in the year he excerpted from Symonds "The prime aim of art is at bottom only presentation" (entry 1861). In the same year he noted approvingly the concept of "spiritual naturalism" (entry 1886); a decade later he assented to the idea that "An artist aims at the spirit of things" (entry 2151); a few years later still he cut out from a newspaper Chesterton's argument that Maeterlinck's position in modern life is due to his "great glorification of the inside of things at the expense of the outside" (entry 2333). Almost two decades after that he excerpted from the *Observer* the opinion that Chekhov never forgot that "what we see is less important than what we do not see" (entry 2447). In 1910 he quoted Goethe's pronouncement that "Art is called art because it is not nature" (entry 2375); two years later he re-copied the same statement; a decade later he entered "There is no such thing in art as nature" (entry 2421). Then, finally, in 1926, in one of his last entries, he added, after a quotation from Shaw on realism and the theatre, his own comment "Realism – the opposite of art" (entry 2456).

Thus for about half a century Hardy expressed and collected anti-realistic opinions. It is only to be expected of course that an artist should be concerned about aesthetic theory; and it is not surprising that an author of Hardy's symbolic art should be interested in the case against realism. What is surprising, however, is his constant reiteration in his "Literary Notes" – and I have quoted only a few – of the same points, whether they focus on his favourite "idiosyncratic mode of regard" or anti-realistic pronouncements in general. For this was really just a constant battering against what was already then an open door. Since Hardy's notes here are of an ideological nature – and not stylistic excerpts, not, that is, a collection of mere felicitous expressions – it seems possible that they reveal an even greater insecurity on Hardy's part in aesthetic matters than has earlier been suspected.

As we have just seen, there is in both Hardy's religious and aesthetic thought a core of fixed ideas which changed very little or not at all over a period of nearly half a century. This I strongly suspect will also be the case with other aspects of his thought once his "Literary Notes" have been studied in more detail. So, when Hardy protests against "objectless consistency" in his "General Preface to the Novels and Poems", and assures us that his sentiments "have been stated truly to be mere impressions of the moment, and not convictions or arguments" (Orel, p. 49), we should be aware of the limited validity of this assurance. It is not that we should question his truthfulness, but that we should allow for the possibility that he may have been far more consistent than he himself was aware of.

The "Literary Notes", then, offer different approaches to Hardy's art and thought. Individual entries provide us with glimpses into his workshop. The whole collection of notes suggests the overall outline of his intellectual background. In so doing, the "Literary Notes" can extend our insight into Hardy the writer as well as Hardy the man.

NOTES

1. "Literary Notes", entry 1443. Part of the "Literary Notes" have been published in *The Literary Notes of Thomas Hardy*, vol. I, ed. Lennart A. Björk (Göteborg, 1974). The reference is here to the numbering of entries for the complete edition now being prepared for publication. Subsequent references to the "Literary Notes" will be made parenthetically in the text and refer to the entry numbers.
2. See, for instance, extracts from Marie Liechtenstein, *Holland House* (London, 1874) in entry 1454 and "Facts", pp. 180–3; W. R. Frith, *My Autobiography and Reminiscences* (London, 1887) in entry 1475 and "Facts", pp. 187, 190–1.
3. *Thomas Hardy's Personal Writings* ed. Harold Orel (London, 1967) pp. 112–13, 114. Subsequent references to this work will be made parenthetically in the text and refer to this printing.
4. For the dating of the notes see "Introduction" to the *Literary Notes*, pp. xxxiii ff.
5. For a rewarding discussion of Hardy's use of reference and allusion, see M. A. Springer's unpublished dissertation, "Allusion in Thomas Hardy's Early Novels: A Stylistic Study" (Indiana University, 1969).
6. Springer, p. 223.
7. See F. B. Pinion, "A hundred years ago: Hardy at Oxford", *The Thomas Hardy Society Review* (1975) pp. 15–16, and *Thomas Hardy: Art and Thought* (London, 1977) pp. 187–9.
8. An entry dated 2 July, 1865. Hardy changed the third word of the entry: "is", to "was". For Hardy's other references to Newman in *Jude*, see *Literary Notes*, entry 2n.
9. "whoso prefers either Matrimony or other Ordinance before the Good of Man and the plain Exigence of Charity, let him profess Papist, or Protestant, or what he will, he is no better than a Pharisee."
10. See also "Introduction" to *Literary Notes*, pp. xx–xxiii and entry 101n.
11. See, for instance, Walter F. Wright, *The Shaping of the Dynasts* (Lincoln, Nebraska, 1967); Michael Millgate, *Thomas Hardy: His Career as a Novelist* (London, 1971); Robert Gittings, *The Older Hardy* (London, 1978).
12. For a sound discussion of Hardy's views on Christianity, especially in his later years, see Harold Orel, *The Final Years of Thomas Hardy* (London, 1976) pp. 108–20.

13. Penelope Vigar, *The Novels of Thomas Hardy: Illusion and Reality* (London, 1974), esp. pp. 1–57.
14. For further documentation see Lennart A. Björk, "Hardy's reading", in *Thomas Hardy: The Writer and his Background*, ed. Norman Page (London, 1980) p. 105.

Three Unpublished Letters by John Addington Symonds

Hardy and Symonds seem never to have met. Phyllis Grosskurth mentions their correspondence in the closing years of Symonds' life as evidence of his interest in 'the young English writers who were emerging at the end of the century' (*John Addington Symonds* [1964], p. 305) – rather oddly, since the two men were exactly the same age and Hardy was a well-established author of nearly forty-nine when the correspondence began. The three letters below, overlooked by the editors of Symonds' collected letters, record the reactions of an appreciative early reader of *The Return of the Native* and *Tess of the d'Urbervilles* who found in Hardy's work support for his own deeply-felt convictions about the 'peasantry'. They are printed here by kind permission of Symonds' granddaughter, Dame Janet Vaughan; I am also grateful to Mr R. N. R. Peers, Curator and Secretary of the Dorset County Museum, for supplying me with photocopies of the letters, which are in the possession of the Museum.

There is a brief reference in the *Life* (p. 218) to the first of these letters, and Hardy's interesting reply to it is given in the first volume of Purdy and Millgate's edition of *The Collected Letters of Thomas Hardy* (pp. 190–1). Robert Gittings quotes briefly from the first and third letters in *The Older Hardy* (p. 69) but gives the date of the third letter incorrectly (p. 221, note 19). As Lennart Björk's edition of *The Literary Notes of Thomas Hardy* testifies, Hardy had known Symonds' writings long before they corresponded; in particular he made extensive notes on Symonds' *Studies of the Greek Poets*, 2nd series (1876).

Am Hof,
Davos Platz,
Switzerland.
April 9, 1889

Dear Mr. Hardy

I take it that you will think it somewhat queer to have some one writing to you at this time of day in praise of your "Return of the Native", and in gratitude for the pleasure it has given him.

I am a belated reveller indeed. I ought to have drunk long ago at the pure fount of pathos and humour which welled from your genius in this book. But I am glad that I came so tardily to its perusal, when time and experience enable me to feel its vigour and its freshness and its charm.

Mrs. Leslie Stephen, chaffing me on a visit here about my passion for the natives of Davos, promised to send me your idyll – so full of comedy and tragedy blent in a picture of real human life. She fulfilled her promise, true and noble woman as she is. I have enjoyed two days of delightful comradeship with the peasants you Shakespearianly portray.

I should ask: "are they in fact so loveable, so full of human pith and sap, as Hardy paints them?" if my own experience of the Graubünden mountaineers – people whom I have come to love, and from whom I have learned much – did not carry conviction to my heart.

I see the artist's touch upon his subject. But I recognize his sincerity of observation.

To my mind, your book breathes the right democratic spirit, which is rare in contemporary work. I thank you for that loyal knight in humble garb, the reddleman. You have shown what all have not eyes to see, that beauty and heroism and the virtues of ancient story or romance lie at our doors – upon the common paths we tread. And this with humour, with the Virgilian lachrymae rerum.

I do not know whether you meant to teach this lesson, or whether there are many who will learn it from your writings. Life in the exile of these Alps has taught it me; and I feel grateful to the artist who genially suggests the truth by which society must be guided in the future – the perception of beauty in simplicity and the recognition of dignity in lives apart from class-competition.

Forgive me for intruding on you with this dithyramb, and believe me very respectfully yours

John Addington Symonds

Am Hof,
Davos Platz,
Switzerland.
Jan. 6, 1892

Dear Mr. Hardy

I was prevented by an attack of my old enemy (in the lungs) from responding at once to your kind letter, and am not yet very fit to do so.

I hope that this delay will not have cooled down your intention of sending me your book. I admire your work so deeply and feel the truth of your touch on human nature so keenly that a book of yours coming to me as your gift has a peculiar value.

You are almost the only man living who in the English tongue can command the tragic passions. And what I admire most is that Virgil's lachrymae rerum are always felt, even when the tragic thrill is sternest, most acute.

I have just finished a long and arduous piece of work. It is a life of Michelangelo Buonarroti: begun against the grain (because the subject seemed to me so worn, and carried through with great labour (for the same reason).

What I have discovered of new about him is principally in the psychological region, and will probably be unacceptable to the public as it dispels some romantic illusions.

I hope to come to England next summer, and shall look about seriously for some quiet healthy home to settle in ere long – somewhere on the Southern Coast. I will not forget what you tell me about Portland.

For myself, I could be content to live on here. But my wife and daughters naturally want to be in England. This is a very austere climate, lacking all amenities of life except the sun.

A friend of mine, a fine young peasant, was swept away in an avalanche two days ago, while trying to save a friend. His body will not reappear until next May.

Believe me most sincerely yrs
    J. A. Symonds

Am Hof,
Davos Platz,
Switzerland.
January 17, 1892

Dear Mr. Hardy

I have been lying in bed with a bad attack of bronchitis during the last three days; and now I write to you from the same place to say how much the reading of "Tess" has occupied and interested me.

I happen to have two personal reasons for starting with an interest in the book. It so happens, to begin with, that I am one probably among very few of your readers for whom the d'Urberville motif will possess actuality. I represent an old Norman family, once potent in the counties of Essex, Herts. and Norfolk but now where still extant reduced to very modest gentry. Our name rhymes with Byron in one version of the Roll of Battle Abbey:

> Belle et Biroun
> Sans Peur et FitzSimoun.

Edward III chose one of the family, Sir Richard FitzSimon, to be a Companion of the Garter when he founded the Order.

I was brought up among the memories of pedigrees and heraldries, referring to bygone Plantagenet splendours.

Let that pass. I only mention it because perhaps no one else will tell you that this part of your fabric had its veracity for him.

But what you directly say and indirectly make us feel (in this book not perhaps more than in the others) about peasants, touches me still more deeply. The whole tenour of my life has been altered by coming to live with peasants here. The sense of contentment they at last have given me, is only saddened by the regret of having learned the lessons and the lovelinesses of the life too late. We have a very fine and happy race of peasants here, all of them landowners and politically equals.

So you see my *Stimmung* for your book was appreciative.

The way you have drawn a fine and sensitive woman's character marred by fateful contact with two wretched specimens of the male sex is magnificent. In art I find one want. We do not know clearly what the first seduction of Tess by Alec was worth to herself – *how* she became his mistress, after he found her asleep at the woodside. Here the frankness of Guy de Maupassant would have been helpful to the problem.

Then I protest against such a loathsome male as you have made Angel. I cannot use another epithet. I wonder what you really meant him to be, what impression he was intended by you to produce? I should have liked to kick or curse the fellow at almost every turn of his gauche, middleclass, maudlin career. Alec is not quite so repulsive.

You generally succeed better with your serious women than your serious men, I think. The quartette of dairymaids in love with Angel at Talbothays would indeed by charming truly, if he were not such a consummate ass and prig. Of course you meant him to be something of that. But did you mean him to be as much that as you have made him?

Well: I must stop. Writing makes me cough, and I am very weak.
Yours most sincerely,
J. A. Symonds

P.S. January 19. I have looked this over which I wrote when I was very ill and feverish. I am still too weak to begin another letter. But I feel that I have been unjust to my own impressions about Angel, and more than unjust to your presentment of him. The character is intelligible, and that ought to suffice. My vehemence please take as a sign of the intense interest I took in the novel.

Thomas Hardy, Donald Davie, England and the English

John Lucas

I

Over the last twenty or so years Thomas Hardy's reputation has risen at an astonishing rate. I can indicate the nature of this rise by saying that if I think back to the latter half of the 1950, when I was an undergraduate, I recall how very cool were the literary and academic worlds towards "the good little Hardy". Indeed, James's famous remark was thought to say it all. There were few critical studies, of the novels or the poetry, and I do not imagine that Hardy was taught on many undergraduate courses. You might know why R. G. Collingwood thought that the ending of *Tess of the d'Urbervilles* spoilt an otherwise impressive novel, and any anthology of twentieth-century poetry would be likely to include "The Darkling Thrush" and a few other poems; but that was more or less that. Not any more, however. Hardy has replaced Jane Austen as the novelist students will have read all or most of, the critical studies pour from the presses, and as for his poetic work, it is almost certain to feature prominently in any course on modern poetry.

Yet here of course the difficulties start. Is Hardy really a modern poet at all? Is he a great one? Or even a master? And if he has had an important influence on later English poets (and Auden and Larkin, at least, have been quick to insist on his significance for them) has that been a good or a bad thing? More particularly, does Hardy offer a valuable challenge to these and other poets, or is he their excuse for not doing better, working harder, struggling with great intensity to make it new? These questions are at the very heart of Donald Davie's *Thomas Hardy and British Poetry* (1973), a book which, like everything else that Davie has written, is packed with interesting, challenging ideas; and which is also often muddled and infuriating. Yet perhaps this has to be so. For the book is very much a personal record of Davie's fight to establish what he wanted (and wants?) to be his own priorities; and I strongly suspect that it was written at a time of some crisis, a crisis which was certainly within Davie himself and which he thought was also within England. Hence the muddle. For Davie is compelled to speculate on links between the two which may not always be there, or which, if they were there, were so in ways different from the ones he imagined. As a result, the priorities he seeks to establish don't emerge with any great clarity, they can't be easily defended, and it is even possible that they can't be fully understood.

I grant that to say this may seem merely impertinent, an intrusion into areas which are strictly private. Yet one can hardly avoid the fact that *Thomas Hardy and British Poetry* must have been written at the period when Davie was deciding to leave England in order to work in the United States; and it is clear from pronouncements he made at that time that he saw England as somehow finished. America called because in America he could practise his art as poet and critic with a seriousness and dedication which in England had become virtually impossible, since in England the very terms "seriousness" and "dedication" would be likely at best to provoke a wry smile, at worst a hoot of dismissal. Is this to state the matter too baldy? I do not think so. For if we recall the time when the book had its inception, the late 1960s, we will remember that it was among other things the period of student unrest, of sit-ins, riots, book-burnings; it was the period of Danny the Red, of Tariq Ali and *Red Mole*, of *Oz* and its trials; it was a period in which, if the worst seemed to have all the passionate intensity, then some of the best had to demonstrate conviction. And Donald Davie's conviction was that if the great Anarch was about to let universal darkness fall on England he must escape to a world elsewhere. It is this, I believe, which explains the almost hysterical note that sometimes intrudes into the book. To give just one example. Davie speaks of "English intellectuals of the Left making the late Stephen Ward (one of the minor actors in the Profumo scandal) into love's martyr, happy to overlook the squalid tastelessness of his life as a procurer for the sake of the humaneness that (arguably) shone through it" (p. 71). Now this won't at all do. It is true that Ward – whom I may say I never heard an intellectual of the left refer to as love's martyr – *ought* to have been a minor actor in the scandal. But in fact his desertion by the rich and famous who had used his services turned him into the fall-guy and caused his suicide (whereas they themselves were well enough protected by the establishment to be able to escape). That they could do so understandably angered many people, and not, I believe and hope, merely those on the left. Davie goes on to say that you won't find "moral fastidiousness" in British politics of the left or the right, not until you get to the far right – "as the case of D. H. Lawrence shows". And I think the kindest way to treat that remark is to assume it was written in haste and out of great anger.

Much of the anger is quite justified. Donald Davie was writing at the time when many intellectuals felt a sense of acute dismay at the goings-on of the Wilson government. This government had, after all, come to power mouthing the words of the great men of the British labour movement, and what had resulted? A shallow, largely cynical or philistine acceptance of tawdry glitter in civic life; a materialism which found expression in the high-rise blocks of town-planners, and the bulldozing of inner cities; above all, perhaps, an open contempt for the ideals of education and the life of the mind which had been at the heart of the socialism identified with R. H. Tawney. The 1960s witnessed a disaster for English education, one we are still living through and from which we may never entirely recover. I write as a socialist, and I cannot look back on the 1960s without thinking that during these years a great tradition was systematically betrayed. "The tigers of wrath are wiser than the horses of instruction". Blake's proverb was everywhere spray-gunned or chalked on walls. It meant that all respect for learning, for wisdom and its concomitant, memory, were suspect, derided. What made it worse was that this was being done in the name of *socialism*! And this appalling preference for ignorance was actively encouraged by well-meaning liberal educators who were terrified of alienating the young by requiring them to *know*, to *remember*, to fill their minds with *facts*.

The nature of this disaster is conveniently indicated by the famous debate between F. R. Leavis and C. P. Snow about the two cultures, and in Harold Wilson's promise of "a technological revolution". (Snow became a member of Wilson's government.) In many ways the debate was trivial, but in one way at least it proved crucial for the 1960s. Snow and his supporters looked forward to the displacement of the humanities from the centre of education. For Leavis, on the other hand, and *his* supporters – among whom Davie would surely want to be included? – such a displacement must be ruinous because, *pace* Snow and Wilson, technology had already been tried and had been found wanting. It had proved insufficient to nourish the creative human spirit. I do not mean to say that I agree with this, or even with the terms of the debate, but I think it important to note that such a conviction is deeply embedded in *Thomas Hardy and British Poetry*. For Davie's procedure is to identify some symptoms of what he believes to be England's serious, even terminal, malaise, and then look for a root cause. The result is that when he writes about Hardy it is as though he sees him as the poet-spokesman of the technological revolution; an embodiment of all those forces whose sudden-as-it-might-seem eruption in the 1960s spelt anarchy. Such anarchy could be literal and take political shape – as it did, for example, on Davie's own university campus at Essex, or it could be implicit – as it was, or was held to be, in the general capitulation before youth culture and the acceptance of "pop" in art, poetry, and music: but no matter what shape it took the anarchy didn't so much presage the technological revolution as show itself to be that revolution's malformed child. Only a society which did not take humane education at all seriously could encourage the illiterate in their illiteracy, or say that anyway none of it mattered, the important thing was to get rid of élitist, out-moded views of art in favour of a cultural free-for-all of doing your own thing.

Now all this may seem very strange. Does the road from Hardy lead to Roger McGough? Well, in perfectly obvious senses, no. But in one sense at least it does, or so Donald Davie implies. He takes Hardy as the starting-point for an investigation of the dangerous consequences that modesty breeds. Hardy is absolutely different from Yeats, Eliot, Pound, Lawrence, not simply because his politics aren't of the right, as theirs are, not merely because unlike them he is anti-élitist, but because he never claimed very much for his poetry – "all we can try to do is to write a little better on the old themes" he famously told Robert Graves, because he did not make large claims for art as criticism of life, and because he did not write "great" poems. In other words, Hardy encouraged an acceptance of the scaled-down, he thought that small could be beautiful as long as you didn't make too much of the beautiful, and he was prepared to put up with the second-best. This, at least, is what Davie argues, and he goes on to assert that it is this which has bedevilled English poetry throughout the twentieth century and which reaches its logical conclusion in the fulsome praise accorded to the Liverpool pop poets and the fact that Larkin put them into his *Oxford Book of Twentieth-Century English Verse*. (Davie doesn't say that in *Thomas Hardy and British Poetry*, but he has argued it subsequently, and the argument fits perfectly well with all he says in his book.)

It is easy to imagine Davie agreeing with Nietzsche's Zarathustra, who gazed at a row of new houses and asked himself what they meant:

> Verily, no great soul put them up as its likeness. . . . And these rooms and chambers – can *men* go in and out of them? . . . And Zarathustra stood still and reflected. At last he said: "Everything has become smaller! Everywhere I see lower gates: those who are my kind probably still go through, but they must stoop. Oh, when shall I get back to my homeland, where I need no longer stoop – no longer stoop *before those who are small*? [Nietzsche's italics]

On this reading, Davie's homeland would be America, because there he can find the matter of art taken with that passionate intensity which frees it from the grasp of trend-spotters, philistines, media-men: all those who degrade its worth. (I imagine the very different reception of Charles Tomlinson in the two countries has always been much in Davie's mind.) And it would help to explain why he so frequently invokes the name of D. H. Lawrence in his book. For Lawrence was also a self-imposed exile, one who could be said to have left an England which he saw as given over to littleness and essentially buried under anarchic darkness.

An acceptance of littleness; a taste for modesty. One could not accuse contemporary American poets of living with such things. Self-deprecating modesty is an alien mode for any serious poet writing in America today, as one can see if one looks at an interview with Anthony Hecht that appeared in the magazine *Quarto*. Hecht is a fine poet and in no sense a self-advertiser; and yet in reply to a question about the nature of a writer's responsibility, he says:

> The life of a writer is a life of an extraordinary sort of dedication, and it's worth saying that and repeating it often because most non-writers have no sense of what's entailed in terms of dedication. It becomes more and more, what shall I say, almost religious (though of course I cheapen the word when I use it, I don't mean really religious). But it's a desperate and terrible kind of dedication, the more desperate and terrible because it's so little appreciated. (*Quarto*, September 1981)

"A desperate and terrible kind of dedication." Imagine Philip Larkin talking like that. Or – and here's the nub of the matter – Thomas Hardy. Thus if something is badly wrong with English poetry – and Davie is sure that there is – the root case can be traced back to the particular kind of modesty which Hardy's poetry embodies.

> On every page, "Take it or leave it", he seems to say; or, even more permissively, "Take what you want, and leave the rest". This consciousness of having imposed on his reader so little is what lies behind Hardy's insistence that what he offers is only a series of disconnected observations, and behind his resentment that he should be taken as having a pessimistic design upon his reader, when in fact he so sedulously respects the reader's privilege not to be interested, not to be persuaded. It is on this basis – his respect of the reader's rights to be attentive or inattentive as he pleases – that one rests the claim for Hardy as perhaps the first and last "liberal" in modern poetry. (p. 28)

But Davie hardly means those last words, I think; not unless he specifically wishes to distinguish between the modern and the contemporary. The truth is rather that Hardy inaugurates an attitude to poetry that is harmful both to its practitioners and its readers, and which again may be thought to have come to a head in the 1960s. (For when Davie speaks of Hardy "permissively" allowing his readers to take what they want and leave the rest we can hardly avoid hearing an echo of the 1960s cliché about the permissive society.) The final judgement on him has therefore to be a severe one:

> it begins to look as if Hardy's engaging modesty and his decent liberalism represent a crucial selling short of the poetic vocation, for himself and his successors. For surely the poet, if any one, has a duty to be radical, to go to the roots. So much at least all poets have assumed through the centuries. Hardy, perhaps without knowing it, questions that assumption, and appears to reject it. Some of his successors in England, and a few out of England, seem to have agreed with him. (p. 40)

And Hardy's failings do not end here. Davie contrasts the skills of a craftsman (he seems to believe that Hardy trained as a stone-mason) with those of the engineer; and what he claims to detect in much of Hardy's work is a harsh, metallic brilliance that belongs with the world of engineering. Thus he remarks of "Overlooking the River Stour" that

> The "cunning irregularity" which heedless readers have taken for clumsiness may be in a touch like the crowded stresses and consonants in "the pane's drop-drenched glaze". But once we have taken Hardy's word for it that such effects are the result of "choice after full knowledge", the poem becomes throughout, and all too shiningly, the work of "a superb technician" who dismays us precisely by his *superbia*. The symmetries, stanza by stanza, are all but exact to begin with; once we know that the occasional inexactitude is no less engineered, "engineered" seems more than ever the only word to use. Once again there is an analogy with Victorian civil engineering, which topped off an iron bridge or a granite waterworks with Gothic finials, just as Hardy tops off his Victorian diction with an archaism like "sheen" or "alack". Within its historically appropriate idiom, the poem is a "precision job"; that is to say, its virtuosity is of a kind impossible before conditions of advanced technology. (pp. 22–3)

I do not wish to ask whether Davie is fair to this particular poem (some of his points have been very well answered by Tom Paulin in *Thomas Hardy: The*

Poetry of Perception). I will, however, say that his knowledge of Victorian engineering leaves a good deal to be desired, not simply because waterworks were more often built of brick than of granite, but because they were staggeringly triumphant responses to huge problems of water cleansing and distribution and were the product of wonderful creative energies. Besides, the claim that Hardy's kind of ingenuity is impossible before conditions of advanced technology looks dubious as soon as one thinks of such highly artificial forms as the Pindaric ode (popular in England at the time of Palladianism, so there isn't much of a link there unless one cites the dubious claims of Vanburgh), or of those stanzaic patterns with which major and minor seventeenth-century poets liked to struggle.

Why then should Davie want to see Hardy's poetry in terms of engineering "brilliance"? ("What one hears is not the chip-chip of a mason's chisel, but a clank of iron girders swung down from a crane", he says of "Lines to a Movement in Mozart's E-Flat Symphony"). The answer, clearly enough, is that to do so clinches the argument for Hardy as progenitor of all that is wrong with the spirit of contemporary England and its poetry. It is bad enough that he should be modest and a liberal, but what makes it far worse is that he is on the side of the technological revolution! And driving the final nail into the coffin, Davie calls Hardy a "scientific humanist". Coming across that phrase, and thinking also of his insistence that Hardy was "ambitious technically, and unambitious in every other way", and recalling his account of Hardy's mechanical skills, I find it inevitable that one should make a connection with the young Yeats's passionately voiced hatred of an scientific humanism of Huxley and Tyndall, of his nightmare of the endlessly chattering sewing-machine, and of his view of modern life as a condition where "opinion crushes and rends, and all is hatred and bitterness; wheel biting upon wheel, a roar of steel or iron tackle, a mill of argument grinding all things down to mediocrity" (*Autobiographies*, p. 231; Yeats has modern Dublin specifically in mind in the passage, but what he says there clearly applies to what he thinks of modern life in general). I do not know whether those words were lodged somewhere in the back of Donald Davie's mind when he came to write his account of Thomas Hardy, but they could well have been. Indeed, he has virtually taken over Yeats's terms: for Davie, every bit as much as for Yeats, modern life is characterised by the spirit of scientific humanism, reducing all things, by and because of mechanical means, to an acceptance of the second-best; what we have is a society where littleness and mediocrity triumph, and which is able to claim a modest liberalism as midwife if not parent.

II

So far I have tried to reconstruct the underlying argument of Davie's book, and to explain what its hidden implications are. For it has to be repeated that the argument is very much one to be *inferred*, and is by no means lying out in the open. But now a further problem arises. Just how accurate or telling is this account of Hardy's poetry and of its influence on later poets? (I am not at all clear as to why Davie uses the word British, by the way, since he speaks exclusively of Hardy's influence on English poets, and it would be difficult to imagine how Hardy *could* have influenced Scottish, Welsh or Irish poets. I know that Dylan Thomas said that Hardy was his favourite poet, but that isn't the same thing.) The truth is that Davie's account is both tendentious and procrustean. In the first place, I do not believe that Hardy, any more than any real poet, can adequately be thought of as a scientific humanist. And as it happens, Davie no longer believes it to be so. For in a great essay, "Hardy's Virgilian Purples", which was published in a number of the magazine *Agenda* that was devoted to Hardy (x, 1972), Davie convincingly refutes his earlier contention that Hardy "appears to have mistrusted . . . the claims of poetry to transcend the linear unrolling of recorded time" (*Thomas Hardy and British Poetry*, p. 4), just as he puts paid to the assertion voiced in his book that the ghost of Emma in those late, great love poems is "only subjectively real", is no more than a psychological fancy. In view of what he says in the essay there is really no point in taking issue with the book's untenable argument, that the love poems

> instead of transforming and displacing quantifiable reality or the reality of common sense, are on the contrary just so many glosses on that reality, which is conceived of as unchallengeably "given" and final. This is what makes it possible to say (once again) that he sold the vocation short, tacitly surrendering the proudest claims traditionally made for the act of the poetic imagination. (p. 62)

It is, however, worth suggesting that here again Davie may well be prompted by his own concerns. For in the poem, "Or, Solitude", published in *Essex Poems* (1969), he writes: "The transcendental nature / Of poetry, how I need it! / And yet it was for years / What I refused to credit." But when the poem was first published, in, I think, the *New Statesman*, I recall that the first line was "The metaphysicality / Of poetry". In replacing "metaphysicality" by the more insistent word "transcendental" Davie is utterly rejecting that tradition of commonsensical scientific humanism to which he himself had belonged, and which he saw as reaching back to Hardy.

But not any longer. For in the *Agenda* essay Hardy is specifically linked with Dante and Virgil as a poet of metaphysical insights. What, though, of Davie's other claim that Hardy sold the poetic vocation short? It falls into two parts. The first, which I have already touched on, is that Hardy is too much the engineer and too little the craftsman. I have said why I think it is that Davie chose to level this charge at Hardy; but it isn't at all clear that the charge can be sustained. I agree that there are poems where Hardy's pursuit of form — or rather his determination to make a poem come out in a certain form — may seem perverse. But the fact is that being perverse in this way is undoubtedly an habitual delight for a certain sort of poet — Donne, Browning and Auden come immediately to mind — and to scold them for it feels rather pointless. Besides, Davie himself generously acknowledges that as a prosodist Hardy "was immensely learned, with a learning that seems to be lost beyond recovery". Yet he fails to see that Hardy's characteristic genius is therefore to be accounted for, not by means of analogy with architecture or engineering, but through his extraordinarily subtle ear, his attentiveness to cadence, and the pull of narrative through time. Time rather than space is the element in which Hardy's poems exist, as anyone surely knows who reads them aloud. Davie utterly misses the point when he says that Hardy's "symmetrical stanzas *lie on the page* demurely self-contained" (p. 36). They don't lie there at all, I submit, to anyone who can *hear* the poems, and who can therefore respond to Hardy's "cunning irregularity".

"Cunning irregularity". The phrase comes from a passage in *The Life of Thomas Hardy*, which Davie quotes, but which he doesn't seem fully to understand. This is what Hardy wrote:

> He knew that in architecture cunning irregularity is of enormous worth, and it is obvious that he carried on into his verse, perhaps in part unconsciously, the Gothic art-principle ... of spontaneity, found in mouldings, tracery, and such like — resulting in the "unforeseen" (as it has been called) character of his metres and stanzas, that of stress rather than syllable, poetic texture rather than poetic veneer; the latter kind of thing, under the name of "constructed ornament", being what he, in common with every Gothic student, had been taught to avoid as the plague. He shaped his poetry accordingly, introducing metrical pauses, and reversed beats; and found for his trouble that some particular line of a poem exemplifying this principle was greeted with a would-be jocular remark that such a line "did not make for immortality". (*Life*, p. 301)

Hardy, Donald Davie, England and the English

Stress rather than syllable. It is of the utmost importance, and yet how many commentators of Hardy's poetry have in fact done justice to the subtlety of his ear, have understood his ability to make his poems voice or breathe their meanings through cadences. (It is worth noting that "breathe" is a good Hardy word: you breathe the air and air is a synonym for song, a condition to which many of Hardy's poems move.) The sad truth is that most critics talk of what Hardy's poems are "about" as though how the poems sound had nothing whatever to do with the matter. No doubt this is in great part due to the fact that many of them either began teaching or were taught in the 1960s, when proper respect for, and attentiveness towards, how a poem *sounds* became a matter for scorn. (It is no paradox that that was the decade of large-scale public readings: anyone who remembers the mangling of great poems and the chanting of rubbish that formed the matter of such read-ins will know what I am talking about, just as he will recognise its consequences when he asks any of his students or, God help him, many of his colleagues, to read a poem aloud.) But however one may explain it, the fact is that most critics who write about Hardy are plainly unfit to do so.

I can pinpoint this by referring to a comparatively slight poem, "I Look Into My Glass":

> I look into my glass,
> And view my wasting skin,
> And say "Would God it came to pass
> My heart had shrunk as thin!"
>
> For then, I, undistrest
> By hearts grown cold to me,
> Could lonely wait my endless rest
> With equanimity.
>
> But Time, to make me grieve,
> Part steals, lets part abide;
> And shakes this fragile frame at eve
> With throbbings of noontide.

I had known and loved the music of this poem for years when I had to endure hearing it read by an academic who chose it as an example of Hardy's grim pessimism, and for whom its dignified emphases meant nothing at all. Thus he read the middle stanza with a leaden, metronomic thump, producing a series of steam-hammer iambs. Yet anyone with half an ear must surely notice how in the first line of that stanza the pause on

"I", created by the punctuation, requires that one stress it and so lighten the force of "undistrest"; so that one gets a lovely, quizzical balancing of distress and its opposite: a balancing that can be heard in the echoing vowel sounds ("*grown cold*" is echoed in "*lonely*", "*endless rest*" in "*equanimity*"). And of course the stanza comes to rest with the last word, which takes all three stresses of that line and in its unhurried calm actually embodies what it's about. There are other felicities which one might dwell on: the hovering stresses on "part steals", for example, or the spondee with which the poem concludes and which gives a queer, almost uncanny pulse at its very end. But I will say only that perhaps the most cunning thing about this little poem is that it is written in poulter's measure, that stanza form which we have always been assured – by C. S. Lewis and others – cannot be effectively handled in serious poetry. And it is true that if you look at those Elizabethan poets who used the form the results are mostly dire, though Gascoigne, Turberville and Goodge all produced honourable exceptions. And it is also true that if you look at those eighteenth-century hymn-writers to whom the form was known as 'Short Metre' and who used it for a good many of their hymns, the results are not much better. ("Hosannah to the Son / Of David and of God, / Who brought the news of pardon down, / And bought it with his blood" is a typical example.) But this at least shows where Hardy took much of his inspiration from, and how he modified it. Behind his poetry lies the absorption of and appeal to folk-song, ballad and hymn, to a tradition which is anything *but* those architectural products of engineering that Davie claims to detect as analogue and even inspiration.

The fact is that more than those of any other nineteenth-century poet, more than Hopkins' even, Hardy's poems are for the ear. Ignore that and you lose everything. The man who thumped his way through "I Look Into My Glass" could ignore it because he was helplessly ignorant of how to read poetry. Yet that can hardly be the case with a critic as sensitive and intelligent as Davie. So that if one asks how he came to speak of Hardy's poems as lying on the page one can only reply: by the same route that allowed him not to notice how impossible it is to identify as a scientific humanist the man who wrote such poems as "Friends Beyond", or "Paying Calls", or "During Wind and Rain" or. . . . But of course there are *hundreds* of poems that should have told Davie that his argument was hopelessly awry. If, then, he pressed ahead with it, it must be because the real object of his attack is not Hardy at all, but the plight of English poetry, and beyond that, of England. And this brings us to another major charge he levels at Hardy, that of an improper modesty, a readiness to put up with the second-best, whether in himself or in others; or in what he sees around him.

"Except in the ill-starred and premature *Dynasts*, Hardy the poet comes before us as the 'honest journeyman', highly skilled indeed but disablingly modest in his aims" (*Thomas Hardy*, p. 36). There is not the space here to challenge that dismissive phrase about the *Dynasts*. But I do need to take up the more general and indeed familiar accusation, that Hardy's modesty is a selling short of his vocation. Thus when Hardy "rises dutifully to public occasions, like an unofficial poet laureate", we get "Drummer Hodge", which Davie says is "esteemed by some who would castigate Rupert Brooke's '1914', though the senselessness of war is glossed over by the same means in the one poem as in the other" (pp. 36–7). No, it isn't. For Brooke's "The Soldier", which I assume is the poem to which Davie refers, speaks patriotically of his "richer dust" being forever England in some foreign field; Hardy, on the other hand, speaks with a kind of awed, comic wonder (the tone is difficult to pin down but it certainly *isn't* Brooke's tone!), of Hodge's "homely breast and brain" growing to some southern tree. This is the oddest of transformations, in other words; and there is a genuine and proper slyness in Hardy's handling of his "official" subject which is certainly not to be found in Brooke's sonnet. The poem's modesty therefore implicitly de-mystifies the glorification of war. Such modesty is hardly disabling; on the contrary, whatever else the poem achieves it certainly undercuts conventional patriotism, and sees the death, casual burial and transformation of a common soldier in a deeper, and perhaps darker, comic context.

What is the strategy that lies behind Davie's argument? It amounts to this, I think: that Hardy's modesty is a mode of acceptance, a putting-up with life in England as he finds it. He is a kind of poetical Erastian, whereas the poet with claims to greatness should be a radical, should want to go to the roots and thus confront and question the society he finds himself in. The very first sentence of Davie's book reads: "I have taken it for granted that works of literary art are conditioned by economic and political forces active in the society from which those works spring and to which they are directed, forces which bear in on the solitary artist as he struggles to compose." Hardy, the implication is, struggled too little, was too ready to stand aside and let the forces rush past him. And he has bequeathed the tendency to his followers, so that much English poetry of the twentieth century is bedevilled by its readiness to accept second-best, to duck the awkward questions, confrontations, the really radical issues. Again, I have to add a note of caution. For the truth is that Davie never quite puts this argument together; and it may be that he will protest that I am not being entirely fair to him. Nevertheless, it seems to me that one has to infer such an argument from his book, as is I hope clear from the following astonishing statement, where Davie says that "One recalls the cries of satisfaction with which the modern reader approaches that one of Wordsworth's nature poems, "Nutting", in which the imagery conveys a submerged metaphor of rape. 'All value is in the human, and nowhere else.' It is a possible point of view, and may be sincerely held." (I have to say that I don't recall hearing such cries, but if they exist it is surely for a reason opposite to the one Davie gives: namely, that the rape is seen as a violation of nature, not as confirmation of the overwhelming importance of the human, and therefore Wordsworth has correctly identified an improper human aggressiveness.) But, Davie goes on, this acceptance of the overwhelming importance of the human

> for the English . . . has the great advantage of anaesthetising them to the offensiveness of their own landscapes and removing any sense of guilt at having made them offensive. It is D. H. Lawrence's constant guilt and horror at what the English had made of England which makes it certain that, breeder as he was of his own symbolic horses . . . he certainly counted the cost and mostly he thought it extortionate . . . either we accept that we deserve no better than the gracelessness of scene which surrounds us, or else we shut ourselves off from our neighbours who seem to ask nothing better and are doing their best to make it worse. Like Richard Hoggart as regards literature, Larkin, as regards landscape and architecture and indeed literature also, agrees to tolerate the intolerable for the sake of human solidarity with those who don't find it intolerable at all. Rather than put up with the intolerable, Lawrence forfeited the solidarity – and with a clearer sense of what he was doing, of the price he was paying. (pp. 68–9)

We may seem to have come a long way from Hardy in this series of ill-argued assertions, but we haven't; not really. For it was Hardy, so the submerged argument runs, who initiated a readiness to tolerate the intolerable; and who therefore led English poetry into shared acceptance of that awfulness from which Lawrence recoiled (and Davie after him, we are surely to assume).

Well, it was of course Hardy who famously remarked that natural scenes were of small importance compared with the wear on a threshold made by a human foot, and who to that extent thought that the human must claim primacy over the natural. And Auden, Hardy's admirer, remarked in his "Letter to Lord Byron" that "To me Art's subject is the human clay, / And landscape but a background to a torso". But was Lawrence so different, and if so did he have a clearer sense of the price he was paying?

I do not think so. For the picture that emerges of Lawrence during the war years, when he was planning to leave England, is of a man almost out of control, swayed by angers and contradictory impulses that pushed him to what can only be called the brink of insanity. (The whole thing is thoroughly documented in Paul Delaney's remarkable book, *D. H. Lawrence's Nightmare*.) This is not to say that Lawrence claimed to be unaware of the implications of his decision, but it is to argue that in the event matters turned out to be far more complicated than he persuaded himself they would be. The result was that during those long years of self-imposed exile, when he wandered the world ceaselessly and restlessly, he found himself unable to be at peace in his mind about the England which in *Kangaroo* he had claimed to leave with little or no pain:

> It was a cold day. There was snow on the Downs like a shroud. And as he looked back from the boat, when they had left Folkestone behind and only England was there, England looked like a grey, a dreary-grey coffin sinking in the sea behind, with her dead grey cliffs and the white, worn-out cloth of snow above. (*Kangaroo*, Ch. 12)

There it may seem easy for Lawrence to accept that he was seeing the last of England. But one has only to think of the letter he wrote the young David Chambers in 1928, to realise how little he was able to come to terms with forfeiting that solidarity which Davie says he knowingly and willingly surrendered.

> Whatever I forget, I shall never forget the Haggs – I loved it so. I loved to come to you all, it really was a new life began in me there. The water-pippin by the door – those maiden-blush roses that Flower would lean over and eat and trip floundering around. – And stewed figs for tea in winter, and in August green stewed apples. Do you still have them? Tell your mother I never forget, no matter where life carries us. . . . Oh, I'd love to be nineteen again, and coming up through the Warren and catching the first glimpse of the buildings. Then I'd sit on the sofa under the window, and we'd crowd round the little table to tea, in that tiny little kitchen I was so at home in. . . . If there is anything I can ever do for you do tell me. – Because whatever else I am, I am somewhere still the same Bert who rushed with such joy to the Haggs.

There is surely a pain in that letter which can hardly be thought of as belonging to a man who has a clear sense of what he is doing, of the price he is paying – except in a tragic sense?

And where Lawrence does attempt to be clear-sighted what emerges is a series of simplistic generalisations that imply either an attempt to ease a troubled conscience, or that he has abandoned the difficulties and stresses of real thinking. Such matters are deeply involved in the writing and re-writing of *Lady Chatterley's Lover*, the novel on which he was working during the latter years of the 1920s, and in which he raged at what the English had made of England. In the published version of that novel one has a very powerful and betraying example of Lawrence's wish to trace to one source what he has detected as the symptoms of a terminal malaise. I am thinking in particular of that passage which describes Connie's drive through Tevershall, a journey which fills her with despair over England and its people, "In whom the living intuitive faculty was dead as nails, and only queer mechanical yells and uncanny will-power remained". The passage has been extravagantly admired by F. R. Leavis and others; and it is certainly a clear-sighted statement about the condition of England. Davie could obviously cite it as an – or perhaps *the* – instance of Lawrence's decision not to put up with the intolerable. But to say that is immediately to point to what is wrong with the passage. For the important question is whether Connie's despair amounts to vision. The truth is rather, I suggest, that the clarity of her point-of-view, which is undoubtedly also Lawrence's, depends on wilfil simplification of the actual. This is in no sense radical art: on the contrary, it is simple-minded rant. How can she *know* all this about Tevershall? How can anyone?

Interestingly enough, in the first version of the novel Lawrence deliberately undermines Connie's clear-sighted certainties. For in that version, she has no sooner thought her worst of Tevershall than she remembers that it is where her lover – Parkin, in that version – comes from. Moreover, she doesn't think of the people as being "dead as nails". How can she? Her knowledge of Parkin's belonging with them acts as decisive rebuke to her outsider's view of the matter. Instead, the scene "gave her a certain feeling of blind virility, a certain blind, pathetic forcefulness of life". Lawrence is very careful to make clear that Connie's thoughts are those of a particular individual; they are not to be taken as the truth. Indeed, he stresses how, given her class-prejudices, she *would* think as she does. (Discussions of class and its ideologies play a large part in the novel.) The first *Lady Chatterley's Lover* seems to me far and away the best of the three versions that Lawrence wrote, and this is at least partly because Connie's viewpoint isn't allowed there to operate as an objective account of the truth about England, one in which we can place unquestioning trust. Of course, she feels deeply about England, and her feelings drive her into generalisations. But she is made to see just how rashly simplistic some of them are. Because of that, one therefore has the sense of a real novelistic intelligence at work. In the published version, on the other hand, Lawrence allows Connie's viewpoint to be authoritative, and inevitably you realise that a number of crass simplicities have taken the novel over and reduced it to rant; and they are such simplicities as may be found in Davie's statements about "the gracelessness of scene around us . . . [and] neighbours who seem to ask nothing better and are doing their best to make it worse". As soon as you put the matter that way you have outlawed yourself from a due seriousness of purpose. For now everything can be seen – clearly, no doubt – as a series of distemper-board headlines.

If we need further evidence that this was the way that Davie was thinking during the latter part of the 1960s, we can turn to his poem "Thanks to Industrial Essex", a poem which invokes the "hatred" that infects *Lady Chatterley's Lover*:

> Thanks to industrial Essex,
> I have spun on the greasy axis
> Of business and sociometrics;
> I have come to know the structures
> Of public service
> As well as I know the doves
> Crop-full in mildewed haycocks.
> I know that what they merit
> Is not scorn, sometimes scorn
> And hatred, but sadness really.
>
> Italic on chalky tussocks,
> The devious lovely weasel
> Snakes through a privileged annex,
> An enclave of directors.
> Landscapes of supertax
> Record a deathful failure
> As clearly as the lack
> Of a grand or expansively human
> Scale to the buildings of Ilford.
>
> The scale of that deprivation
> Goes down in no statistics.

If this is to be radical, to go to the roots, then give me Erastianism. For in spite of the last two lines, with their confident, Pound-like assumption that in England now quantification of life has taken over from quality – so that public services are defined as structures – what we have is a series of bland and blank statements with no particularity to them. Except, that is, for the doves in the mildewed haycocks, who symbolise a lost glory; oh, and the weasel, of course, a last flicker of the natural life that is fugitive in a world of directors. But for the rest, we must make do with the simple, untested *Telegraph*-ese of "the lack / Of a grand or expansively human / Scale to the buildings of Ilford." The poem's title snarls defiance at thanks. "Thanks to Essex, *this* is what I have to live with . . .". I cannot take that seriously, any more than I can take seriously the anger of Charles Tomlinson's poem "On the Hall at Stowey", which is about the final decay of a great house and what is symbolises:

> Five centuries – here were (at the least) five –
>   In linked love, eager excrescence
> Where the door, arched, crowned with acanthus,
>   Aimed at a civil elegance, but hit
> This sturdier compromise, neither Greek, Gothic
>   No Strawberry, clumped from the arching-point
> And swathing down, like a fist of wheat,
>   The unconscious emblem for the house's worth . . .
>
> Five centuries. And we? What we had not
>   Made ugly, we had laid waste –
> Left (I should say) the office to nature
>   Whose blind battery, best fitted to perform it
> Outdoes us, completes by persistence
>   All our negligence fails in. Saddened,
> Yet angered beyond sadness, where the road
>   Doubled upon itself I halted, for a moment
> Facing the empty house and its laden barns.

"On the Hall at Stowey" is the kind of poem that would obviously appeal to those who know of the tradition of country-house poems; it is very self-consciously a literary poem. No harm in that, perhaps; but where a tradition is uncritically invoked and set against what "we" have done, then the dangers abound. For this is not radicalism at all; it is a mere echoing of cliché ("But to have gathered from the air a live tradition . . ."). And if there is to be anger then it had better be a good deal more self-critical and enquiring than either Davie or Tomlinson shows himself capable of being. It had better be the anger of Yeats ("And maybe the great grandson of that house, / For all its bronze and marble, 's but a mouse"), which has an acute historical dimension to it, doesn't seek refuge in convenient commonplaces about past and present, and accepts a measure of guilt for what was engendered in the "great" past. Davie refers to Lawrence's "guilt and horror", and the horror is there, right enough: not only in Lawrence, but in Davie and Tomlinson too. Hence, no doubt, the anger. But where is the guilt? It does not exist, I suggest, for in Tomlinson's poem "we" is an unexamined term that may as well be read as "you" (after all the speaker of the poem knows the greatness of the past and is thus not guilty of ignorant vandalism). And where there is no self-criticism, no enquiry into the adequacy of one's clear-sightedness, there can be no generosity of vision, without which art becomes rhetoric. At the end of his essay on Dickens, George Orwell wrote of how he imagined Dickens's face: "He is laughing, with a touch of anger in his laughter, but no triumph, no malignity. It is the face of a man who is always fighting against something, but who fights in the open and is not frightened, the face of a man who is *generously angry*" (Orwell's italics). Generous anger is the very opposite of those commonplace clarities that between them confuse the purpose of *Thomas Hardy and British Poetry*. And although I would not claim Hardy as a poet of generous anger, his modes of acceptance amount to a comprehending generosity of vision that seems to me far more valuable for English poetry than the alternatives that Davie prescribes.

A Survey of Recent Hardy Studies

Richard H. Taylor

At the still point of the Hardy world is the enduring art of a man who was, as Lord David Cecil said at the 1978 Hardy Festival, "tender-hearted and not very hopeful": a gentle and exact description. Dr Robert Gittings has recently taken a rather different view of Hardy's personal qualities. Gittings's appearance on the biographical stage has been greeted by some as if he were the villain of a Victorian melodrama. The role is not, in a sense, inappropriate since this least villainous of men does pose a skilful challenge to the status quo. Instead of twirling a waxen moustache, however, he has come on propounding a revisionist view of Hardy's character: in contrast to Cecil's (and the prevailing) view of Hardy as "a good man as well as a great man", Gittings depicts a mean-spirited and small-souled author. When one of our most distinguished biographers compounds indefatigable scholarship with what appears to be personal animosity toward his subject, the result is bound to be controversial, and I shall return to it later.

Since new biographies have also now expounded the lives of both Emma and Florence Hardy, and as primary documents such as letters and notebooks are becoming increasingly available in print, our knowledge of the external details of Hardy's life is being constantly enriched. Yet none of these enterprises leads us unfalteringly to a clear understanding of his mind, his most personal impulses. What emerges from the craft of the biographer and editor is inevitably a mediated and selective vision of the subject, whose inner life, if it is to be found anywhere, is most faithfully implicit in his art.

Hardy's art is flourishing on a mighty scale. He is now surely the most popular novelist of quality in the English-speaking world, and he is at last escaping from Leavisite hostility (and its legacy of critical timidity) into recognition as a great poet. The release of his writings from copyright on 1 January 1979 has generated a gallimaufry of new editions to exploit the lucrative Hardy market, among them some long-needed critical editions from Hardy's old and new publishers. Textual studies have been neglected in the past and some admirable work is now being done in this field.

A Survey of Recent Hardy Studies   153

It is with these accomplishments and other critical work on Hardy that I shall be concerned in this review essay. In future issues of the *Annual* I shall survey the work done in the single year prior to publication. In this first issue, however, I shall discuss some of the major critical activity between 1978 (the fiftieth anniversary of Hardy's death) and the time of writing. This essay and bibliography will supplement a reader's guide and bibliography that I contributed to *Thomas Hardy: The Writer and his Background* (1980), edited by Norman Page, describing Hardy studies up to 1978. The sectional organisation will broadly follow the pattern established in that volume and anticipate a similar pattern in *Thomas Hardy: A Secondary Bibliography*, which I am currently compiling. Fuller details of essays, mentioned in this survey by title and date only, will be found in the bibliography that follows.

(Hardy's work stimulates so much critical attention that it is impossible to keep abreast of it all, but this yearly survey will aim to be as inclusive as possible. Any details, copies or offprints of books or articles would be gratefully received. Could readers kindly send any such contributions to Dr Richard H. Taylor, c/o Miss Julia Tame, The Macmillan Press Ltd., 4 Little Essex Street, London WC2R 3LF?)

EDITIONS

Some five years before the expiry of the Hardy copyrights, Macmillan London issued their largely admirable New Wessex Edition of Hardy's works in hardback and paperback, shrewdly anticipating the inevitable 1979 *melée* by seeking to establish a prolonged and authoritative presence in a field that had long been their sole fief. Wearing belt and braces for the occasion, the firm also published another sound edition of the major works, destined for a slightly different market – the Macmillan Students' Hardy, very capably edited by James Gibson.

And now, in case belt and braces were not enough, Macmillan have published two compilation volumes: *A Thomas Hardy Omnibus* (1978), containing four novels and *Wessex Tales* and weighing in (one reviewer reported) at "3 lb 7 oz exactly", and *The Bedside Thomas Hardy* (1979), with extracts from ten novels, seventeen short stories and forty poems, selected and introduced by Edward Leeson. The latter makes a good introduction and in its wide range may repel an early invader of Macmillan's kingdom, Geoffrey Halson's *Thomas Hardy Selection* (1979) in the Longman Imprint series, a similar but more limited compilation for secondary school pupils. It offers good value, though: Halson gives a proper sense of Hardy's variety and his book is very much cheaper.

It is in the publication of individual novels, however, that Macmillan face some of their stiffest new challenges. The New English Library edition of five novels (1979) is new only to the United Kingdom: in the Signet Classics series NEL have plucked from the past the New *American* Library issues of 1959–64. The afterwords are all valuable, though not (by now) unfamiliar. A more determined offensive has been mounted by Penguin Books, who have published a new series of crisply introduced editions of the major novels and stories (seven in 1979, one in 1981), and I believe that this series will join the New Wessex Edition as market leaders. The latest addition to the series is *The Woodlanders* (1981), with an introduction by Ian Gregor and notes by James Gibson. Susan Hill includes eleven stories in *The Distracted Preacher and Other Tales* (1979), an excellent edition with a wise introduction ("we should not go to Hardy at all if we do not want to be told a rare tale, to be amazed, disturbed and intrigued"). One critic demonstrates his longevity in the field: A. Alvarez, whose 1961 afterword to *Jude* now appears as a Signet Classic in Britain, also contributes an introduction to the 1979 Penguin *Tess*. Alan Chedzoy pleasingly introduces *FFMC* and *MC* to the Collins Classics series, and there is a welcome addition to another established series in Norman Page's Norton Critical Edition of *Jude* (USA 1978, UK 1980): a shrewd selection of critical materials, a full text and an excellent introduction make this the most useful edition of the novel currently on the market.

James Gibson's *The Complete Poems of Thomas Hardy: A Variorum Edition* (1979) is a major publishing event, the first variorum edition of any of Hardy's work and a task carried out with meticulous care and loving exactness. (See Textual Studies, where Dale Kramer's *variorum* edition of *The Woodlanders* (1981) is also discussed.) David Wright's *Selected Poems by Thomas Hardy* (1979) represents Penguin English Library's challenge to the existing Macmillan selections by T. R. M. Creighton, James Gibson and John Wain (who edited two selections, one with Eirian Wain). The institutional nature of the Penguin imprint will assure it a wide readership which will be well served by the acuity of Wright's judgement and the generosity of his selection. *Thomas Hardy: Selected Poems* (1981), edited by James Reeves and Robert Gittings, is a late entrant in the stakes. Its principal virtue is a charming and sensitive introduction by the late James Reeves, whose valedictory publication this is. Hardy is seen steadily and seen whole by Reeves, yet the selection is rather slight, though more expensive for about one hundred poems than James Gibson's forthcoming paperback edition of *The Complete Poems*, containing nearly one thousand. It is pleasant to see Hardy's own selection, *Chosen Poems*, in print again with a brief introduction by Francine S. Puk (1979), but the production is rather unattractive — unlike Trevor Johnson's Folio Society edition, *Poems by Thomas Hardy* (1979); though the woodcuts by Jacques Hnizdovsky are variable in quality, Johnson's introduction is typically perceptive.

TEXTUAL STUDIES

There have been too many works of critical exegesis and too few attempts to explore the text of Hardy's work, so this remains a potentially exciting area of scholarly discovery. Even now the advances, individually distinguished, are being made haphazardly. Macmillan have been fainthearted over giving adequate attention to textual matters in the New Wessex Edition, preferring to keep to the old Wessex Edition even though it is demonstrably no longer to be regarded as authoritative. The welcome accorded to Dale Kramer's *variorum* edition of *The Woodlanders* must be tempered by the knowledge that the Oxford University Press has sought to devise no common editorial policy for this and the planned editions of *Tess* and *UGT*; nor is there a commitment to extend the series to other novels.

That textual study is not just the endeavour of scholars in the dessicated mould of Browning's grammarian is implied in the fascinating work of Simon Gatrell, whose "Hardy the Creator: *FFMC*" (1979) heralds a series of essays which seek to make a comparative study of all Hardy's texts to discover "the kinds of things he was interested in altering, heightening, deleting, augmenting", including style and punctuation. Gatrell believes that we shall thus better understand Hardy as a creative artist, and that "the most rewarding way to penetrate his amply shielded personality may be through the creative mind at work". In another striking essay, "Hardy, House-Style, and the Aesthetics of Punctuation" (1979), Gatrell demonstrates that Hardy's punctuation was regularly vandalised on the whims of compositors: the printed version of *UGT* has 1281 more commas than appear in Hardy's manuscript, yet his dashes were frequently removed (and with them the ingenuous breathlessness of Fancy Day). Much of the punctuation that we have long accepted is not Hardy's own and the implications of this are considerable. We can at least hope that Gatrell shares the grammarian's pertinacity.

That is a quality prominent in James Gibson's *The Complete Poems of Thomas Hardy: A Variorum Edition* (1979), a major work of meticulous scholarship and the product of many years of thorough research into virtually every extant manuscript and all subsequent revisions to printed texts. (It is unfortunate that private owners like Frederick B. Adams Jr and

Richard L. Purdy should not have felt able to allow Gibson to see their manuscripts: such proprietorial restrictiveness cannot be in the best interests of scholarship.) Gibson's excellent introduction gives a lucid account of Hardy's methods of writing. Hardy's revisions are prolific and Gibson's editorial judgements are always reliable, authoritatively establishing the comparative importance of variations in substantives and accidentals. All uncancelled variants are recorded and all cancelled variants "which, either for reasons of meaning or style, seem to be of interest or importance" are given. Gibson says that his admiration for Hardy's "creative genius, his integrity, the quality of his feelings, and the professionalism of his approach to his writing has grown with the years and made the labour eminently worthwhile". Gibson's own professionalism is a fine tribute to his author, and it will greatly enhance appreciation of Hardy's poetry.

Hardy's assiduous alterations are seen, too, in Dale Kramer's critical edition of *The Woodlanders*, where the editor collates nine versions through which the text has evolved, including the manuscript, printer's copy, and proofs revised by Hardy. (Printers' interference with punctuation is shown to have been as extensive as Gatrell implied.) Kramer's introductory analysis of his material is convincing and he establishes a sound text, with lengthy appendices devoted to variants. Hardy is discovered polishing his style, refining his characterisation, or simply in flight from Mrs Grundy. This is a severe edition, not designed for the general reader but giving, for the first time, full details of the textual evolution of one of Hardy's novels.

BIBLIOGRAPHIES AND HANDBOOKS

This essay and serial bibliography will draw each year upon such reliable serials as the *Victorian Studies* and *PMLA* bibliographies as well as other sources. They will supplement Richard H. Taylor, "Thomas Hardy: A Reader's Guide" and "Thomas Hardy: A Select Bibliography" (1980, see above), which identify several generations of Hardy critics "on their progress from moral stricture and classical apotheosis, via philosophical postulation and agrarian history, to psychic analysis and once again the text itself". That essay also appraises critical editions, handbooks, editions of notebooks and letters, and biographical studies, from Hardy's own time to 1978.

Guidance into the rich pastures of Hardy scholarship becomes increasingly essential and an attractive new handbook engagingly collates much basic information about Hardy and his work. Alan Hurst's *Hardy: An*

Illustrated Dictionary (1980) comprises an alphabetical dictionary, a survey of Hardy's Wessex, a finding list of Hardy's characters, and suggestions for further reading. There is some overlap with Frank Pinion's famous *Hardy Companion*, but new material includes notes on theatrical, film and television adaptations. The dictionary entries, ranging over Hardy's writings and life and a wide variety of associated people, places and issues, are thoughtfully compiled, and the book contains a pleasant selection of photographs.

BIOGRAPHY, LETTERS AND NOTEBOOKS

John Fowles recently expressed an uncompromising view of Hardy as a man with some "very serious faults, a rotting carcass from which the honey came"; in 1942 Edmund Blunden, who had met Hardy, described him as "one of the kindest and brightest of men". Gertrude Bugler, who probably knew Hardy even better, has said that "he was not the grim, cynical man often pictured" (1964) and that "he had a very keen sense of humour and I was not the only one who heard him laugh" (personal letter, 1977). If he laughs now it may be with ironic "laughter in the wind", to use his own phrase, over the inability of his biographers to give a balanced account of him. Hardy knew what would happen, sooner or later, after his death, and ghosted his biography over Florence's name, sketching a modest and deliberately pedestrian self-portrait: an aniseed trail to divert subsequent biographers. (William E. Buckler, in "Thomas Hardy's Sense of Self" (1980), shows how, in his disguised autobiography, Hardy "builds a self-image that is overwhelmingly poetical". Hardy's entire imaginative tendency is poetic and his greatest fulfilment was achieved through his dedication to poetry after 1895. *The Life of Thomas Hardy* is full of prose poems that themselves chronicle Hardy's return to poetry: it is "the muted, oblique narrative fulfilment of the myth of that return".)

There is, in the *Life*, no sense of the grim cynic, the rotting carcass, and nor is there in the biographies of the 1930s to the 1950s, which range from the hagiography of Weber to the benevolence of Blunden, Evelyn Hardy, Holland and Rutland. But in the 1960s more scratchy impressions of a tight-fisted snob, an evasive and sometimes rude recluse, began to emerge as those who knew Hardy (often fairly slightly) as an octogenarian were interviewed in a series of monographs. To these partial but insidious new images a dimension of scandal was added in 1966 by Deacon's and Coleman's now discredited allegations that Hardy had fathered the child of his cousin Tryphena Sparks. "Some monstrous calumnies are afloat!" Hardy, like Mrs Charmond, might have said.

Nothing so dramatic is advanced by Robert Gittings, whose *Young Thomas Hardy* (1975) rebuts those notions and gives a clear account of Hardy's formative experiences. But now, in *The Older Hardy* (1978) (*Thomas Hardy's Later Years* in the USA), Gittings has explored Hardy's life from 1876 until his death, and parades his subject's disagreeable idiosyncrasies. In his middle age and in his eighties, Gittings implies, Hardy was in the grip of sexual fantasies about women, yet he was neglectful of the feelings of either his first or his second wife. Hardy's retreat into the gloom of Max Gate is described and what remains with the reader is an impression of his meanness, his deceitfulness, and the vicariousness of his living through his art rather than through his demonstrable feelings. This is a shock in view of his aesthetic commitment to lovingkindness and compassion. Edward Clodd said of Hardy (who was his friend) that he had "no largeness of soul", and this feeling permeates Gittings's view of his subject. We are all, as George Eliot said, "mixed human beings", and we must not expect those whom we admire to be made of any other stuff; and exposure of a subject's "mixedness" is a proper pursuit of the biographer. Yet at last, despite an admirable impulse to arrive at an objective view of Hardy through irrefutably thorough research, Gittings errs as far on the side of censure as earlier writers may have erred on the side of indulgence. Gittings, too, despite providing an absorbing read, misses the balanced view. The case against accepting Gittings's Hardy is elegantly put by T. R. M. Creighton (*Powys Review*, 7 (1980) 100–3), who is severely doubtful about Gittings's interpretation of his "imposing fabric of evidence".

A less ambitious and more gentle picture of Hardy is drawn by Anna Winchcombe in *Thomas Hardy: A Wayfarer* (1978), a concise and pleasing biography for school pupils. And a more sympathetic view of him also emerges from Denys Kay-Robinson's *The First Mrs Thomas Hardy* (1979), a pioneering biography of Emma. Kay-Robinson's plausible thesis is that a deep and consistent love united the Hardys and that their division was wrought by each mistakenly assuming the other's emotional defection. Emma could be a scatterbrained fool, unreasonably jealous of Hardy's success, yet she was loyal, loving, afraid of losing Hardy's affection and often pathetically trying to retrieve it: her derided poetry, Kay-Robinson suggests, may have been written with this in mind. Hardy, appalled by Emma's rejection of his views on religion and marriage, absorbed in his poetry and in his lionised social life, retreated unwillingly from her, his love frustrated rather than dead. So his powerful reaction to her death was not "a turnabout" but an involuntary release of repressed emotions. Bertha Newcombe, a friend of the Hardys, summed up Emma in a 1900 letter: "It is pathetic to see how she is struggling against her woes.

A Survey of Recent Hardy Studies

She ... is a great bore, but ... so kind and goodhearted, and one cannot help realising what she must have been to her husband." Such an understanding is made real by Kay-Robinson's tolerant biography and it is good to see Emma so kindly rehabilitated.

While Hardy himself canonised the memory of Emma, Robert Gittings and Jo Manton now virtually canonise the memory of his second wife, Florence. Kay-Robinson identifies no villain in his analysis of a marriage but sees a well-founded love thwarted by ordinary human misunderstandings and failures of communication. For Gittings and Manton, in *The Second Mrs Hardy* (1979), Hardy is again the villain, the deceptive, immature, selfish husband. An illumination of the shadowy Florence is welcome. Her image long distorted by Somerset Maugham's fictional misrepresentations in *Cakes and Ale*, or feinted by her pretended authorship of Hardy's biography, Florence is now shown in clearer focus. Though characterised by moderate talents, lacklustre disposition and a penchant for elderly professional men (including J. M. Barrie), she is championed by her biographers against her churlish husband. After some years of elementary teaching, she pursued her literary ambitions through local journalism and children's stories. In her determination to rise in the world she was distinctly tenacious, but her marriage to Hardy was not just opportunism or social pragmatism (and we are told that they did have sexual relations despite the disparity in their ages). Inescapably trained to submissiveness in all her life-roles, Florence was the companion and amanuensis that Hardy needed, though Gittings and Manton convict him of rewarding her with negligence. Volubly jealous of Emma's memory, Florence suffered from the "ruthlessness of the creative mind at work" as Hardy looked back. But Gittings and Manton must know that Hardy looked inwards too, and many poems of self-criticism show that he was never quite the indifferent egotist evoked here. Like many a widow, Florence discovered herself after Hardy's death, in a brief career of local good works and general acclaim. Hers is a sad, quiet and unexciting story, but one which is valuably told.

It is surveyed again in Marguerite Roberts's *Florence Hardy and the Max Gate Circle* (1980), which mainly comprises closely packed primary documentation adroitly held together by an unobtrusive narrative. This makes the monograph a rich source in itself. Dr Roberts has one advantage over Gittings and Manton since she met her principal subject, Florence, several times in London and Dorchester from 1934. The monograph also describes Hardy's social relations with the group of men (such as Barrie, Sydney Cockerell and T. E. Lawrence) who congregated around the Hardys at Max Gate. This is a generous tribute to the "melancholy" Florence's loyal support of the aged Hardy, and it echoes the question posed about her by

Hardy's literary executrix: "Did she, as Irene Cooper Willis thought, pay the price for Hardy's happiness in his last years?"

Miss Cooper Willis's own 1940 *Essay on Thomas Hardy* is at last published in full for the first time, with introduction and notes by F. B. Pinion (1981). This too reflects on Emma ("She was not intellectually gifted, but was decidedly an individual in a quaint way, and very kind-hearted") and Florence ("the expression in [Hardy's] face changed after his second marriage") as well as Hardy. This valuable essay is not entirely biographical: it also contains some astringent writing on Hardy's thought. Pinion's notes are concise and often as stimulating as this: "The *Life* should be regarded as complementary to his poems, and not a single independent work."

One of the most interesting of the Toucan Press monographs has been published in a new, expanded edition: *Thomas Hardy and the Hardy Players* (1980) by Norman J. Atkins, who played Alec in the 1924 production of *Tess*. Visits to Max Gate and meetings with Hardy are recalled with attractive fluency and humour. There are some delightful verbal snaps, such as Hardy laconically remarking of Henry James: "He kept on writing – but I really was not interested."

James himself is invoked by Miss Cooper Willis, when she applies his comment on Emerson's letters to those of Hardy's which appear in the *Life*: "They read like a series of beautiful circulars." This impression may be confirmed by the appearance of Volume II of *The Collected Letters of Thomas Hardy* (1980), superbly edited by R. L. Purdy and Michael Millgate. This covers the years 1893–1901, when Hardy was a controversial writer of the first rank. They are not, as one reviewer alleged in a piece entitled 'The Letters of a Grey Little Man', "exceedingly dull letters". They are sometimes Pooteresque in domestic matters (common enough, I fancy) but absorbing to those who care about the details of a life. Hardy is courteous but concise with his "business" correspondents – publishers, editors, admirers, and inviters of all kinds. His passing comments on other writers lose nothing by their compression (Tennyson was "a great artist, but a mere Philistine"). But he is more expansive in his correspondence with women, particularly those who had beauty – Agnes Grove or the cool Florence Henniker: many of these letters are poignant and revealing. There is warmth, too, in the briefer letters to Emma, despite received views of their mutual hostility in this period.

There is value, at a time when biographical heresies are being expounded or rebutted, in having such primary material made dispassionately available. Another source is Richard H. Taylor's edition of *The Personal Notebooks of Thomas Hardy* (1979), which draws together four notebooks in which "there is much to delight the reader responsive to the nuances of Hardy's imagination". "Memoranda I" and "Memoranda II" contain notes broadly divisible into three categories – literary and antiquarian, social, personal; the "Schools of Painting" notebook (the earliest extant one) represents a stage in Hardy's self-help education; the "Trumpet-Major notebook" is "unique in containing extensive notes that were used in the writing of a specific novel".

Possibly the most interesting feature of this book is the inclusion (as an appendix) of the first full publication of the passages that appeared in the *Life* typescripts but which were omitted from the published version. The introduction to this section includes an account of the writing of the *Life*, Hardy's "authorised version", and of the involvement of Barrie and T. E. Lawrence. The largest generic group among the omitted passages contains Hardy's acerbic rejoinders to critics, but there are many other interesting details which Hardy, or (later) Florence or Barrie, decided to delete; Florence struck from the record several complimentary references to Emma and to other women who caught Hardy's eye, including the admission that "some of his best poems were inspired by" Florence Henniker. There are some printing errors. Full annotations, and general and textual introductions, are given in both parts of the book, which reveals a reticent and sensitive author "in his private workshop".

CRITICAL STUDIES: NOVELS AND STORIES

In "Hardy and the Lay Reader" (1981) Frank Brown makes a deft plea for Hardy to be rescued from the critics, who "have created their own private battlefield to which they admit neither Hardy nor the lay reader". Are these subjective critics out to enlighten, or do they "fragmentise" their subject – reveal what suits their purpose, conceal what does not suit their personal book – and then "selectively reassemble" him? The lay reader is in danger of being "ironed flat" by the critics' "isms" and "ologies", the imposition of their own patterns rather than the discovery of Hardy's. Brown's sharp essay is salutary, a fitting prologue to the question: how *is* Hardy faring in the hands of the academic critics?

Not well, according to C. H. Salter, whose *Good Little Thomas Hardy* (1981) must make its author a strong contender to inherit the villain's cloak from Gittings. Salter's views have something in common with Brown's, but the perspective is different: whereas Brown implies that Hardy's genius has been diminished by the cantering of critics on hobbyhorses, Salter argues that it has been grossly inflated. According to his book's blurb, Salter "sweeps away what he considers to be excessive claims made by Hardy's recent and early critics and by the writer himself". He does so in a waspish, provocative, excitable style which makes strong reading. Hardy is, Salter argues, much too tentative and past-oriented to be a modernist, despite his claims to be an advanced thinker; and his social criticism is weak, out-of-date, incidental and flawed. Any notable influence of Victorian ideologies is denied, including the ideas of Darwin. (Roger Robinson argues quite differently in "Hardy and Darwin" (1980), where he identifies Hardy as "the greatest artist of the Darwinian crisis", especially in *Tess*, which is "not a version of Darwinism but a work made up of deeply-felt responses to it".) Comte, Arnold, Mill, Spencer and Leslie Stephen are shown to have had little intellectual influence, while eighteenth-century sources of Hardy's agnosticism, and of his themes, style, characters and language, are identified.

Salter makes too large a meal of Hardy's repetitiousness in subject-matter and themes ("a sign of limited power of invention") and in style and rhetoric (his "range of self-expression is limited" too). Assiduously collected examples give Salter's thesis an illusory force that is surely dispelled by his own much later remark that "more important than [Hardy's] repetition of idiosyncratic ideas is the fact that he had them". Yet Hardy is seen as derivative too, because of his dull exploitation of other writers through plodding quotation or plagiarism. Even in the greatest novels "there are serious faults of narrative and motivation", the range of characters is narrow, and critical claims to have identified form, poetic structure, mythic patterning in Hardy's fiction are rejected; Hardy is seen as a self-indulgent writer who could not have achieved such consistencies.

Among critics who engage Salter's fire are Bailey, Beatty, Björk, Brooks, Gregor, Hyman, Lerner, Hillis Miller, Pinion, Southerington, Lionel Stevenson and Merryn Williams; their ideas are variously "wrong . . . insensitive . . . erroneous . . . absurd". The author admits that his is "a largely negative, destructive approach", and the affection behind his iconoclasm has to be inferred from his display of impressive intimacy with Hardy's work. This spiky book will give workers in the Hardy industry a shot in the arm, or perhaps the backside. Its conclusions may be hard to agree with but it is by no means the least interesting study to have appeared.

More positive propositions are advanced by John Bayley in *An Essay on Hardy* (1978). This urbane study takes us into the texture of Hardy's writing, where Hardy's inconsistencies are shown as virtues as well as defects. A "radical disunity" is perceived in Hardy's style: "as with the poems, component parts of the prose seem unconscious of each other's presence." This terminology of dissonance provides an exciting new way of appreciating Hardy. It derives from a duality within Hardy, a tension between "Hardy conscious and unconscious". The conscious author is "laborious in the pursuit of literature and the exploitation of verbal effect and allusions", and his unconscious self is manifest in what slips through into the work from Hardy "off duty". What we respond to, as readers, is "the alternation between the two". In his sophisticated and sympathetic way, Bayley shows that Hardy's text is really "an affair of collaterals, effects not isolated from but independent of each other".

This provides a framework for analysis of major novels and various poems – "The Darkling Thrush" is given a fine new reading and is shown to give us a clue to Hardy's whole process through "the separation . . . between the things seen in it, and the images and interpretations made out of them" – as well as the neglected early novels. Two of these (*HE* and *AL*) Bayley describes as "more characteristic, more concentratedly Hardyan, than the last two great, and also more dynamically doctrinaire, novels"; these latter are abstracted from the unconscious Hardy. The book is full of such radical claims (elsewhere Bayley asserts that "Hardy never ever wrote anything better" than the first half of *Two on a Tower*) and they are all substantiated within the terms of its subtle arguments.

Hardy's "style of separation" is most inspired in the scenes involving Tess's confession, but in *Tess*, though separation is still a key, "now its equanimity is lost": "Hardy's apprehensions of Tess *do* seem aware of each other". And when, in *Jude*, Hardy strikes off in "an entirely new direction" in his fiction by writing schematically in terms of contrasts, the productive tensions of disunity are lost in an abdication of the unconscious Hardy. By now, his fiction is all too consistent. Bayley's dissatisfaction with this is clear: "Nothing could be less suited to Hardy's genius than this new approach."

Nothing could be *more* suited to Hardy's genius than Bayley's own new approach. It is the most distinguished, and often brilliant, study of Hardy that has appeared for many years, and its provocative subtlety is done no proper justice by this summary account. Bayley's title is disarmingly modest, and so is Joan Grundy's description of herself in *Hardy and the Sister Arts* (1979) as "a gate-crasher upon an already crowded party". In fact she is a welcome guest as she arrives laden with new perceptions about Hardy's affinities with the other arts. Hardy's writing has "the simplicity and complexity of life itself, of the actual process of living; and it has it in part at least because Hardy's method of creation involves the fusion of several different arts to create an illusion of living". Grundy's argument convinces the reader that Hardy's response to the other arts is much more deeply felt than the frequently aired view of him as a show-off autodidact implies.

Grundy starts from the sonnet "Rome: The Vatican: Sala Delle Muse" and Hardy's comment on it in the *Life*: "probably few literary critics discern the solidarity of all the arts." She proceeds to demonstrate Hardy's indebtedness to the pictorial arts, the theatre (particularly Victorian melodrama), the cinema's liberating effects ("Painting could suggest movement but not create it: theatre could create movement but only within a relatively limited area"), music and dance. Surely she is not accurate, though, when she says of Hardy's characters that "we are taken into their situations rather than into their minds: we know how life *felt* to them . . . rather than what they themselves are psychologically and morally" and that they are not "primarily psychological and moral entities". In his exploration of "the hobble of being alive", in the phrase that Grundy takes from Hardy succinctly to describe the fundamental issue of his fiction, Hardy makes psychological and moral developments and disturbances central, as Rosemary Sumner's new study (discussed later) emphasises. This seems to be the only flaw in a convincing, wide-ranging and important study.

Hardy is seen in the context of other practitioners of his own art in a series of useful essays, though a full study of Hardy in his literary context yet remains to be written. In his forthcoming *George Eliot Companion* (1982), F. B. Pinion writes on Hardy's indebtedness to Eliot and, in "'Infected by a Vein of Mimeticism': George Eliot and the Technique of *FFMC*" (1978), Lawrence Jones discusses her influence on a single novel. The two novelists are again drawn together by Jones, this time along with Lawrence, in "Imagery and the 'Idiosyncratic Mode of Regard': Eliot, Hardy and Lawrence" (1981). A specific novel-to-novel comparison between Dickens and Hardy is made by Philip Collins in "Pip the Obscure: *Great Expectations* and Hardy's *Jude*" (1978), while Janet B. Wright submits the same novel to a wider contextual study in "Hardy and his Contemporaries: The Literary Context of *Jude*" (1980), proving interestingly that "Hardy was not only aware of the critical controversy surrounding the 'fiction of Sex and the New Woman' in the early 1890s, but was also familiar with a large number of the novels of this type which were being published". Pierre Coustillas, in "Gissing on Hardy: A Novelist's View of a Contemporary Writer" (1980), provides some fascinating material from Gissing's paper, in which the younger novelist frequently writes to or comments (in mixed terms) on the older. Hardy would not have enjoyed it all since he resented the patronising criticism of fellow-writers. Chesterton's famous description of Hardy as "a sort of village atheist" inspired Hardy to dictate on his deathbed an acerbic "Epitaph" for Chesterton. Brocard Sewell has now written "Thomas

Hardy and G. K. Chesterton: A Study of Two Temperaments'' (1978-9), provoking responses by John Sullivan and Peter Hunt.

Hardy's admiration for a largely forgotten writer, Charlotte Mew, has been too little documented, though he told Vere Collins in 1921 that "Miss Mew is far and away the best living woman poet – who will be read when others are forgotten", and later arranged a civil list pension for her, so it is pleasing to see Mary C. Davidow's "Charlotte Mew and the Shadow of Thomas Hardy" (1978). A major writer is found to share some of Hardy's practice by John Peck in "Hardy and Joyce: A Basis for Comparison" (1981). Hardy anticipates Joyce in three areas: both show how to relate a large form (such as epic or tragedy) to life, both scrutinise various styles that can be employed in a narrative, and both encourage us to consider how the individual written word relates to the world. Three writers who show regional affinities with Hardy are the subjects of recent essays. Unexpected but apt analogies with the American novelist Ellen Glasgow are made by Velma Richmond in "Sexual Reversals in Thomas Hardy and Ellen Glasgow" (1979), while James W. Tuttleton confines himself to one of her novels in "Hardy and Ellen Glasgow: *Barren Ground*" (1979). It is more usual to find writers from Hardy's own region considered together with him, as in David A. Cook's "Powys, Hardy and Wessex" (1978) and R. G. King-Smith's "William Barnes and Thomas Hardy" (1978).

The regional qualities of Hardy's writing, and the ways in which he aesthetically exploited the region while remaining "unrestrained by Wessex limits", have been sensitively treated in several studies, including W. J. Keith's "A Regional Approach to Hardy's Fiction" (1979) and George Wing's "Hardy and Regionalism" (1980). Hardy knew the dangers: as Keith points out, he said of Barnes that "his place-attachment was strong almost to a fault". Both Keith and Wing agree that Hardy is not a "regional novelist" in any restrictive sense; rather, as Keith says, he introduces new elements into the genre "which not only counteracted its limitations but even turned them into strengths" by relating his "cirumscribed scene" to the larger world. Both writers indicate how Hardy responds to the social tendencies of the age, an issue more generally raised by Merryn and Raymond Williams, who show, in "Hardy and Social Class" (1980), that Hardy's fiction evidences "the arbitrariness, the coldness, the irresponsible power of a social class system" and that it remarkably explores "a new kind of consciousness" beyond this system. Keith describes how "a sense of the growing importance of social distinctions that inevitably weaken the cohesion of a local community" develops in Hardy's portrayal of Wessex; as Wing puts it, "a blight . . . seems gradually to spread over the region". The accompanying restlessness culminates in *Jude*, where, according to Keith, "regionalism receives its *coup de grâce*; Jude is deprived of both his context and his roots".

This conclusion is shared by Andrew Enstice in *Thomas Hardy: Landscapes of the Mind* (1979), a study which traces "the development from particular to more flexible landscapes" in Hardy's fiction. Enstice argues that in most of his novels Hardy creates "enclosed landscapes", and he shows how the author shapes a fictional Wessex out of his native region. For Enstice, too, the process culminates in *Jude*, where the enclosed landscape of the community is abandoned and the individual is alienated in an anonymous land; it is a place where "the new landscapes of the novel are ones of the mind – the author's, the reader's, and Jude's" and where we see only "the contours of the individual's own mental landscape as he struggles".

The mental landscapes of Hardy's characters are traversed in a number of essays and one full-length study. Among the essays three may be mentioned. Peter Casagrande, in "A New View of Bathsheba Everdene" (1979), challenges the common view of Bathsheba as "a vain, egotistical girl" who is matured by misfortune and suffering into "a wise, sympathetic woman". Through exploring her "subtler psychology", Casagrande reveals Hardy's ambivalence towards her and identifies her as an "unconscious agent of evil". Leon Waldoff's "Psychological Determinism in *Tess*" (1979) discusses the extent of Tess's responsibility for her fate in terms of "a psychological condition . . . intuited by Hardy", an irreconcilable conflict, identified by Freud, between affectionate and sensuous feelings. Angel and Alec respectively represent these polarities and Tess is caught between them. The "decisive determinant" is the peculiar sexual attitude of Angel. The question of sexual neurosis is also discussed by Rosemary Sumner in "Hardy as Innovator: Sue Bridehead" (1979).

Sumner's essay is now subsumed into her *Thomas Hardy: Psychological Novelist* (1981), a bracing account of Hardy's understanding of psychological currents well in advance of their definition by Freud, Jung, Adler and later psychological writers. This is an impressive contribution to the genre of psychoanalytical criticism since, in her illustration of Hardy's ability (in Forster's phrase) to "let a bucket down into the subconscious", Sumner never subjugates text to theory. Sympathy and common sense enrich her analysis of Lesbianism in Cytherea and Miss Aldclyffe, repression in Boldwood, aggression and schizophrenia in Henchard, and inhibitive sexual neuroses in Knight, Angel and Sue. Sumner achieves a more thorough and complex view than usual of both Sue and Jude, and draws piquant analogies with Freud's "*Civilised*" *Sexual Morality and the Neuroses*.

Throughout the book "Hardy's fascination with unusual states of mind and strange ways of thinking and feeling" is kept in view. In "Barbara of the House of Grebe" (1890) he is shown to have experimented with aversion therapy; the book is full of disclosures as interesting as this. Less unusual circumstances and characters are treated equally sensitively. Grace, torn between "modern nerves and primitive feelings", is shown in her "unstateable" quality to anticipate one of Lawrence's contributions to the novel, the idea that characters, like human beings, can never be fully known. The idea of Hardy "going in the same direction as Lawrence, who said he was trying 'to make new feelings conscious'", and of Hardy anticipating the instinctual life of Lawrence's characters, is not new but it is presented with unusual clarity. The dynamic of Hardy's fiction is towards a change in people's attitudes in favour of tolerance, an acceptance of the unknowable, an understanding of man's unconscious drives and needs and a consequent erosion of "the war between flesh and spirit". Sumner's humane study will enrich our perceptions of how Hardy achieved this through his profound understanding of individual psychologies.

An effective introductory study of Hardy's novels and poems is found in Lance St John Butler's *Thomas Hardy* (1978), which views its subject from several perspectives and throws up some lively ideas. It is a measure of Hardy's variousness that anthologies of essays can continue to be published without seeming unduly stale or repetitious in their contents, though the danger is there and needs to be monitored. Three such miscellanies have recently appeared: *The Novels of Thomas Hardy*, edited by Anne Smith, and *Critical Approaches to the Fiction of Thomas Hardy*, edited by Dale Kramer, both in 1979, and *Thomas Hardy: The Writer and his Background*, edited by Norman Page, in 1980. The first two collections contain studies unified by no common theme or approach, and each contains individual essays of distinction. On balance, Kramer's anthology makes the more substantial contribution to Hardy scholarship. Its high standard is well matched by Page's collection (as a contributor I had better declare my interest), which in cohesiveness benefits from the guiding principles of an established series designed to present "major authors in their intellectual, social, and artistic contexts". This aim is soundly accomplished in a distinctive volume.

Several essays, in addition to those mentioned elsewhere, in these various volumes deserve more than the cursory notice that space affords. James Gibson's "Hardy and his Readers" (1980) is a lively and often amusing account of the substantial influence of Grundyism on Hardy's writing. This is an important essay, as is Norman Page's "Hardy and the English

Language'' (1980), a rare and valuable example of close scholarly attention to Hardy's style in prose and poetry: in contrast to the usual easy critical sneers, Page finally endorses the "extraordinary vitality" of Hardy's writing. There are distinguished essays (all 1979) on individual novels, by the late Juliet Grindle on *MC*, Barbara Hardy on *UGT*, Robert Heilman on *RN*, and Patricia Gallivan on the influence of Victorian psychological theories on *Jude*. Elaine Showalter's "The Unmanning of the Mayor of Casterbridge" is a closely argued feminist critique (as are, elsewhere, Mary Jacobus's 1978 essay, "Tess: The Making of a Pure Woman", and, in a 1978 case of Bridehead revisited, Kathleen Blake's depiction of Sue as "The Woman of the Feminist Movement").

Three serial publications also contain collections of essays. The *Thomas Hardy Year Book* continues to appear, usually two years after its cover date, and it has become a tidied-up and tighter publication containing a useful selection of essays. These are listed individually in the bibliography, as are those in two journals which have each devoted a full issue to Hardy: *Inscape* (University of Ottawa, 1980), edited by Keith Wilson and David Shore, and *Cahiers Victoriens & Edouardiens* (Université Paul Valéry, Montpellier, 1980), edited by Annie Escuret. Both issues may be strongly recommended for their thoughtful studies of Hardy's poetry and prose. *Inscape* includes two essays by writers who have developed their themes into forthcoming full-length studies: Marlene Springer writes persuasively on "The Uses of Allusion in Thomas Hardy's *RN*" and Kristin Brady's "Ancient and Modern: A Double Perspective in Thomas Hardy's 'The Fiddler of the Reels'" offers a stimulating short analysis. (Elsewhere, in "Conventionality as Narrative Technique in Hardy's 'On the Western Circuit'" (1978), Brady exposes Hardy's skilled use of literary conventions to keep his audience while subtly challenging the laws and customs of his time. It is good to see the stories, at last, getting their due in studies by Brady and others, and Brady's *The Short Stories of Thomas Hardy* may be anticipated with pleasure.) *Cahiers* has eleven essays by British and French critics: of special interest are F. B. Pinion on "Hardy's Literary Imagination", Jean Brooks on "*The Dynasts* as Total Theatre" (an excellent essay), and Annie Escuret's "*Tess des d'Urberville*: le Corps et le Signe". Simon Gatrell, in "Hardy and his Critics", gives details of Hardy's responses to his biographical critics (especially Chew, Hedgcock, Brennecke).

The *Thomas Hardy Society Review*, published annually under the shrewd editorship of F. B. Pinion, maintains a consistently high standard and several of its essays are cited elsewhere in this survey.

CRITICAL STUDIES: POETRY

James Gibson's edition of *The Complete Poems of Thomas Hardy* (1976) has, for the first time ever, made all Hardy's poems attractively and reliably accessible. I suspect that it has generated a considerable increase in enthusiasm for this side of Hardy's work, a keenness evidenced by much increased scholarly activity (about sixty essays have appeared in the period under review). Hardy, who regarded himself primarily as a poet, would have welcomed this.

Gibson is also co-editor, with Trevor Johnson, of a substantial addition to Macmillan's Casebook series: *Thomas Hardy – Poems* (1979). The editors have assembled a discriminating selection of the criticism of three-quarters of a century, from the dyspeptic reaction of the *Saturday Review* (1899) to *Wessex Poems* ("it is impossible to understand why the bulk of this volume was published at all – why he did not himself burn the verse") to more generous and acute recent writings by Hynes, Larkin, Creighton, Kenneth Marsden, Jean Brooks and others. There is a selection of Hardy's own comments on his poetic art, and the editors' introduction is an excellent survey of critical responses to that art. I am sure that the editors would welcome the correction of a printing error (which occurred beyond their control) in their epigraph to the book – quoted from Hardy, it should read: "But criticism is so easy, and art so hard."

The most striking individual essay to have appeared lately is Samuel Hynes's "The Hardy Tradition in Modern English Poetry" (1980). Hynes identifies and defines a "Hardy tradition", one that is quite distinct from Eliot's, and expounds a view that is, I believe, widely held by individual readers, though rarely committed to print. Claiming that "much modern poetry is traditional and continuous with the past, and that the apocalyptic uniqueness of modern experience has been exaggerated", Hynes shows how a line of continuity stretches, more surely from Hardy than from Eliot or other "Major Moderns", into the present: Frost, Edward Thomas, Lawrence, Blunden, Day Lewis, Grigson and Larkin all belong to it. Hardy is "a great poet in an old and central tradition", and one who is more often read voluntarily "by people who simply enjoy reading poetry" than any of the more complex modern poets.

The Poetry of Thomas Hardy (1980), edited by Patricia Clements and Juliet Grindle, is a welcome anthology of new essays that will enhance that enjoyment. It offers a series of mature impressions. The patronising view of Hardy as a clumsy autodidact has gone, and good riddance. An altogether brisker and more artful figure is defined in Isobel Grundy's spirited defence of his linguistic experiments ("for his purpose of seeking to make us wonder at the usual, Hardy's harshness of style is invaluable'') and Ronald Marken's essay on his use of rhyme. S. C. Neuman explores the contrapuntal play between prosody and lexical content in his poetry, and Patricia Clements excitingly discusses the ways in which Hardy's poetic "exploration of reality" imposes order on life: the mind stiffens experience with pattern, but Hardy's poetry repeatedly submits the mind's formalisations "to correction in the fire of sensory apprehension". Other notable essays include those by Jeremy Steele (on Hardy's empathy with Sophocles), Glen Wickens (a fine essay demonstrating the deliberate inconsistency of Hardy's Spirits in *The Dynasts*), Simon Gatrell (on the motif of travel and pilgrimage) and Patricia Ingham (meticulously true to Hardy in her account of his imagery of time). Gatrell and Ingham invoke some of Hardy's most appealing poems as his pilgrimage through time is unrolled: "Yes: I have re-entered your olden haunts at last; / Through the years, through the dead scenes I have tracked you."

This process of return to the past, through reverie, is the plot that Dennis Taylor finds most interesting in Hardy's poetry. The speaker often views a scene, absorbs its pastness, loses himself in reverie, and is recalled abruptly to present reality: "The central issue in Hardy studies is what happens to an experience as it is made into literature, the experience remembered, the literature reread, a similar experience undergone, the whole made into more literature." The development of this pattern of thought and feeling in Hardy's lyric poems is the main theme of *Hardy's Poetry 1860–1928* (1981), an impressive study of Hardy's process of poetic self-discovery in the context of nineteenth-century intellectual history: "gradually Hardy discovers the deep connections between the plot of his own life and the plot of Victorian life" and his "lyric vision climaxes in the image of a grotesque nightmare apocalypse haunted by a changed world" (Emma's death and the Great War). Taylor's rhetoric and scholarship are not epideictic but they are tightly woven; so much so, perhaps, that the exposition of his thesis is rather tortuous. Ultimately his theory, that Hardy "makes his lyric poem the model of a man's life: the way the lyric speaker forms his thoughts within the few moments of a reverie recapitulates the way a man has thought over a lifetime; the smaller interruption of the reverie portends the larger interruptions of life", seems too schematic. But even if its central thesis is not wholly accepted, this book is shot through with stimulating criticism. Taylor's chapter identifying an imagery of patterns throughout Hardy's work is outstanding, and he gives a neat account of traditions that contributed to Hardy's lyric (including Gothicism, romantic aesthetics, theories of the grotesque, the ballad, and developments in philosophy and epistemology).

Affinities with, rather than influences from, other traditions or writers have been noticed by various critics. One of the most unexpected is found in Ernest L. Fontana's "Zen in Thomas Hardy's 'Moments of Vision'" (1980), where Fontana claims that the poems which Paul Zietlow categorises with the title of one of Hardy's poetry volumes "bear a remarkable resemblance to the qualities of Japanese Zen poetry of perception, technique and mood". Cornelia Cook, in "Thomas Hardy and George Meredith" (1980), uses Hardy's friendship with Meredith as a peg on which to hang an instructive comparison of the two in terms of philosophy, style and use of language. Ross C. Murfin, in *Swinburne, Hardy, Lawrence and the Burden of Belief* (1978), holds Hardy and the others rather unsteadily in focus in an argument that is at times almost swallowed up by the metaphors through which he expresses it.

A tauter series of studies is found in a Hardy commemorative issue of *Victorian Poetry* (1979), imaginatively edited by Frank R. Giordano Jr. Among the informative essays are those by William E. Buckler on the "Poems of 1912-13", Frank Giordano on the country songs, Trevor Johnson on the anthologist's Hardy, and Kathryn King and William W. Morgan on the Boer War poems. To give this issue an additionally interesting dimension, two portraits of Hardy and his *Wessex Poems* illustrations are reproduced and a series of poems *about* Hardy (by Day Lewis, Gittings, Richards and Sassoon) are included.

Over fifty years ago Hardy complained, with good reason, about the "curiously blundering reception" of his poetry: "There were those prose works standing in a row in front, catching the eye at every attempt to see the poetry, and forming an almost impenetrable screen." At last the screen is being lifted and the new editions, and the diversity of refreshing studies, that are now appearing may begin to atone for the blunders of the past.

Dennis Taylor, *Hardy's Poetry, 1860–1928* (Macmillan, 1981) pp. xx + 204.
Patricia Clements and Juliet Grindle (eds), *The Poetry of Thomas Hardy* (Vision Press, 1980) pp. ix + 194.

Reviewed by P. N. Furbank

Dennis Taylor is by no means the first to take "pattern" as a key to Hardy's verse. It was once used as not so much a key as a stick to beat Hardy with. Taylor quotes R. P. Blackmur's complaint, that Hardy's poetry reveals an "absolutist, doctrinaire . . . totalitarian, frame of mind. . . . If you had the pattern, everything else followed right"; and Samuel Hynes wrote that form in Hardy's poems was something accidental, a framework chosen at random, "as though the receptacle had been constructed first and then an idea had been dropped into it". What can be claimed for Dennis Taylor's book is that he has explored the topic of "pattern" more thoroughly and variously than his predecessors, and this makes his book one to be respected and reckoned with.

His approach is partly historical. He explores "pattern", and paradoxes about pattern – do we find pattern or do we impose it? – as a ruling idea for the Victorian age generally. He reminds us, very relevantly, of its importance for George Eliot, both as scientific model and as ethical metaphor. He mentions Hardy's interest in electrical engineering, with its "coils", current-patterns and "electric ropes". He argues, though I think without proving, that Hardy was influenced by Darwin's diagramme of diversifying species and genera, and shows Hardy perceiving a "seared and cynic face" in the patterns of his own family-tree. Most important, he examines the complex of Hardy's thoughts and feelings towards Gothic architecture and church-restoration. "Gothic", at any rate in Hardy's view of it, is pre-eminently an architecture of pattern, and Hardy's "The Abbey Mason", which Ezra Pound called "Hardy's personal aesthetic", relates directly to a Victorian debate about the origins of Gothic forms.

"Nobody but those who have had to carry church-restorations out", said Hardy in 1896, "knows the difficulties of such problems – whether to preserve the venerable *lines*, or the venerable *substance*, when you cannot do both." The remark is for us a kind of gloss on his interest in *skeletons*. The thought at work is that the skeleton or pattern embodies truth, but a truth only perceived when it is too late. Knowing the truth is a posthumous activity. And from here there is a natural transition of ideas, made by Taylor, to verse-pattern. Hardy, as we know, loved the pattern-aspect of verse-form, obtruding it rather than hiding it in his poems, and constructing skeleton verse-forms to be provided with flesh later. And the crown of his achievement, according to Taylor, was a certain *genre* of poem, the "meditative lyric", in which the verse-pattern, apparently rigid and formulaic, quietly prepares a surprise of the kind, and the scale, that life itself provides. Much of the first section of Taylor's book is an attempt to define this *genre*. He takes as a model of it, and of the mode of thought it is designed to express, the poem "Copying Architecture in an old Minster" – summarised by Taylor thus:

A man sits in an old church and sketches on a large architectural pad. He begins to muse about the many dead who lie buried there under stone effigies. He then thinks about the world outside the church, a world full of war and personal tragedy. He thinks also about himself and the gloomy setting of the church seems to harmonise with his reflections. Suddenly he looks up. His pencil and pad have slipped to the floor. It is much later. He feels stiff. He looks outside and discovers that the late evening fog has come up and engulfed the church.

This is a central type of experience in Hardy's poetry. As he meditates about the world, the world changes around him and intrudes on the meditation.

Another, and perhaps the greatest example of all, of this *genre*, according to Taylor, is "During Wind and Rain". And certainly from his own slant Taylor manages to point out quite a few new things (new anyhow to me) about that much-discussed poem. One is, says Taylor, to posit a speaker looking out at a graveyard during the advancing stages of a storm and remembering the advancing stages of a human lifetime. And when the speaker sees the sick leaves reeling down, he then remembers a scene where they were cleaning up leaves . . . and so on. "We discover that we have been following two journeys, both conditioned and interrupted by the changing elements. The smaller experience of the speaker caught in an evolving reverie recapitulates the larger experience of a lifetime caught in an evolving life-style."

I am ready to grant Taylor his genre and furthermore his view that this genre, painfully and fumblingly approached by Hardy, was perfected under the shock of Emma Hardy's death. The thought for which it became the vehicle was that something, an anonymous "It", has crept up upon the dreamer, sunk in his forty-year-old reverie: ". . . the image of his early love had become a 'phantom horsewoman', a *personne supplémentaire*, which had persisted long after the couple themselves had changed." Here, too, says Taylor, convincingly, is the source of Hardy's "grotesque" – a concept he again sets in the context of Victorian thought. The grotesque, for Hardy, results when reality intrudes upon a too-long-cherished reverie. And here, too, he suggests, can be found a justification for Hardy's linguistic archaisms: rigidity and obsoleteness in phraseology can be made to mirror the Rip Van Winkle fixatedness of the dreamer.

What Taylor wants to say further is that, contrary to accepted views, Hardy *matured* as a poet, and this maturing is defined by increasing mastery of this genre, the "meditative lyric". Here I think he is pushing things rather. By this theory some of one's very favourite poems, like "The Last Chrysanthemum", "The Darkling Thrush" and "The Self-Unseeing", published moreover when Hardy was past sixty, would have to qualify as "immature" – which hardly seems right. I think there is some assumption at work that if you are going all out to praise a writer you must credit him with "development" as well as everything else. But because Yeats, Rembrandt and Beethoven so obviously had a "development", it does not follow that we think less of Chardin or Hardy if they did not. And Taylor's third and final section, much concerned with the "development" of Hardy's war-poetry and attitudes to war, is not convincing to me, for the same reason in reverse. His theory is that Hardy learned to repent of his early patriotic passions as he learned to repent of, or saw the sinister consequences of fixation upon, his early romantic love-emotions: "Hardy approached nearer to the realisation that there was an intimate connection between the way the imagination works and the way war is created." The snag is, one is only mildly interested in the "maturing" of Hardy's views of war, as exemplified in the progress from "Leipzig" and "The Sergeant's Song" to "And there was a Great Calm". For the theory to work, "And there was a Great Calm" would have to be a high point in Hardy's art, and I don't think it is quite that. It is a fine poem, containing as it does that extraordinary stanza about the "weft-winged engines", but, as you might say, a fine "magazine" poem – precarious in its effect and somewhat queered by those bugbears, those comic-opera Eumenides, the Sinister Spirit and Spirit of Irony.

The Poetry of Thomas Hardy, edited by Patricia Clements and Juliet

Grindle, contains eleven essays, rather akin in style to Dennis Taylor's book. There are none of those swingeing revaluations and devaluations of earlier years – Donald Davie's seems to have been the last – and a rough consensus, it seems, has been arrived at as to what sort of thing Hardy's poetry is. Many of the perceptions in these essays fit neatly into Dennis Taylor's. For instance, Taylor's discussion of "pattern" is glossed by Patricia Clements, discussing Hardy's preoccupation with repetition and return: "however persuaded Hardy's returning characters (or his readers) may be that what is before them is what should be there, they are forced finally to see something which is not part of the lawful assembly, to recognise a moment at which the tracing and the experience do not match." It is glossed, too, by S. C. Neuman's laborious but persuasive analysis of "The Master and the Leaves", which shows how the rigid stanzaic pattern "says" things quite at odds with the poem's ostensible content.

Here again are efforts to justify Hardy's archaisms, but as always – as it seems to me – they are doomed to partial failure. Patricia Ingham, in "Hardy and 'The Cell of Time'", relates Hardy's use of archaic language to his conception of human time as imprisoning and denaturing. An archaism is a sterile form, and "Such sterility fits perfectly where man is seen in an artificial and virtually inescapable trap". And the same is true, she says, of the "ere"s, "yea"s and "blent"s which sprinkle his poems, and she quotes: "And hammerings, / And quakes, and shoots, and stifling hotness, blent / With webby waxing things and waning things." But, we object, "blent" reads most naturally and vigorously here and calls for no special pleading. And vice-versa, often as Hardy uses an archaism with deliberate artistic purpose, just as often he does it just to tease, he does it out of mere bad habit.

The editors have evidently insisted on close reading and scrupulous documenting of critical *apercus*, and it is not for a reviewer to complain, for he would infallibly complain of their absence. All the same, seeing Hardy's poems deployed in one formation and then another on the parade-ground, one shares the emotions of royalty on the saluting-stand – one's eyes have a tendency to glaze. I think this happens mainly with essays, however good, which deal with an arbitrarily-chosen topic or a topic chosen for its own limited sake. Maybe it is stupid always to be looking for the "key" to Hardy, but this does lure one on, and one is less impelled to read on when this lure is absent. I am thinking for instance of Simon Gatrell on the theme of *travelling* in Hardy's verse. He is sensible and acute and manages a very deft turn in his concluding sentence, but somehow, as soon as one has grasped the subject, one sees how it will go – how, in a sense, it will *have* to go. One murmurs to oneself, "What about the theme of *rain* in Hardy's verse: an essay there too . . .?" – and indeed maybe someone has written it. In a slightly different way, the problem arises with Cornelia Cook on "Thomas Hardy and George Meredith". Someone had to do it, and it is well done, but given the commission one could have done it oneself, if not so competently; nothing unguessed-at emerges, or indeed was likely to emerge.

I found I was most engaged by the essay I had most disagreements with, Patricia Ingham's subtle "Hardy and 'The Cell of Time'". Rather against the current trend, she finds in "Poems of 1912–13" not so much the crown of Hardy's achievement as a triumphant exception. These poems, she says, convey a "sense of release" from what otherwise was an "obsession" with Hardy, a feeling of imprisonment in a narrow "cell of time", a conviction that human time, unlike the grandeur of geological time, is a benumbing, denaturing and reductive force. The phrase in her title comes from the poem. "After the Last Breath" and is contrasted by Ingham with "She opened the door or Romance to me, / The door from a cell / I had known too well. . . ."

Of these three thoughts about Hardy and human time – that he thought it treadmill-like, that he thought it "denaturing", and that he thought it "claustrophobic" – the first two seem right and the last wrong to me; and it is curious to see this last thought distorting her response to poems. She cites the lovely poem "Old Furniture", which was quite new to me, saying of it that the furniture "mocks" the human beings whose memory it recalls and that the poem captures the "undoing" effect of time, along with "the sense of being trapped within the permanently furnished room". But surely what the poem breathes is affection for rooms, not claustrophobia, affection for old furniture, and affection for the past users of furniture. It is a sneaking affection, if you like, such as the "world" and the Webbs would have come down upon severely, regarding it as effete; but where do traps or claustrophobia come in? How do they come in, again, in "Who's in the next room?"? What worries the speaker, surely, is that he is *not* as secure as he thought he was in his own cosy room?

More generally, is there not something, as it were, ungrateful in describing themes of Hardy's as "obsessions"? (Patricia Clements does not go so far as Patricia Ingham and calls Hardy's preoccupation with repetition and return "almost obsessive".) Would one speak of Yeats as being "obsessive" on the subject of towers and winding-stairs? I think one would, rather, praise the creativity which enabled him to give himself such "obsessions" – and likewise with Hardy.

Jeannette King, *Tragedy in the Victorian Novel: Theory and Practice in the Novels of George Eliot, Thomas Hardy and Henry James* (Cambridge University Press, 1978) pp. viii + 182.

Reviewed by Juliet McMaster

In her preface to *Tragedy in the Victorian Novel* Jeannette King acknowledges that this book emerged from a thesis; but the reader need have no apprehensions that its content will be the expected "Piled higher and Deeper" that the letters PhD have been said to stand for. It is not the intensely researched narrow piece of learning, on a topic so original that no one wants to know about it, that we have unfortunately come to expect of theses. It rather errs in the other direction. King's topic is the large and much worked-over one of tragedy in the novel, and the novelists she treats are George Eliot, Hardy and James, who can hardly be said to have been neglected. A treatment of such a subject in 182 pages can't but be superficial; and, unless it were actually perverse, it would be surprising if it were very new. In fact its procedures are conservative, and the readings of the novels treated as tragic are brief and sensible if not startling. It comes out as a kind of guide for undergraduates, who will be glad of some painless critical theory on tragedy and the novel, and some quick thematic runovers of long novels like *The Mill on the Floss*, *Tess of the d'Urbervilles*, and *The Wings of the Dove*. Perhaps it has already found that market, as it reached paperback a year after the hard-cover publication.

The book begins with a consideration of the contemporary critical context for these novelists, and the general failure of reviewers to recognize the potential for tragedy in the novel because of their preoccupation with Aristotelian terms. There is some useful examination of the problems inherent in the translation of tragedy from drama to prose fiction. Can the tragic hero be reincarnated in a medium that by tradition has explicitly rejected heroism? Can the dignity of the tragic protagonist be located in the labouring-class people that both Goerge Eliot and Hardy often chose as characters? Can the universality we expect of tragedy be reconciled with the particularity that has been the novelist's concern?

King finds the answers to these questions to be yes, with certain qualifications.

Her discussion of the theoretical issues is weakened by her frequently expressed assumption that tragedy exists in life apart from its artistic rendering. Walpole's epigram, "This world is a comedy to those that think, a tragedy to those that feel", attests that comedy and tragedy exist rather as modes of perception than as independent chunks of reality. King talks of "the depiction of contemporary tragedy" (p. 44), as though what a writer of tragedy needed to do were to get out there with his notebook like a reporter and take it down. Such an assumption inevitably weakens her ability to deal with tragedy as what it is – strictly an art form.

The book is short, for instance, on any sustained consideration of rhetoric. The question of audience (or reader) reaction is largely ignored, though one would have thought that an acid test of tragedy through all metamorphoses would remain its capacity to move us to pity and terror. (King mentions "awe and reverence" once, and "sympathy" often, but sympathy is not a response peculiar to tragedy; "pity" she reserves as a non-tragic response to pathos.) The power to move resides in the rhetoric, both of the narrator and of the characters themselves. But we nowhere have a sustained analysis of a single scene that would demonstrate how the novel can move us as tragedy does.

A partial reason for this lack of any detailed consideration of rhetoric is King's assertion that "inarticulacy" is appropriate to the medium in an age where expression can no longer be direct, eloquent and complete. The tragic novel, unlike the tragic drama, deals with what George Eliot calls "the roar on the other side of silence", and silence becomes the new eloquence. Of course this concept could be interestingly applied to James's characters, with their pregnant pauses and "silences of deeper import"; but there are clearly dangers in making a virtue of inarticulacy. The example provided is hardly convincing. Hetty Sorrel, on trial for child murder, says nothing, and we are told, "her silence in the dock is pathetic, because she does not realise that she is letting slip by the opportunity to save herself" (p. 55). In fact, as the accused she would not have been allowed to say anything anyway, so her silence in the circumstances is not particularly indicative of anything except George Eliot's knowledge of normal trial procedure.

King is on surer ground when she moves from the form to the traditional subject matter of tragedy, and its successful adaptation in the novel. Like Aeschylus and Euripides, George Eliot, Hardy and James were all in their different ways concerned with free will and destiny, and the chapter on this subject covers the expected ground, and uses the familiar quotations.

George Eliot is the sternest moralist of the three, insisting on individual responsibility though recognizing some impelling circumstances. Hardy's characters are more completely the helpless victims of Fate, Nature, and chance. It is difficult to say much that is new on this subject.

The second half of the book is a treatment of each of the three novelists in turn, with a section on each of the novels that can be considered as tragedies. In her discussion of George Eliot, King concludes that Hetty and Casaubon, who prompt the reader's pity for a character not particularly admirable, are cases of "pathetic tragedy" rather than tragedy itself. Women are particularly useful vehicles of pathos, in that society and their biological functions have doomed them to a passive role in life, the role of sufferer. (King's interpretation makes George Eliot sound more resigned to long-suffering womanhood than she was, I think. According to George Eliot, we hear, "a woman's love is essentially Christian, in that it is a love which is unconditional and merciful, as opposed to the love of the Old Testament God of justice, which must be earned" [p. 77]. But when Romola and Dorothea discover their husbands don't deserve their love, they don't go on loving them, and they would be fools if they did. They go on being dutiful; but that's another matter.) The one Eliot novel that lives up to the name of tragedy is *The Mill on the Floss*, and Maggie is a heroine successfully conceived in Aristotelian terms.

Hardy, King shows, incorporates more of the formal characteristics of classical tragedy into his novels, as well as of the thematic concerns. He uses the concept of *peripeteia*, and incorporates Nemesis in the form of the past that relentlessly returns to confront the protagonist in his new present. He also follows Aristotle in placing more emphasis on action than on character. His definition of tragedy, "the WORTHY encompassed by the INEVITABLE", works in his novels as in classic and Shakespearean tragedy. He observes, in his own characteristic ways, the unities of time and place. He also adheres to classical precepts on tragic form, says King, in his "Ideals of unity and organic structure" (p. 100). But here, as elsewhere, she alienates to tragedy what could be said of any work of art. "Really, universally," she quotes James, "relations stop nowhere, and the exquisite problem of the artist is eternally but to draw, by a geometry of his own, the circle within which they shall happily *appear* to do so" (p. 130). James is talking here not just of the tragedian but of all artists. *The Return of the Native*, *The Mayor of Casterbridge*, *Tess*, and *Jude* each receive an individual treatment, sensible but not surprising, of about six pages.

The recurrent themes in James's work that are most suitable for tragic development are the wasted life and the conflict of freedom with form.

These are followed convincingly through individual treatments of *The American*, *The Portrait of a Lady*, and *The Wings of the Dove*.

This book is worth knowing about, and it treats some interesting questions about the relation of a high mimetic form, tragedy, with a low mimetic form, the novel. It will be informative for the beginning student of the novel who wants to explore its analogies with other forms. But the scholar will not find much to challenge or advance his views on the subject.

R. L. Purdy, and M. Millgate (eds), *The Collected Letters of Thomas Hardy*, vol. 2, 1893–1901 (Clarendon Press, 1980) pp. x + 309.

Reviewed by Norman Page

The first two of the projected seven volumes of this handsome edition cover between them sixty-one years of Hardy's life, the opening volume (the title of which rather oddly carries the dates 1840–92) including letters of the thirty-one years from 1862 to 1892, and the second volume presenting the letters of the next nine years. By the end of the second volume Hardy is already an old man with his career as a novelist behind him; but there are plenty more letters to come and the remaining volumes will each span on average little more than five years. It follows that we must not expect to learn from this edition much that is new concerning Hardy's early years; and that may be a matter for regret but should occasion no surprise, since the famous are not only apt to write more letters than the obscure but tend to have their letters more zealously preserved.

Nor should we be surprised that these letters contain few revelations. Leaving aside the destruction of private papers before and after Hardy's death, which no doubt ensured that (as with Jane Austen) the letters we should most like to have went up in smoke, anyone with the faintest understanding of Hardy's temperament knows that reticence, not self-revelation, was his ticket. Reading the letters of, say, Keats or Flaubert or Lawrence creates the illusion of reading a substantial and satisfying work of autobiography; reading Hardy's letters offers no more than marginal annotations to a biography that must largely be supplied from other sources. Even in the most personal of his letters, Hardy did not seize his pen and pour out his thoughts and feelings, hopes and fears; nor did he often take evident pleasure, as a good letter-writer must, in conveying to a correspondent the flavour of an experience through the written word. There is very little humour (one would never guess from the letters that Hardy could be a delightfully funny writer), and a very striking feature is the flatness of style: the high art of the novels and poems permitted linguistic adventurousness and experiment, but as a letter-writer Hardy takes no risks. He hides his feelings behind clichés as other men hide behind newspapers.

Several reviewers of the first volume of this collected edition found Hardy's correspondence unexciting stuff and coupled admiration for the way in which the editors had discharged their heavy and complex duties with doubts whether the task was worth undertaking in the first place. But comparison with other editions in progress, such as those of the letters of Dickens and Lawrence, though perhaps inevitable, are ill-advised: Hardy would have had to be quite a different man from the man he was to write letters as attractive as those of Dickens or Lawrence, and if he had been a different man he could not have written the major novels and poems that are his. It is true that many, perhaps most, of the letters so far printed are not really very interesting: 'Forgive an uninteresting letter,' Hardy wrote to Mrs Henniker on one occasion, and this edition requires the reader to exercise such forgiveness continually. The editorial policy of printing everything that has survived has inevitably involved the inclusion of many trivial items, for Hardy was not a man able, or at any rate willing, to stamp his individuality on a Christmas card or a note declining an invitation. There seems too (to get the grumbles out of the way all at once) something disproportionate in the scrupulous presentation of these documents exactly as they were written, as if they were poems whose precise text is a matter of intense interest. For example, Hardy's odd contractions – 'Litre' for 'literature', 'sincly' for 'sincerely', and so on – have been retained, though it is hard to imagine a reader who would not have been perfectly happy for such matters to have been silently regularized. The notes record minor slips of the pen: if Hardy writes 'the the' instead of 'the', the fact is noted, though it is again hard to imagine the reader who is likely to find such information of the slightest interest. Hardy is a great writer, but, whatever interest they may possess, his letters do not belong to literature; and such veneration for their text seems, according to one's mood, slightly absurd or irritating.

And yet, though these are far from being great letters, one is glad to have them. Hardy is for many readers so fascinating an author that almost any addition to our knowledge of him will be welcomed; he is also such a complex and often baffling figure that any crumb of information may turn out to contribute to our understanding. The job of editing his letters needed doing, and in most respects has been done extremely well. The annotation presents succinctly a good deal of precise information, much of it not easy to come by elsewhere; one regrets, however, that, although each volume contains an index of recipients, a proper index will not be available until the distant day when the final volume appears. In the meantime, the reader who has not made his own index as he goes along must hunt impatiently throughout the volumes for that suggestive reference to Sappho or Poe or Zola or Havelock Ellis that he recalls encountering. Even an index of names in each volume would have been better than nothing, with a full cumulative index in the final volume.

Apart from the merely formal notes, the letters fall into two main categories: business and personal. Not surprisingly, the latter are the more interesting and provide a fragmentary account of Hardy's day-to-day existence during his later years. Those to women are usually more relaxed in tone than those written to men. The business letters show Hardy acting as his own literary agent and to have been notably shrewd and clear-headed over contracts, copyrights, royalties, and so forth. He tutors Florence Henniker in what he calls 'the tricks of the trade', warning her against the wiles of publishers; and the material evidently exists for a useful monograph on Hardy as a professional author.

In the second volume, the principal recipients are (in descending order of prominence) Mrs Henniker, Edmund Gosse, Clement Shorter, Agnes Grove, Emma Hardy and Sir George Douglas. Not all of these personal letters are equally interesting (the ones to Agnes Grove, for instance, are uniformly dull); and not all of them are new to the student of Hardy. The jacket-description tells us that most of the letters are here published for the first time, and no doubt this is true, mathematically speaking; but the fact remains that many of the most interesting letters have already been printed. The letters to Mrs Henniker, the largest group in the volume, were published in 1972 under the editorship of Evelyn Hardy and F. B. Pinion; and most of the letters to Emma Hardy were published by Carl J. Weber as long ago as 1963 (Purdy and Millgate print two letters from this period not given by Weber). What has been done is to propose new dates, based on more detailed biographical knowledge, for many of the numerous letters undated by Hardy: of the twenty-five letters to Emma, Purdy and Millgate's conjectural dating differs from Weber's in no fewer than seventeen instances.

It is in the letters to Mrs Henniker that Hardy comes closest to speaking out; their acquaintance began early in the period covered by this volume, and it is striking that almost one-third of the letters to Mrs Henniker were written in the first year of their friendship. The letters to Emma are, quite undramatically, surprising: they contain, to my mind, no hint of strain in the relationship between Hardy and his first wife, but seem to be exactly the kind of letters one would expect a man to write, during short absences from home, to a woman to whom he had been married for twenty years or more. They are full of domestic trivia, showing Hardy's interest in their shared life and sometimes his concern for Emma's health and comfort; they also show his parsimony, notably in a hilarious passage that debates the momentous question whether she should bring to London in her luggage a sixpenny bottle of almond oil and risk its breaking (which 'would ruin everything').

During the years from 1893 to 1901, as well as meeting Mrs Henniker, Hardy published *Jude* and *The Well-Beloved*; he turned away from fiction and published his first two volumes of verse; Victoria died; the Boer War was fought; and Hardy discovered a new enthusiasm for bicycling. The record provided by the surviving letters contains some gaps; for example, Hardy makes few references to *Jude* during the period of its composition, though it is interesting to find that, having been distinctly lukewarm about embarking on this novel (p. 43), he has some eight months later become 'more interested in this Sue story than in any I have written' (p. 84). Later he confesses that he had 'been intending for years to draw Sue' (p. 102), and such comments help to render more intelligible the thematic shift in the novel from a 'story of a young man who could not go to Oxford' to a 'Sue story'. A more comprehensive confession is that to Mrs Henniker in 1893: 'Would that I could write all my books over again: I might make them worth reading' (p. 32). A review of *The Well-Beloved* leaves him 'much surprised and distressed', and he adds that 'After such a cruel misrepresentation I feel inclined to say I will never write another line' (p. 156). This, from the usually low-keyed Hardy, is strong language; and indeed it is in his reactions to criticism that we find some of the strongest emotions that he is prepared to express in his letters. When *Wessex Poems* appears he observes to Lionel Johnson: 'what an appalling lack of insight into, or rather feeling for poetry of any sort prevails among reviewers outside a limited circle' (p. 212); and he tells Edward Clodd that 'nowadays every critikin applies his two foot rule & patent compasses to new verse' (p. 217). Again the intensity of the reaction takes one by surprise. There are several interesting comments on *Wessex Poems*: for example, the declaration that 'I have been going to publish it for years' (p. 206), and the implausible disclaimer that 'The sketches are *quite* unimportant – as, indeed, are the poems' (p. 205). At about the same time he tells Gosse that 'in the full tide of a fashion which seems to view poetry as the art of saying nothing with a mellifluous preciosity, the principle of regarding form as second to content is not likely to be popular' (p. 208). To William Archer he writes:

> As to a novel from me, I don't incline to one. There is no enlightened literary opinion sufficiently audible to tempt an author, who knows that

in the nature of things he must always come short of real excellence. . . . And zest is quenched by the knowledge that by printing a novel which attempts to deal honestly and artistically with the facts of life one stands up to be abused by any scamp who thinks he can advance the sale of his paper by lying about one. (p. 206)

A similar point is made to Mrs Henniker nearly two years later: 'I am of opinion that the present condition of the English novel is due to the paralysing effect of English criticism upon those who would have developed it . . .' (pp. 269–70).

The possibility of war in 1899 struck Hardy as 'a justification of the extremest pessimism' (p. 229), since it was evidence of man's failure to progress from barbarism to enlightenment; when war appeared inevitable, however, his attitude changed: 'the sooner we get at it, & get it done, the better' (p. 232). Early in 1900 he visited the Dorchester barracks and saw soldiers – Drummer Hodge and his kind – about to embark for South Africa ('my thoughts are all Kahki [sic] colour'). Later in the year he comments, characteristically but disturbingly, on the 40 000 slain: 'Could we ask them if they wish to wake up again, would they say Yes, do you think?' (p. 269). He is, however, honest enough to confess that he takes 'a keen pleasure in war strategy & tactics, following it as if it were a game of chess' (p. 248). *The Dynasts* is, of course, just round the corner.

During the years covered by this volume Hardy spends a good deal of time in London: he clearly dislikes it, continually grumbles about it, but keeps going there none the less. In the summer of 1893 he finds the capital 'dreary and oppressive', but the social magnet is evidently strong and his letters show him mingling with titled folk and even royalty (he notes with satisfaction that he and Prince Christian of Schleswig-Holstein are both suffering from 'a touch of rheumatism' – enough, it seems, to make the whole world kin). In 1899 he tells Mrs Henniker: 'I do not know when we shall go to London; for myself I would rather go into a monastery' (p. 219), but within a few weeks he is installed in a Kensington flat: presumably Emma has won the day. He believes London to be unhealthy, with a 'malignant quality' in its air; and he is often unwell there. It is true that the prolonged sojourns for the London season enabled him to see friends who might not often have travelled down to Dorset, and he spent much time at the Athenaeum and Savile clubs. He also enjoyed the London concerts, and a remark in 1899 reminds one how starved of music it was possible to be in the pre-gramophone age: 'the chief objection to a country life is that difficulty of hearing good music when one wishes to' (p. 225). But a suggestive clue to the deeper roots of his regular metropolitan martyrdom occurs in another letter to Mrs Henniker: 'the ordinary Dorset landowners only tolerate an author; they do not associate with him . . .' (p. 144). In London society Hardy was accorded a recognition withheld by the squirearchy of late-Victorian Dorset.

The Hardy of these letters is low-spirited and often ailing, if not hypochondriac. 'I am in up & down spirits – *down* as a rule', he tells Mrs Henniker in 1898 (p. 202), shortly before the publication of *Wessex Poems*. Influenza, neuralgia, toothache, chills on the liver, headaches, loss of appetite: one's notes on Hardy's health during this period read like the advertisement for a patent medicine. At one point minor aches and pains become universal, and he writes to Emma from London that 'Lilian has earache &c: everybody has aches in fact' (p. 257). Elsewhere, 'I feel a dyspeptic headache gradually brewing' (p. 149); 'a 3 days' headache came on' (p. 184). Significantly, these periods of indisposition usually occur in London, though in 1899 at Max Gate he is, for no evident reason, 'as weak as a cat' (p. 226), and in the following year he has 'no energy . . . to write anything' (p. 264). What comes as a surprise is the energy he finds, in his late fifties, for the new pursuit of bicycling. In 1897 long rides in fine autumn weather as far afield as Wells and Glastonbury make him 'almost forget books' (p. 180); by 1900 he can refer to 'the invaluable but now vulgar bicycle' (p. 253). There are some brief but vivid glimpses of the lost world of England's empty, dusty roads; the first reference to a motor-car is in 1899.

Though these letters help to fill out our knowledge of Hardy's life and personality, then, they contain few surprises. If the nuggets are far from numerous, however, one is glad to have them; and the formal shell occasionally cracks as Hardy delivers himself, without fuss, of a startling observation, such as the quiet comment not long after the publication of *Jude* that 'I don't see any possible scheme for the union of the sexes that would be satisfactory' (p. 122). Visiting Belgium in 1896 after a twenty-year absence, he asks himself 'why am I here again, & not underground!' (p. 130). There are a few memorable vignettes – of Hardy, for instance, pacing up and down during a gale murmuring Shakespeare's 'Thou God of this great Vast, rebuke these surges . . .'; recalling his youth when he read Swinburne's poems as he walked along the crowded London streets; and attending Gladstone's lying-in-state in Westminster Hall. (How entirely characteristic that on such an occasion he should have noted, counterpointing the solemnity of the historic scene, the disparaging remarks made by two carpenters in the throng on the quality of the coffin!) One is grateful, too, for some scraps of information concerning Hardy's reading: to know, for instance, that he read Symons' *The Symbolist Movement in Literature* soon after it appeared (even though he found it 'disappointing'). There are a few epigrams and dicta that stick in the mind: Tennyson is 'a great artist, but a mere Philistine of a thinker' (p. 183); Herbert Spencer's *First Principles* acted upon Hardy as 'a sort of patent expander when I had been particularly narrowed down by the events of life' (pp. 24–5); frost 'has always a curious effect upon my mind, for which I can never account fully – that something is imminent of a tragic nature' (p. 211); and the wistful remark, in congratulating a correspondent on the birth of a son, that 'My children, alas, are all in octavo' (p. 102). Had Hardy often written thus, his letters would make more engrossing reading. In 1901, after describing at length to Florence Henniker the death of a favourite cat, he adds self-defensively: 'You will think I am telling you rather small news, but everything in my life has been small lately, in the ordinary sense' (p. 283). These letters are in the main a record of the 'small news' of a man who was simultaneously writing masterpieces but was usually unprepared to allow his letters, even those written to his closest friends, to express the idiosyncratic sensibility and the range and depth of feelings and ideas that are to be found in his published work. If this sounds like a paradox, another confession to Mrs Henniker goes some way towards providing an explanation:

> I have been thinking that the sort of friend one wants most is a friend with whom mutual confessions can be made of weaknesses without fear of reproach or contempt. What an indescribable luxury! Do you want such an one for yourself? – I wonder if I shall ever find one. (p. 48)

Such moments, all too rare in the letters so far published in this edition, transmit to us Hardy's very self and voice.

REVIEWS IN BRIEF

Winifred Hughes, *The Maniac in the Cellar: Sensation Novels of the 1860s* (Princeton University Press, 1980) pp. x + 212.

This study contains two general chapters; one each on Charles Reade and Wilkie Collins; one shared by Miss Braddon and Mrs Henry Wood; and a final chapter on 'Influences of the Sensation Novel' which includes a section on Hardy. This last offers a lively discussion of *Desperate Remedies*, which Professor Hughes finds a 'staggeringly uneven work' and 'an extreme example of the genre' wherein 'the sensation novel finally runs amuck'. She then proceeds to a discussion of the element of melodrama in Hardy's major novels, showing their affinities with popular fiction of the 'sensation' school – for example, the resemblance between the plot of *Tess* and that of M. E. Braddon's *Aurora Floyd*. Professor Hughes suggests that Hardy's temperament and outlook found the melodramatic mode congenial, and that 'in his hands melodrama becomes the expression of an arbitrary unverse'.

Alan Hurst, *Hardy: An Illustrated Dictionary* (Kaye & Ward, 1980) pp. 215.

The bulk of this book consists of an alphabetical list of entries referring to works, characters, places and people connected (sometimes rather tenuously) with Hardy and on such topics as 'Animals', 'Dance' and 'Films'. There are also 140 black and white photographs, some of them not much better than the average holiday snapshot. A typical couple of pages includes about thirty lines on *The Well-Beloved*, entries on H. G. Wells (on the strength of his review of *Jude*) and 'Wessex' ('a tousled brown and white Caesar terrier . . .'), an aerial view of Wareham and a photograph of the dog's tombstone in the pets' graveyard at Max Gate. Some of the entries are so brief as to be pointless (for example, five lines on 'Diction' and the same on Shakespeare). There is also a brief chronology of Hardy's life and a list of characters in the novels. Except in point of price, Mr Hurst's book is in no respect a serious rival to F. B. Pinion's *A Hardy Companion*, which discharges a similar function with much greater thoroughness.

David Lodge, *Working with Structuralism: Essays and Reviews on Nineteenth- and Twentieth-Century Literature* (Routledge & Kegan Paul, 1981) pp. xii + 207.

Professor Lodge's collection includes three pieces on Hardy that have already appeared in one form or another. '*The Woodlanders*: A Darwinian Pastoral Elegy' is an abridged version of his introduction to the New Wessex edition of the novel; and 'Thomas Hardy as a Cinematic Novelist' and 'Pessimism and Fictional Form: *Jude the Obscure*' are reprinted from the collections of essays recently assembled by, respectively, Lance St John Butler and Dale Kramer.

N.P.

A Hardy Bibliography, 1978–81

Richard H. Taylor

Note: Place of publication is London unless otherwise stated. These abbreviations have been used:

Cahiers	*Cahiers Victoriens & Edouardiens* (Montpellier)
CLQ	*Colby Library Quarterly*
CQ	*Critical Quarterly*
DR	*Dalhousie Review*
ELH	*Journal of English Literary History*
ELN	*English Language Notes*
ELT	*English Literature in Transition*
JENS	*Journal of the Eighteen Nineties Society*
MLQ	*Modern Language Quarterly*
NCF	*Nineteenth-Century Fiction*
NQ	*Notes and Queries*
PS	*Prose Studies*
RES	*Review of English Studies*
THSR	*Thomas Hardy Society Review*
THYB	*Thomas Hardy Year Book*
TLS	*Times Literary Supplement*
TSLL	*Texas Studies in Literature and Language*
VN	*Victorian Newsletter*
VS	*Victorian Studies*

Titles of novels are abbreviated as follows: *AL* (*A Laodicean*), *DR* (*Desperate Remedies*), *FFMC* (*Far from the Madding Crowd*), *HE* (*The Hand of Ethelberta*), *Jude* (*Jude and Obscure*), *MC* (*The Mayor of Casterbridge*), *PBE* (*A Pair of Blue Eyes*), *RN* (*The Return of the Native*), *Tess* (*Tess of the d'Urbervilles*), *TM* (*The Trumpet-Major*), *TT* (*Two on a Tower*), *UGT* (*Under the Greenwood Tree*), *The W* (*The Woodlanders*), *WB* (*The Well-Beloved*).

1. EDITIONS AND TEXTUAL STUDIES

(a) *Editions*

POETRY

The Complete Poems of Thomas Hardy: A Variorum Edition, ed. James Gibson (Macmillan, 1979).

A Dorset Collection: Poems by Thomas Hardy, music by Dennis Cooper (Broadstone, Dorset: Dennis Cooper, 1979).
The Gates Along the Path: Poems by Thomas Hardy, illus. Norman Stevens (Terra Nova Editions, 1979).
Landscape Poets: Thomas Hardy, intro. Peter Porter, photographs by John Hedgecoe (Weidenfeld & Nicolson, 1981).
The New Wessex Selection of Thomas Hardy's Poetry, chosen by John and Eirian Wain, intro. John Wain (Macmillan, 1978).
Poems by Thomas Hardy, with prints by David Imms (Rothwell, Northants: David Imms, 1978).
Poems by Thomas Hardy, ed. Trevor Johnson, wood engravings by Jacques Hnizdovsky (Folio Society, 1979).
Poems of Thomas Hardy and William Barnes, music by Dennis Cooper (Broadstone, Dorset: Dennis Cooper, 1979).
Selected Poems by Thomas Hardy, ed. David Wright, Penguin English Library (Harmondsworth: Penguin Books, 1979).
Thomas Hardy's Chosen Poems, ed. Francine Shapiro Puk (New York: Ungar, 1978).
Thomas Hardy: Selected Poems, ed. James Reeves and Robert Gittings (Heinemann, 1981).

OMNIBUS VOLUMES (PROSE AND POETRY)

The Bedside Thomas Hardy, ed. Edward Leeson (Macmillan, 1979). [Several short stories, 40 poems, extracts from most of the novels.]
Thomas Hardy Omnibus, intro. Edward Leeson (Macmillan, 1978). [*FFMC, MC, The W, Wessex Tales, Tess.*]
A Thomas Hardy Selection, ed. Geoffrey Halson (Longman, 1979). [Poems, stories, extracts from novels.]

PROSE

Short stories:
The Distracted Preacher and Other Tales, ed. Susan Hill, Penguin English Library (Harmondsworth: Penguin Books, 1979).
Our Exploits at West Poley, intro. R. L. Purdy (OUP, 1952; rev. edn, with illustrations by John Lawrence, 1978).

Editions of individual novels:
Far from the Madding Crowd
(1) Afterword James Wright, Signet Classics (New English Library, 1979 [1960]).
(2) Ed., intro. and notes Ronald Blythe, Penguin English Library (Harmondsworth: Penguin Books, 1979).
(3) Intro. Jane Carruth, illus. Jenny Thorne (Maidenhead: Purnell Books, 1979).
(4) Intro. Alan Chedzoy, Collins Classics (London and Glasgow: Collins, 1980).

Jude the Obscure
(1) Ed. Norman Page, Norton Critical Edition (New York: Norton, 1978; UK: 1980).
(2) Afterword A. Alvarez, Signet Classics (New English Library, 1979 [1961]).
(3) Ed., intro. and notes C. H. Sisson, Penguin English Library (Harmondsworth: Penguin Books, 1979).

The Mayor of Casterbridge
(1) Afterword Walter Allen, Signet Classics (New English Library, 1979 [1962]).
(2) Ed., intro. and notes Martin Seymour-Smith, Penguin English Library (Harmondsworth: Penguin Books, 1979).
(3) Intro. Alan Chedzoy, Collins Classics (London and Glasgow: Collins, 1980).

The Return of the Native
(1) Afterword Horace Gregory, Signet Classics (New English Library, 1979 [1959]).
(2) Ed., intro. and notes George Woodcock, Penguin English Library (Harmondsworth: Penguin Books, 1979).

Tess of the d'Urbervilles
(1) Afterword Donald Hall, Signet Classics (New English Library, 1979 [1964]).
(2) Intro. A. Alvarez, ed. and notes David Skilton, Penguin English Library (Harmondsworth: Penguin Books, 1979).

Under the Greenwood Tree
Ed., intro. and notes David Wright, Penguin English Library (Harmondsworth: Penguin Books, 1979).

The Woodlanders
(1) Intro. Ian Gregor, ed. and notes James Gibson, Penguin English Library (Harmondsworth: Penguin Books, 1981).
(2) Ed. Dale Kramer (OUP: Clarendon Press, 1981). [Textual edition.]

(b) *Textual Studies*

Gaskell, Philip, *From Writer to Reader: Studies in Editorial Method* (OUP, 1978). [Editorial problems in nineteenth-century works, including *The W.*]
Gatrell, Simon, 'An Examination of Some Revisions to Printed Versions of *The Dynasts*', *Library*, 6th series, 1 (1979) 265–81.
Gatrell, Simon, 'Hardy, House-Style, and the Aesthetics of Punctuation' in Smith (ed.), pp. 169–92 (see 4a below).
Gatrell, Simon, 'Hardy the Creator: *FFMC*' in Kramer (ed.), pp. 74–98 (see 4a below).
Millgate, Michael, 'The making and unmaking of Hardy's Wessex Edition' in Jane Millgate (ed.), *Editing Nineteenth-Century Fiction* (New York: Garland, 1978) pp. 61–82.
[See also James Gibson's *variorum* edition of *The Complete Poems* and Dale Kramer's textual edition of *The W.*]

2. BIBLIOGRAPHIES, HANDBOOKS, TOPOGRAPHICAL STUDIES

(a) *Bibliographies*

Carter, Kenneth, 'Thomas Hardy in Dorset County Library: Part 1', *THSR*, 1, no. 6 (1980) 169–71, and 'Part 2 – The Lock Collection', *THSR*, 1, no. 7 (1981) 204–7.
Taylor, Richard H., 'Thomas Hardy: A Select Bibliography' in Page (ed.), pp. 259–72 (see 4a below).

(b) *Handbooks*

Hurst, Alan, *Thomas Hardy: An Illustrated Dictionary* (Kaye & Ward, 1980).

(c) *Topographical studies*

Clarke, E. R., *Mellstock and Around: Map of Hardy's Inner Wessex* (Cerne Abbas: M. Y. Horton, 1980).
Curl, James Stevens, 'Thomas Hardy's Casterbridge: Dorchester', *Country Life*, CLXV (1979) 2023–4. (See also letter from Edward Brooks, CLXVI (1979) 174.)
Daiches, David, and John Flower, *Literary Landscapes of the British Isles: A Narrative Atlas* (Paddington Press, 1979): includes chapter on Hardy's Wessex.
Edwards, Anne-Marie, *Discovering Hardy's Wessex* (BBC Publications, 1978).
Hallett, Ray, 'Following Hardy into Wessex', *Country Life*, CLXVII (1980) 466–7.
The Heart of Hardy's Wessex [Ordnance Survey map, with Hardy names and index added.] (Bournemouth: Wessex Heritage Tours, 1980).
Skilling, Ruth, *The Country of Hardy's 'Mellstock' Poems* (Dorchester: Thomas Hardy Society, 1980).
Worth, James W., *Thomas Hardy's Wessex* (Pitkin Pictorials, 1978). [Photographs of Hardy locations with commentary on Hardy's life and work.]

3. BIOGRAPHICAL DOCUMENTS

(a) *Biography*

FULL-LENGTH BIOGRAPHY

Gittings, Robert, *The Older Hardy* (Heinemann, 1978). [In US: *Thomas Hardy's Later Years.*]
Winchcombe, Anna, *Thomas Hardy: A Wayfarer* (Dorchester: Dorset County Library and the Thomas Hardy Society, 1978).

RELEVANT BIOGRAPHY AND AUTOBIOGRAPHY

Gittings, Robert, and Jo Manton, *The Second Mrs Hardy* (Heinemann, 1979).
Kay-Robinson, Denys, *The First Mrs Thomas Hardy* (Macmillan, 1979).
Roberts, Marguerite, *Florence Hardy and the Max Gate Circle* (St Peter Port, Guernsey: Toucan Press, 1980; first published as issue 9 of the *THYB*).

With reference to Florence Emily Hardy, *The Life of Thomas Hardy*:
Buckler, William E., 'Thomas Hardy's Sense of Self: The Poet Behind the Autobiographer in *The Life of Thomas Hardy*', *PS*, III (1980) 69–86.

SHORT ACCOUNTS AND RECOLLECTIONS

Ahman, Suleiman M., 'Hardy and Liverpool', *THSR*, I, no. 4 (1978) 119–23.
Atkins, Norman J., *Thomas Hardy and the Hardy Players* (Guernsey: Toucan Press, 1980). [Expanded version of 1962 monograph.]

Baker, Kenneth, 'Thomas Hardy's Life as a Literary Source', *THYB*, 8 (1978) 10–15.
Beatty, C. J. P., *Thomas Hardy's Career in Architecture (1856–1872)* (Dorchester: Dorset Natural History and Archaeological Society, 1978).
Brewin, Arthur, 'Two Visits to Max Gate', *THSR*, I, no. 6 (1980) 171–4. [Recollections of visits to Florence Hardy.]
Bugler, Gertrude, 'More Than a Monkey-Puzzle: Hardy's House at Sturminster', *THSR*, I, no. 6 (1980) 187.
Cox, J. S. and G. S. (eds), *Thomas Hardy's Life in Pictures* (St Peter Port, Guernsey: Toucan Press, 1978). [92 illustrations.]
Coxon, Peter W., 'Recollections of Thomas Hardy in St Andrews', *THYB*, 8 (1978) 10–15.
Dorset Evening Echo (19 August 1978): 'Thomas Hardy Festival', 32-page supplement with contributions by various hands.
Evans, Ray, 'Hardy Growing Up', *Festival Handbook 1978*, 15–17.
Gittings, Robert, 'The Love Life of Thomas Hardy', *The Sunday Times* (19 February 1978) 33–4. (Extracted from *The Older Hardy*.)
Hardy, Evelyn, 'Hardy's Emma at Home', *Country Life*, CLXIV (1978) 1760, 1762.
Harris, Margaret, 'The Lives of Thomas Hardy', *Quadrant*, 148 (1979) 26–30.
Knight, Ronald D., *Thomas Hardy and Edmund Gosse* (Weymouth: R. D. Knight, rev. edn 1978).
Pinion, F. B., 'A Sorrow of the Past', *THSR*, I, no. 5 (1979) 163–4. [On Hardy's final minutes as described in *Personal Notebooks*, pp. 202, 287.]
Rabiger, Michael, 'More About Thomas Hardy in London', *THYB*, 8 (1978) 16–18.
Taylor, Richard H., 'Hardy's Disguised Autobiography', *THSR*, I, no. 4 (1978) 104–9.
Willis, Irene Cooper, *An Essay on Thomas Hardy*, ed. F. B. Pinion (Dorchester: Thomas Hardy Society, 1981).
Winchcombe, Anna, 'The Author with Durability', *Dorset*, 69 (1978) 9–10.
Winchcombe, Anna, 'The Birthplace Remains', *Festival Handbook 1978*, 14.

(b) *Letters*

Purdy, Richard Little, and Michael Millgate (eds), *The Collected Letters of Thomas Hardy* (OUP: Clarendon Press, vol. I (1840–92) 1978, vol. II (1893–1901) 1980).
Sampson, Edward C. and Cynthia R., 'A Forgotten Letter by Thomas Hardy', *NQ*, n.s. XXXV (1978) 321–2.

(c) *Notebooks*

Taylor, Richard H. (ed.), *The Personal Notebooks of Thomas Hardy* (Macmillan, 1979).

4. CRITICAL STUDIES OF THE NOVELS AND STORIES, AND GENERAL ESSAYS AND ARTICLES

(a) *Book-length studies and collections of essays*

Bayley, John, *An Essay on Hardy* (Cambridge University Press, 1978).
Butler, Lance St John, *Thomas Hardy* (Cambridge University Press, 1978).

A Hardy Bibliography, 1978-81 195

Cahiers Victoriens & Edouardiens [Special issue: *Studies in Thomas Hardy*, ed. Annie Escuret] 12 (1980) (Montpellier: Université Paul Valéry, 1980).*

Cox, J. S. and G. S. (eds), *The Thomas Hardy Year Book*, No. 7: 1977 (1979) and no. 8: 1978 (1980) (Guernsey: Toucan Press).*

Enstice, Andrew, *Thomas Hardy: Landscapes of the Mind* (Macmillan, 1979).

Festival Handbook 1978 (Dorchester: Thomas Hardy Society, 1978).*

Grundy, Joan, *Hardy and the Sister Arts* (Macmillan, 1979).

Inscape Critical Series [Special issue: *Thomas Hardy*, ed. David R. Shore and Keith G. Wilson], XIV (1980) (Ottawa: University of Ottawa, 1980).*

Kramer, Dale (ed.), *Critical Approaches to the Fiction of Thomas Hardy* (Macmillan, 1979).*

Page, Norman (ed.), *Thomas Hardy: The Writer and his Background* (Bell and Hyman, 1980).*

Salter, C. H., *Good Little Thomas Hardy* (Macmillan, 1981).

Smith, Anne (ed.), *The Novels of Thomas Hardy* (Vision Press, 1979).*

Sumner, Rosemary, *Thomas Hardy: Psychological Novelist* (Macmillan, 1981).

Walbank, Christopher, *Thomas Hardy* (Glasgow: Blackie, 1979).

(* = Individual essays listed separately in appropriate sections of this bibliography.)

(b) *Articles, essays and parts of books*

Arkans, Norman, 'Hardy's "Religious Twilight"', *TSLL*, XXI (1979) 413-32.

Bies, Werner, 'Thomas Hardy and Literary Competitions in *The Academy*', *THSR*, I, no. 7 (1981) 223-4.

Björk, Lennart A., 'Hardy's Reading' in Page (ed.) pp. 102-27.

Black, Edward, 'Poetry and Prose', *THSR*, I, no. 7 (1981) 228-33. [Poetic quality of Hardy's prose.]

Brown, Frank H., 'Hardy and the Lay Reader', *THSR*, I, no. 7 (1981) 214-18.

Buck, Thomas, 'Thomas Hardy and Ultima Thule', *THSR*, I, no. 5 (1979) 138-41.

Caless, Bryn, 'The Psychological Significance of Critical Passivity in Protagonist Characters', *JENS*, IX (1978) 5-9.

Canham, Stephen W., 'Love and Passion in the Novels of Thomas Hardy', *Inscape*, XIV (1980) 109-19.

Chellapan, V., 'Hardy and the First Cause', *Journal of English Studies* (India), I (1978) 11-15.

Collins, Philip, 'Hardy and Education' in Page (ed.) pp. 41-75.

Cook, David A., 'Powys, Hardy and Wessex', *Powys Newsletter*, V (1978) 19-23.

Coustillas, Pierre, 'Gissing on Hardy: A Novelist's View of a Contemporary writer', *Cahiers*, 12 (1980) 1-18.

Cox, Gregory Stevens (ed.), '*The Mumming Play of St George*', *Cahiers*, 12 (1980) 57-72. [Incorporated by the Hardy Players in their 1920 adaptation of *RN*, which quotes fragments of the play; also performed by them in a longer version in 1923, of which this is the text.]

Davidow, Mary C. 'Charlotte Mew and the Shadow of Thomas Hardy', *Bulletin of Research in the Humanities*, LXXXI (1978) 437-47.

Dorset: The County Magazine, 69 (1978) 1-15, 37-8.

Efron, Arthur, 'Thomas Hardy's Bulging Autograph', *Paunch*, LII (1978) 12-28.

Enstice, Andrew, 'The Fruit of the Tree of Knowledge' in Smith (ed.) pp. 9-22.

Essex, Ruth, 'Hardy's Spiritual Orphans: An Introduction to the Parentless Universe of his Wessex Women', *Festival Handbook 1978*, 60-5.

Fleishman, Avrom, *Fiction and the Ways of Knowing* (Austin: University of Texas Press, 1978) *passim*.
Gatrell, Simon, 'Hardy and the Critics', *Cahiers*, 12 (1980) 19–44.
Gibson, James, 'Hardy and his Readers' in Page (ed.) pp 192–218.
Grice, Elizabeth, 'Under the Greenwood Tree', *The Sunday Times* (27 August 1978). [Report on the Hardy Festival.]
Hardy, Evelyn, 'Stinsford Churchyard' [poem], *THSR*, I, no. 6 (1980) 174–5.
Hawkins, Desmond, '"By Truth Made Free": A Reassessment of Thomas Hardy', *Contemporary Review*, CCXXXII (1978) 209–12.
Hawkins, Desmond, 'The Yellow Birds', *THSR*, I, no. 5 (1979) 136–8. [Bird imagery.]
Hynes, Samuel, 'Sad Hearts and Hiding Places', *TLS* (10 March 1978) 283–4. [Review article.]
Ingham, Patricia, 'Hardy and *The Wonders of Geology*', *RES*, XXXI (1980) 59–64.
Jackson, A. M., 'The Evolutionary Aspect of Hardy's Modern Men', *Revue Belge de Philosophie et d'Histoire*, LVI (1978) 641–9.
Jones, Lawrence, 'Thomas Hardy After Fifty Years', *Southern Review* (Adelaide), XI (1978) 316–24. [Review article.]
Jones, Lawrence, 'Imagery and the "Idiosyncratic Mode of Regard": Eliot, Hardy and Lawrence', *Ariel*, XII (1981) 29–49.
Jung, George, 'Chance in Hardy and Contemporary German Novelists', *THSR*, I, no. 7 (1981) 223.
Keith, W. J., 'A Regional Approach to Hardy's Fiction' in Kramer (ed.) pp. 36–49.
Kendrick, Walter M., 'The Sensationalism of Thomas Hardy', *TSLL*, XXX (1980) 484–503.
Kincaid, James R., 'Hardy's Absences' in Kramer (ed.) pp. 202–11. [Intentional gaps in narration.]
King, Jeannette, *Tragedy in the Victorian Novel: Theory and Practice in the Novels of George Eliot, Thomas Hardy and Henry James* (Cambridge University Press, 1978) pp. 97–126.
King-Smith, R. G., 'William Barnes and Thomas Hardy', *THYB*, 8 (1978) 18–20.
Knowles, Stewart, 'Will the Madding Crowd Ruin Hardy?' *TV Times*, 18–24 February 1978. [Article in conjunction with TV dramatised documentary: see Section 8 below.]
Langbaum, Robert, 'Modern Ideas and Old Observations', *TLS*, 28 July 1978, 859. [Review article.]
Larkin, Philip, 'Things Noticed', *New Statesman*, 4 May 1979, 642–3. [Review article.]
May, Derwent, 'Thomas Hardy Revisited', *Saturday Review*, 22 July 1978, 40–3.
Miles, Rosalind, 'The Women of Wessex' in Smith (ed.) pp. 23–44.
Osawa, Mamoru, 'Hardy Studies in Japan', *THSR*, I, no. 6 (1980) 180–4.
Page, Norman, 'Hardy and the English language' in Page (ed.) pp. 151–72.
Peck, John, 'Hardy's Novel Endings', *JENS*, IX (1978) 10–15.
Peck, John, 'Hardy and Joyce: A Basis for Comparison', *Ariel*, XII, 2 (1981) 71–85.
Pettit, Charles P. C., 'From Magazine Serial to Limited Edition', *Festival Handbook 1978*, 48–52.
Pinion, F. B., 'Thomas Hardy', *Blackwood's Magazine*, CCCXXIII (1978) 4–14. [Hardy's Scottish links and his significance today.]
Pinion, F. B., 'Hardy's literary imagination', *Cahiers*, 12 (1980) 45–56.
Pinion, F. B., 'Thomas Hardy' in *The Novel to 1900* [Macmillan Reference Books] (Macmillan, 1980) pp. 134–8.
Pinion, F. B., 'George Eliot and Thomas Hardy' in *A George Eliot Companion* (Macmillan, 1982) pp. 244–52. [Hardy's indebtedness to George Eliot.]

Richmond, Velma Bouregois, 'Sexual Reversals in Thomas Hardy and Ellen Glasgow', *Southern Humanities Review*, XIII (1979) 51–62.
Robinson, Roger, 'Hardy and Darwin' in Page (ed.) pp. 128–50.
Schwartz, Daniel R., 'Beginning and endings in Hardy's major fiction' in Kramer (ed.) pp. 17–35.
Sewell, Brocard, 'Thomas Hardy and G. K. Chesterton: a study in two temperaments', *Chesterton Review*, V (1978–9) 104–20. (Responses by John Sullivan and Peter Hunt, 258–68.)
Spear, Jeffrey L., 'Robinson, Hardy and a Literary Source of "Eros Turannos"', *CLQ*, XV (1979) 58–64.
Taylor, Richard H., 'Thomas Hardy: A Reader's Guide' (with a select bibliography) in Page (ed.), pp. 219–72.
Tomalin, Claire, 'Hardy's Perennial', *Radio Times*, 21–7 January 1978.
Tristram, Philippa, 'Stories in Stones' in Smith (ed.) pp. 145–68. [Hardy's use of architectural motifs and themes in his writing.]
Tuttleton, James, W., 'Hardy and Ellen Glasgow: *Barren Ground*', *Mississippi Quarterly*, XXXII (1979) 577–90.
Van Tassel, Daniel E., 'Clym, Gabriel, and Bathsheba: Hardy's Use of scriptural names', *THSR*, I, no. 4 (1978) 125–7.
Weatherby, H. L., 'Hardy Criticism in a New Phase', *Sewanee Review*, LXXXVI (1978) 298–306.
Weatherby, Harold L., 'Victorian Wessex', *Southern Review*, XV (1979) 300–12.
Weiner, Seth, 'Thomas Hardy and His First American Publisher: A Chapter from the Henry Holt Archives', *Princeton University Library Chronicle*, XXXIX (1978) 134–57.
Williams, Merryn and Raymond, 'Hardy and Social Class' in Page (ed.) pp. 29–40.
Williamson, Eugene, 'Thomas Hardy and Friedrich Nietzsche: The Reasons', *Comparative Literature Studies*, XV (1978) 403–13.
Wing, George, 'Hardy and Regionalism' in Page (ed.) pp. 76–101.

5. CRITICAL STUDIES OF THE POETRY

(a) *Book-length studies and collections of essays*

Clements, Patricia, and Juliet Grindle (eds), *The Poetry of Thomas Hardy* (Vision Press, 1980).*
Gibson, James, and Trevor Johnson (eds), *Thomas Hardy – Poems: A Selection of Critical Essays*, Macmillan Casebook Series (Macmillan, 1979).
Giordano, Frank R., jr (ed.), *The Poetry of Thomas Hardy: A Commemorative Issue* [of *Victorian Poetry*, XVII, 1–2 (1979)].*
Taylor, Dennis, *Hardy's Poetry 1860–1928* (Macmillan, 1981).
(* = Individual essays listed separately in 5(b) below.)

(b) *Articles, essays and parts of books*

Alexander, Michael, 'Better Than Beer, More Lasting Than Bronze', *Cahiers*, 12 (1980) 219–26. [Review essay.]

Arkans, Norman, 'Hardy's Poetic Landscapes', *CLQ*, xv (1979) 19–35.
Arkans, Norman, 'Vision and experience in Hardy's Dream Poems', *MLQ*, XLI (1980) 54–72.
Bayley, John, 'Hardy's Poetical Metonymy', *Essays and Studies*, XXXI (1978) 115–30.
Benvenuto, Richard, 'The Small Free Space in Hardy's Poetry', *VP*, xvii (1979) 31–44.
Bies, Werner, 'A Note on Hardy, W. B. Yeats, and the Brownings', *THSR*, I, no. 6 (1980) 193.
Buckler, William E., 'The Dark Space Illumined: A Reading of Hardy's "Poems of 1912–13"', *VP*, xvii (1979) 98–107.
Clements, Patricia, '"Unlawful Beauty": Order and Things in Hardy's Poems' in Clements and Grindle (eds) pp. 137–54.
Collins, Michael J., 'A Note on Hardy's Rhythmic Technique', *THYB*, 8 (1978) 36–7.
Cook, Cornelia, 'Thomas Hardy and George Meredith' in Clements and Grindle (eds) pp. 83–100.
Davies, Cecil W., 'Order and Chance: The Worlds of Wordsworth and Hardy', *THYB*, 8 (1978) 40–50.
Davies, H. Neville, 'Thomas Hardy's "In the Cemetery", line 4', *NQ*, n.s. XXV (1978) 322–3.
Eakins, Rosemary L., 'The Mellstock Quire and Tess in Hardy's Poetry' in Clements and Grindle (eds) pp. 52–68.
Evans, Ray, 'The Setting of Hardy's Elegy on Swinburne in *Satires of Circumstance*', *THSR*, I, no. 7 (1981) 221–3.
Fontana, Ernest L., 'Hardy's "The Shadow on the Stone"', *Explicator*, XXXVII, no. 1 (1978) 17–18.
Fontana, Ernest L., 'Zen in Thomas Hardy's *Moments of Vision*', *Inscape*, XIV (1980) 160–5.
Ford, Mary, 'The View from Wessex Heights: Thomas Hardy's Poetry of Isolation', *DR*, LIX (1980) 705–16.
Gatrell, Simon, 'Travelling Man' in Clements and Grindle (eds) pp. 155–71.
Gibson, James, 'The Posthumous Poems', *Festival Handbook 1978*, 55–9. [On *Winter Words*.]
Giordano, Frank R., jr, Introduction to *The Poetry of Thomas Hardy: A Commemorative Issue*, *VP*, XVII, 1–2 (1979) ix–xi.
Giordano, Frank R., jr, 'A Reading of Hardy's "A Set of Country Songs"', *VP*, XVII (1979) 85–97.
Grundy, Isobel, 'Hardy's Harshness' in Clements and Grindle (eds) pp. 1–17.
Haarder, Andreas, 'Fatalism and Symbolism in Hardy: An Analysis of "The Grave by the Handpost"', *Orbis Litterarum*, XXXIV (1979) 227–37.
Hardy, Evelyn, 'Hardy's Last Poem: Some Revelations', *THSR*, I, no. 4 (1978) 127–8. [On 'He Resolves to Say No More'.]
Harrison, Anthony H., 'Hardy's Poetry: The Uses of Nature', *Ball State University Forum*, XIX (1978) 63–70.
Harvey, Geoffrey, 'Thomas Hardy's Poetry of Transcendence', *Ariel*, IX, 4 (1978) 3–20.
Hazen, James, 'Hardy's War Poetry', *Four Decades of Poetry 1890–1930*, II (1978) 76–93.
Humm, Maggie, 'Illustrations for *Wessex Poems*', *VP*, XVII (1979) 135–54. [On Hardy's sketches.]
Hynes, Samuel, 'The Hardy Tradition in Modern English Poetry' in Page (ed.) pp. 173–91.
Ingham, Patricia, 'Hardy and the "Cell of Time"' in Clements and Grindle (eds) pp. 119–36.
Johnson, Trevor, '"Pre-Critical Innocence" and the Anthologist's Hardy', *VP*, XVII (1979) 9–29.

Jones, Bernard, 'Hardy and the End of the Nineteenth Century', *THSR*, I, no. 7 (1981) 224–8. [On 'The Darkling Thrush'.]
Jones, Lawrence, 'Leslie Stephen and "Nature's Questioning"', *THSR*, I, no. 6 (1980) 190–3.
King, Kathryn, and William W. Morgan, 'Hardy and the Boer War: The Public Poet in spite of himself', *VP*, XVII (1979) 66–83.
Kirkup, James, 'Hardy the Poet', *Eigo Seinen* [*The Rising Generation*] (Tokyo), 124 (1978) 422–4.
Lentz, Vern B., and Douglas D. Short, 'Thomas Hardy's "Ah, Are You Digging On My Grave?" and Child no. 78, "The Unquiet Grave"', *THYB*, 8 (1978) 37–9.
McCarthy, Robert, 'Hardy and "The Lonely Burden of Consciousness": The Poet's Flirtation with the Void', *ELT*, XXIII (1980) 89–98.
McCarthy, Robert, 'Hardy's Baffled Visionary: a reading of "A Sign-Seeker"', *VP*, XVIII (1980) 85–90.
Mahar, Margaret, 'Hardy's Poetry of Renunciation', *ELH*, XLV (1978) 303–24.
Marken, Ronald, '"As Rhyme Meets Rhyme" in the Poetry of Thomas Hardy' in Clements and Grindle (eds) pp. 18–32.
Murfin, Ross C., *Swinburne, Hardy, Lawrence and the Burden of Belief* (University of Chicago Press, 1978) *passim*.
Neuman, S. C., '"Emotion Put Into Measure": Meaning in Hardy's Poetry' in Clements and Grindle (eds) pp. 33–51.
Ousby, Ian, 'Past and Present in Hardy's "Poems of Pilgrimage"', *VP*, XVII (1979) 51–64.
Potter, Vilma Raskin, 'Poetry and the Fiddler's Foot: Meters in Thomas Hardy's work', *Musical Quarterly*, LXV (1979) 48–71.
Press, John, 'W. B. Yeats, Thomas Hardy and Philip Larkin', *Aligarh Journal of English Studies*, III (1978) 153–65.
Pritchard, William H., 'Hardy's Winter Words', *Hudson Review*, XXXII (1979) 369–97.
Rehder, Robert M., 'Hardy's Lyrics: Visions of Moments', *Cahiers*, 12 (1980) 201–10.
Richards, I. A., 'Some Notes on Hardy's Verse Forms', *VP*, XVII (1979) 1–8.
Richards, Max, 'Hardy's Poetry: Voice and Vision', *Critical Review* (Melbourne), XXI (1979) 24–35.
Siemens, Lloyd, '"A Full Look at the Worst": Hardy and the Poetry of Optimism', *Wascana Review*, XIII, no. 1 (1978) 3–17.
Siemens, Lloyd C., 'Hardy's Poetry and the Rhetoric of Negation', *DR*, LVIII (1978) 69–78.
Simpson, Peter, 'Hardy's "The Self-Unseeing" and the Romantic Problem of Consciousness', *VP*, XVII (1979) 45–50.
Stallworthy, Jon, 'Read by Moonlight' in Clements and Grindle (eds) pp. 172–88.
Steele, Jeremy V., 'Thoughts from Sophocles: Hardy in the '90s' in Clements and Grindle (eds) pp. 69–72.
Tarr, Rodger L., 'Hardy's "Channel Firing"', *Explicator*, XXXVI (1978) 17–18.
Taylor, Dennis, 'Victorian Philology and Victorian Poetry', *VN*, 53 (1978) 13–16.
Wesling, Donald, 'Hardy, Barnes, and the Provincial', *VN*, 55 (1979) 18–19.
Wirdnam, Richard, 'The Dance Poems of Thomas Hardy', *THSR*, I, no. 6 (1980) 176–80.

6. STUDIES OF SPECIFIC WORKS

(See also 1(a) above.)

Desperate Remedies
Jones, Lawrence, '*Tess* and the "New Edition" of *DR*', *CLQ*, xv (1979) 194–200.
Wickens, G. Glen, 'Hardy's *DR*', *Explicator*, xxxix (1980) 12–14.

The Dynasts
Brooks, Jean R., '*The Dynasts* as Total Theatre', *Cahiers*, 12 (1980) 137–78.
Buckler, William E., '"The Thing Signified" in *The Dynasts*: A Speculation', *VN*, 57 (1980) 9–14.
Buckler, William E., 'Thomas Hardy's "Chronicle-Piece" in "Playshape": An Essay in Literary Conceptualization', *VP*, xviii (1980) 209–27.
Gatrell, Simon, 'An Examination of Some Revisions to Printed Versions of *The Dynasts*', *Library*, 6th series, i (1979) 265–81.
Orel, Harold, '*The Dynasts* Undesired', *Festival Handbook 1978*, 24–7.
Orel, Harold, 'What *The Dynasts* Meant to Hardy', *VP*, xvii (1979) 109–23.
Vaché, Jean, 'Structures Métaphoriques dans *Les Dynastes*', *Cahiers*, 12 (1980) 179–200.
Wickens, G. Glen, 'Hardy's Inconsistent Spirits and the Philosophic Form of *The Dynasts*' in Clements and Grindle (eds) pp. 101–18.
Wilson, Keith, '"Flower of Man's Intelligence": World and Overworld in *The Dynasts*', *VP*, xvii (1979) 124–33.

Far from the Madding Crowd
Casagrande, Peter J., 'A New View of Bathsheba Everdene' in Kramer (ed.) pp. 59–73.
Eastman, Donald, 'Time and Propriety in *FFMC*', *Interpretations*, x (1978) 20–33.
Gatrell, Simon, 'Hardy the Creator: *FFMC*' in Kramer (ed.) pp. 74–98.
Giordano, Frank, R., jr, 'Farmer Boldwood: Hardy's Portrait of a Suicide', *ELT*, xxi (1978) 244–53.
Hopkins, V. T., 'Hardy and Ainsworth: The Storm', *THSR*, i, no. 4 (1978) 109–12.
Jones, Lawrence, '"A Good Hand at a Serial": Thomas Hardy and the Serialization of *FFMC*', *Studies in the Novel*, x (1978) 320–34.
Jones, Lawrence, '"Infected by a Vein of Mimeticism": George Eliot and the Technique of *FFMC*', *Journal of Narrative Technique*, viii (1978) 56–76.
Madden, O. E., 'William Boldwood', *THSR*, i, no. 6 (1980) 193.
Millar, A. R., '*FFMC*: Let's Indulge in a Homeric Fallacy or Two', *CRUX: A Journal on the Teaching of English*, xiii, 3 (1979) 41–3.
Ousby, Ian, 'Love-Hate Relations: Bathsheba, Hardy and the Men in *FFMC*', *Cambridge Quarterly*, x (1981) 24–39.
Senechal-Teissedou, J., 'Focalisation, regard et désir dans *FFMC*', *Cahiers*, 12 (1980) 73–84.
Thompson, Geoffrey, 'Toller Whelme, Waterston House, and *FFMC*', *THSR*, i, no. 6 (1980) 196–8.

Jude the Obscure
Adewoye, Sam, 'Human Responsibility in Thomas Hardy's *Jude*', *Nigerian Journal of the Humanities*, ii (1978) 87–101.
Benvenuto, Richard, '*The Odd Women* and the foreshadowing of *Jude*', *CLQ*, xiv (1978) 191–7.
Blake, Kathleen, 'Sue Bridehead: The Woman of the Feminist Movement', *Studies in English Literature*, xviii (1978) 703–26.
Collins, Philip, 'Pip the Obscure: *Great Expectations* and Hardy's *Jude*', *CQ*, xix (1978) 23–35.

Conroy, Christopher, 'Place and Movement in *Jude*', *THSR*, I, no. 5 (1979) 154–7.
Dobrinsky, Joseph, 'Un Inédit de Thomas Hardy: quatre schémas pour une adaptation dramatique de *Jude*', *Etudes Anglaises*, XXXII (1979) 198–205.
Efron, Arthur, 'A Blue, Moister Atmosphere: Life Energy in *Jude*', *International Journal of Life Energy* (Toronto), I (1979) 175–84.
Findlay, L. M., 'D. G. Rossetti and *Jude*', *Pre-Raphaelite Review*, II (1978) 1–11.
Gallivan, Patricia, 'Science and Art in *Jude*' in Smith (ed.) pp. 126–44.
Horne, Lewis B., 'Symbol and Structure in *Jude*', *Literatur in Wissenschaft und Unterricht* (Kiel), XI (1978) 199–210.
Horne, Lewis B., 'Pattern and Contrast in *Jude*', *Etudes Anglaises*, XXXII (1979) 143–53.
Horne, Lewis B., 'The Gesture of Pity in *Jude* and *Tender is the Night*', *Ariel*, XI, 2 (1980) 53–62.
King, Jeannette, '*Jude*' in *Tragedy in the Victorian Novel* (1978).
Langland, Elizabeth, 'A Perspective of One's Own: Thomas Hardy and the Elusive Sue Bridehead', *Studies in the Novel*, XII (1980) 12–28.
Lock, Charles, 'Town and Gown: Christminster, the Oxford of *Jude*', *Festival Handbook 1978*, 66–9.
Lodge, David, '*Jude*: Pessimism and Fictional Form' in Kramer (ed.) pp. 193–201.
McMaster, R. D., 'Centre and Periphery: A Rhythmical Motif in *Jude*', *DR*, LVIII (1978) 260–71.
Mulderig, Gerald P., 'Darkness and Discord at Marygreen: A Note on the Opening Chapters of *Jude*', *CLQ*, XV (1979) 201–2.
Page, Norman, 'Marie Bashkirtseff: A Model for Sue Bridehead?', *THSR*, I, no. 6 (1980) 175.
Page, Norman, 'Hardy, Lawrence, and the Working-Class Hero', in *English Literature and the Working Class*, ed. F. G. Tortosa and R. L. Ortega (Seville, 1980) 39–57.
Peck, John, 'Hardy's *Jude*', *Explicator*, XXXIX, 1 (1980) 6–7.
Sumner, Rosemary, 'Hardy as Innovator: Sue Bridehead', *THSR*, I, no. 5 (1979) 151–4.
Van Tassel, Daniel E., '"Gin-Drunk" and "Creed-Drunk": Intoxication and Inspiration in *Jude*', *THSR*, I, no. 7 (1981) 218–21.
Wright, Janet B., 'A Source for Physician Vilbert', *THSR*, I, no. 4 (1978) 118–19.
Wright, Janet B., 'Hardy and His Contemporaries: The Literary Context of *Jude*', *Inscape*, XIV (1980) 135–50.

A Laodicean
Cox, John G., 'John Power was Sir Samuel Morton Petro', *Dorset*, 69 (1978) 15–17.

The Mayor of Casterbridge
Bebbington, Brian, 'Folksong and Dance in *MC*', *English Dance and Song*, XL (1978) 111, 115.
Casagrande, Peter J., and Charles Lock, 'The Name "Henchard"', *THSR*, I, no. 4 (1978) 115–18.
Fussell, D. H., 'The Maladroit Delay: The Changing Times in Hardy's *MC*', *CQ*, XXI (1979) 17–30.
Grindle, Juliet M., 'Compulsion and Choice in *MC*' in Smith (ed.) pp. 91–106.
Higbie, Robert, 'The Flight of the Swallow in *MC*', *'ELN*, XVI (1979) 311–12.
King, Jeannette, '*MC*' in *Tragedy in the Victorian Novel* (1978) pp. 107–12.
Morrison, Blake, 'Hardy Televised: The BBC's *MC* Series', *CQ*, XX (1978) 77–83.
Showalter, Elaine, 'The Unmanning of the Mayor of Casterbridge' in Kramer (ed.) pp. 99–115.

Solimine, Joseph, '"The turbid ebb and flow of human misery": "Love Among the Ruins" and *MC*', *VP*, VIII, 2 (1980) 99–101.

A Pair of Blue Eyes
Ahmad, Suleiman, 'Thomas Hardy's Last Revision of *PBE*', *Papers of the Bibliographical Society of America*, LXXII (1978) 109–12.
Ahmad, Suleiman M., 'Emma Hardy and the MS. of *PBE*', *NQ*, n.s. XXVI (1979) 320–2.

The Return of the Native
Corballis, R. P., 'A Note on Mumming in *RN*', *NQ*, n.s. XXV (1978) 323.
Coxon, Peter, 'Egdon Heath and *King Lear*', *THSR*, I, no. 4 (1978) 112–14.
Giordano, Frank R., jr, 'Eustacia Vye's Suicide', *TSLL*, XXX (1980) 504–21.
Grant, Eric, 'The Heath is the Hero', *Festival Handbook 1978*, 18–21.
Heilman, Robert B., '*RN*:Centennial Observations' in Smith (ed.) pp. 58–90.
King, Jeannette, '*RN*' in *Tragedy in the Victorian Novel* (1978) pp. 102–7.
McKenna, John, 'Clym Yeobright's Eleventh Commandment', *American Notes and Queries*, XVII (1978) 8.
Springer, Marlene, 'The Uses of Allusion in Thomas Hardy's *RN*', *Inscape*, XIV (1980) 120–34.
Wheeler, Michael, *The Art of Allusion in Victorian Fiction* (Macmillan 1979), *passim*.
[Influence of literary passages in 8 novels, including two by Hardy: *RN* and *Tess*.]

Tess of the d'Urbervilles
Beatty, C. J. P., 'A Note on the Source of the Name Stoke d'Urberville', *THSR*, I no. 6 (1980) 198–9.
Begiebing, Robert J., 'The Masque of the Scapegoat in Hardy's *Tess*', *Gipsy Scholar*, V (1978) 69–86.
Bugler, Gertrude, 'Hardy's Dramatization of *Tess*', *THSR*, I, no. 5 (1979) 134–5.
Clark, S. L., and Julian N. Wasserman, 'Tess and Iseult', *THSR*, I, no. 5 (1979) 160–3.
Clark, S. L., and Julian Wasserman, '*Tess* as Arthurian Romance', *Studies in Medievalism*, I no. 1 (1979) 55–64.
Daleski, H. M., '*Tess*: Mastery and Abandon', *Essays in Criticism*, XXX (1980) 326–45.
Eakins, Rosemary L., '*Tess*: The Pagan and Christian Traditions' in Smith (ed.) pp. 107–25.
Ebbatson, J. R., 'Talbothays Garden: A Source?', *THSR*, I, no. 5 (1979) 136.
Escuret, Annie, '*Tess des d'Urberville*: le Corps et le Signe', *Cahiers*, 12 (1980) 85–136.
Fussell, D. H., 'The Sunlit Landscape of *Tess*', *1837–1901: Journal of the Loughborough Victorian Studies Group*, 4 (1979) 70–97.
Grainville, Patrick, 'Tess, l'hérétique', *La Quinzaine Littéraire*, 314 (1979) 14.
Jackson, Arlene M., 'Thomas Hardy, Mrs Bugler, and the *Tess* Woodcuts', *THSR*, I no. 6 (1980) 189–90.
Jacobus, Mary, 'Tess: The Making of a Pure Woman' in Susan Lipshitz (ed.), *Tearing the Veil: Essays on Feminity* (Boston: Routledge, 1978) pp. 77–92.
Jones, Lawrence, '*Tess* and the "New Edition" of *DR*', *CLQ*, XV (1979) 194–200.
King, Jeanette, '*Tess*' in *Tragedy in the Victorian Novel* (1978) pp. 112–20.
Laird, J. T., 'New Light on the Evolution of *Tess*', *RES*, XXXI (1980) 414–35.
McBride, Mary G., '"Appetite for Joy": A Browning Allusion in Hardy's *Tess*', *VP*, VIII, no. 2 (1980) 92–3.
Marken, R. N. G., '"Sick for Home": The Theme of *Tess*', *English Studies in Canada*, IV (1978) 317–29.

Waldoff, Leon, 'Psychological Determinism in *Tess*' in Kramer (ed.) pp. 135-54.
Wheeler, Michael, *The Art of Allusion in Victorian Fiction* (London. Macmillan, 1979). [Influence of literary passages in 8 novels, including two by Hardy: *Tess* and *RN*.]

The Trumpet-Major
Riekert, P., 'The Mural and the Miniature: Public and Private Readings in Thomas Hardy's *TM*', *CRUX: A Journal on the Teaching of English*, XII, no. 2 (1978) 36-42.
Sanders, Andrew, *The Victorian Historical Novel 1840-1880* (Macmillan, 1979). [Includes discussion of *TM*.]
Taylor, Richard H. (ed.), 'The Trumpet-Major Notebook' in *The Personal Notebooks of Thomas Hardy* (1979) pp. xx-xxv (introduction), 115-86 (text).

Two on a Tower
Ward, Paul, '*TT*: A Critical Revaluation', *THYB*, 8 (1978) 29-34.

Under the Greenwood Tree
Edwards Duane, 'The Ending of *UGT*', *THYB*, 8 (1978) 21-2.
Escuret, Annie, '*UGT*: une lecture', *Cahiers*, 7 (1978) 83-122.
Hardy, Barbara, '*UGT*: A Novel About the Imagination' in Smith (ed.) pp. 45-57.
Perry, P. J., 'William Dewy, John Small and the Musical Bull', *THYB*, 8 (1978) 34-5.

The Well-Beloved
May, Charles E., '*WB*: Hardy's Hymeneal Harlequinade', *Victorian Institute Journal*, VII (1979) 1-6.
Ryan, Michael, 'One Name of Many Shapes: *WB*' in Kramer (ed.) pp. 172-92.

The Woodlanders
Austin, Frances, 'Dialogue in *The W*', *THSR*, I, no. 5 (1979) 144-51.
Chalfant, Fran C., 'In Defence of Hardy's Gentleman from South Carolina', *THSR*, I, no. 5 (1979) 142-4.
Cramer, Jeffrey S., 'The Grotesque in Thomas Hardy's *The W*', *THYB*, 8 (1978) 25-9.
Gaskell, Philip, *From Writer to Reader: Studies in Editorial Method* (OUP, 1978). [Editorial problems in several nineteenth-century works, including *The W*.]
Jacobus, Mary, 'Tree and Machine: *The W*' in Kramer (ed.) pp. 116-34.
Riis, Johannes, 'Naipaul's Woodlanders', *Journal of Commonwealth Literature*, XIV (1979) 109-15. [Hardy's novel in Naipaul's *Guerrillas*.]

Short stories
Benazon, Michael, 'Dark and Fair: Contrast in Hardy's "The Fiddler of the Reels"', *Ariel*, IX (1978) 75-82.
Benazon, Michael, '"The Romantic Adventures of a Milkmaid": Hardy's Modern Romance', *English Studies in Canada*, v (1979) 56-65.
Brady, Kristin, 'Conventionality as Narrative Technique in Hardy's "On The Western Circuit"', *JENS*, IX (1978) 22-30.
Brady, Kristin, 'Ancient and Modern: A Double Perspective in Thomas Hardy's "The Fiddler of the Reels"', *Inscape*, XIV (1980) 150-9.
Caless, Bryn, 'The Genesis of "The Distracted Preacher"', *THSR*, I, no. 5 (1979) 157-60.
Carpenter, Richard C., 'How To Read *A Few Crusted Characters*' in Kramer (ed.) pp. 155-71.

Escuret, Annie, 'Une Nouvelle de T. Hardy: "The Waiting Supper"', *Cahiers*, 8 (1979) 39–52.
Larkin, Peter, 'Irony and Fulfilment in Hardy's "A Mere Interlude"', *JENS*, IX (1978) 16–22.
Rees, Joan, 'Hardy and Rossetti' in *The Poetry of Dante Gabriel Rossetti: Modes of Self-Expression* (Cambridge University Press, 1981) pp. 197–8. [On 'An Imaginative Woman'.]
Sumner, Rosemary, 'Hardy Ahead of His Time: "Barbara of the House of Grebe"', *NQ*, n.s. XXVII (1980) 230–1.

Play
Butler, Lance St John, 'Hardy's *Tragedy of the Queen of Cornwall*', *Cahiers*, 12 (1980) 230–1.

7. FILM AND TELEVISION ADAPTATIONS

(a) *Film*

Tess of the d'Urbervilles
(Columbia Pictures, 1979.) Screenplay: Gerard Brach, Roman Polanski, John Brownjohn. Music: Philippe Sarde. Director: Roman Polanski. Cast includes: Nastassia Kinski (Tess), Peter Firth (Angel), Leigh Lawson (Alec), John Collin (Durbeyfield), Rosemary Martin (Mrs Durbeyfield), Sylvia Coleridge (Mrs Stoke-d'Urberville).

(b) *Television*

The Mayor of Casterbridge
(BBC-2 Television Serial, 22 January–5 March 1978.) Dramatised by Dennis Potter in seven episodes. Music: Carl Davis. Producer: Jonathan Powell. Director: David Giles. Cast includes: Alan Bates (Henchard), Anne Stallybrass (Susan), Janet Maw (Elizabeth-Jane), Jack Galloway (Farfrae), Avis Bunnage (Furmity woman), Freddie Jones (Fall).

8. OTHER TELEVISION BROADCASTS

Thomas Hardy – A Man Who Noticed Things
(Independent Television network, Westward Television production, 22 February 1978; dramatised documentary.) Director/producer: John Bartlett. Cast includes: Bartlett Mullins (Hardy), Celia Ryder (Emma Hardy), Roland Viner (young Hardy), Diana Berriman (Emma Gifford), Diane Mercer (Tryphena Sparks). Narrator: Charles Causley. Hardy's poems read by Douglas Leach and Celia Ryder. ['A dramatised documentary on the life of the Dorset novelist and poet Thomas Hardy' (*TV Times*).]

A Haunted Man
(BBC-2 Television, 5 March 1978; dramatised documentary.) Script: Denis Constanduros and Tristram Powell in consultation with Robert Gittings. Executive producer: Bill Morton. Director: Tristram Powell. Cast: Billie Whitelaw (Emma), Cyril Luckham (Hardy). Narrator: Caroline Blakiston. ['Thomas Hardy, famed as a novelist, deeply

reserved and secretive as a man, put his most private feelings into his poems, and the greatest of these were the poems of love and remorse that he wrote after the death of his first wife, Emma. They had fallen in love in Cornwall and ended their days in a grim house outside Dorchester. The romance of their first meeting seemed far away . . .' (*Radio Times*).]

GPSR Compliance

The European Union's (EU) General Product Safety Regulation (GPSR) is a set of rules that requires consumer products to be safe and our obligations to ensure this.

If you have any concerns about our products, you can contact us on

ProductSafety@springernature.com

In case Publisher is established outside the EU, the EU authorized representative is:

Springer Nature Customer Service Center GmbH
Europaplatz 3
69115 Heidelberg, Germany

www.ingramcontent.com/pod-product-compliance
Lightning Source LLC
Chambersburg PA
CBHW031520100426
42873CB00013B/150